Classical
Chinese Poetry

CLASSICAL
CHINESE POETRY

AN ANTHOLOGY

TRANSLATED AND EDITED BY

David Hinton

Farrar, Straus and Giroux
New York

Farrar, Straus and Giroux
18 West 18th Street, New York 10011

Distributed in Canada by Douglas & McIntyre Ltd.
Printed in the United States of America
First edition, 2008

Owing to limitations of space, acknowledgments for permission to reprint
previously published material can be found on page 477.

Library of Congress Cataloging-in-Publication Data
Classical Chinese poetry : an anthology / translated and edited by David Hinton.
        p.   cm.
    Includes bibliographical references and index.
    ISBN-13: 978-0-374-10536-5 (hardcover: alk. paper)
    ISBN-10: 0-374-10536-7 (hardcover: alk. paper)
    1. Chinese poetry—Translations into English.   I. Hinton, David.

PL2658.E3 C645 2008
895.1'1008—dc22

                                                            2008013862

www.fsgbooks.com

10   9   8   7   6   5   4   3   2   1

Contents

Contents

Additional material is available at www.fsgbooks.com/classicalchinesepoetry.

Introduction

THE CHINESE POETIC tradition is the largest and longest continuous tradition in world literature, practiced until recently by virtually everyone in the educated class and stretching from well before 1500 B.C.E. to the present. Remarkably, it has flourished not only in its homeland but also in Korea and Japan, each of which systematically adopted Chinese language and culture and thereafter developed Chinese poetic practice into their own directions. Much later, at the beginning of the modernist revolution, classical Chinese poetry made a surprising appearance in translation far from home when Ezra Pound saw in its concrete language and imagistic clarity a way to clear away the formalistic rhetoric and abstraction that dominated English poetry at the time. And its contemporary voice and sage insight have made it an influential strain of American poetry ever since.

This anthology presents more than three millennia of Chinese poetry from its beginnings sometime before 1500 B.C.E. to 1200 C.E., the centuries during which virtually all of its major innovations took place. In speaking of a Chinese poetic tradition, we are necessarily speaking of the written tradition. Nevertheless, the Chinese tradition was essentially an oral folk tradition for over a millennia, because the major written texts were primarily translations of folk poetry. This fact makes it difficult to assign a firm date for the tradition's origins. Indeed, as the written tradition is quite literally an extension of the oral tradition, its beginnings stretching back almost to the very beginnings of the culture itself. So it is not surprising when literary legend tells us that an especially brief and plainspoken folk-song called "Earth-Drumming Song" (p. 76) originated in the twenty-third century B.C.E.

After a transitional period beginning about 300 B.C.E., a mature written tradition was established around 400 C.E., its poets typically speaking in a personal voice of their immediate experience. These poets belonged to a small, highly educated elite class of artists and scholars that ran the government. From emperor and prime minister to lowly bureaucrat, from regional governor to monk or recluse in distant mountains—they all studied and wrote poetry, and their poetry was widely read among their colleagues. It was shared first on hand-copied calligraphic scrolls, ranging from a small scroll with a single poem to a set of larger scrolls containing a collection of poems, and then, after printing came into common use during the ninth century C.E., in printed books as well. These poems tended eventually to be scattered on the winds of circumstance—war, fire, neglect—with the result that a large share of work by even the most celebrated poets has been lost, and often substantial portions of the collections we now have are of uncertain attribution.

The work of men and women, illiterate peasants and urbane aristocrats, seductive courtesans and august statesmen, shamans and monks and countless literary intellectuals with an astonishing range of unique sensibilities—there is a remarkable diversity in the Chinese tradition, but underlying that diversity lies the unifying influence of the classical Chinese language. Quite different from the spoken Chinese of farm and market, classical Chinese was a literary language alive primarily in a body of literary texts, which means that it remained relatively unchanged across millennia. The most immediately striking characteristic of classical Chinese is its graphic form: it has retained aspects of its original pictographic nature, and so retains a direct visual connection to the empirical world. This was especially true for poetry, which in its extreme concision focuses attention on the characters themselves, and for the original readers of these poems, who were so erudite that they could see the original pictographs even in substantially modified graphs of characters.

The other remarkable characteristic of the language is that its grammatical elements are minimal in the extreme, allowing a remarkable openness and ambiguity that leaves a great deal unstated: prepositions and conjunctions are rarely used, leaving relationships between lines, phrases, ideas, and images unclear; the distinction between singular and plural is only rarely and indirectly made; there are no verb tenses, so temporal location and sequence are vague; very often the subjects, verbs, and objects of verbal action are absent. In addition, words tend to have a broad range of possible connotation. This openness is dramatically emphasized in the poetic language, which is far more spare even than prose. In reading a Chinese poem, you mentally fill in all that emptiness, and yet it remains always emptiness. The poetic language is, in and of itself, pure poetry:

階	下	叢	莎	看	露	光
stairs	below	clump	grass	see	dew	radiance

The grammatical openness is apparent in this line from Meng Hao-jan. And though it is not unusually pictographic, we find many images in the last four characters alone: grass ⧺ (stalks and roots divided by ground level) above water 氵 (abbreviated form showing drops of water; full form 水 from the ancient form, which shows the rippling water of a stream: 災); the eye ◉ (tipped on its side in the second character) shaded by a hand 手 (shown as the wrist and five fingers) for best vision; rain falling from the heavens 雨 that is mysteriously seen only at your feet 足 (schematic picture of a foot below the formal element of a circle, showing heel to the left, toes to the right, leg above, with an ankle indicated to one side); and fire 火 (slightly formalized as the top half of the last character, the horizontal line and above), supported by a person 人 (picture of a person walking, modified slightly in this character to give its base some structural stability, from the ancient form that includes a head: 兄).

These two defining characteristics of the language—empty grammar and graphic form—are reflected in the Taoist cosmology that became the conceptual framework shared by all poets in the mature written tradition. The cosmology must have evolved together with the language during the earliest stages of human culture in China, as they share the same deep structure, and it eventually found written expression in the *Tao Te Ching* (c. sixth century B.C.E.; see p. 36) and the *Chuang Tzu* (c. fourth century B.C.E.). Taoist thought is best described as a spiritual ecology, the central concept of which is Tao, or Way. *Tao* originally meant "way," as in "pathway" or "roadway," a meaning it has kept. But Lao Tzu and Chuang Tzu redefined it as a spiritual concept, using it to describe the process (hence, a *way*) through which all things arise and pass away. To understand their Way, we must approach it at its deep ontological level, where the distinction between presence (being) and absence (nonbeing) arises.

Presence (*yu*) is simply the empirical universe, which the ancients described as the ten thousand living and nonliving things in constant transformation, and absence (*wu*) is the generative void from which this ever-changing realm of presence perpetually arises. This absence should not be thought of as some kind of mystical realm, however. Although it is often spoken of in a general sense as the source of all presence, it is in fact quite specific and straightforward: for each of the ten thousand things, absence is simply the emptiness that precedes and follows existence. Within this framework, Way can be understood as the generative process through which all things arise and pass away as absence burgeons forth into the great transformation of presence. This is simply an ontological description of natural process, and it is perhaps most immediately manifest in the seasonal cycle: the pregnant emptiness of absence in winter, presence's burgeoning forth in spring, the fullness of its flourishing in summer, and its dying back into absence in autumn.

At the level of deep structure, words in the poetic language function in the same way as presence, the ten thousand things, and the emptiness that surrounds words functions as absence. Hence, the language doesn't simply replicate but actually participates in the deep structure of the cosmos and its dynamic process; it is in fact an organic part of that process. And the pictographic nature of the words, enacting as it does the "thusness" of the ten thousand things, reflects another central concept in the Taoist cosmology: *tzu-jan*, the mechanism by which the dynamic process of the cosmos proceeds, as presence arises out of absence.

The literal meaning of *tzu-jan* is "self-ablaze," from which comes "self-so" or "the of-itself." But a more revealing translation of *tzu-jan* is "occurrence appearing of itself," for it is meant to describe the ten thousand things arising spontaneously from the generative source (*wu*)—each according to its own nature, independent and self-sufficient; each dying and returning into the process of change, only to reappear in another self-generating form. This vision of *tzu-jan* recognizes the earth, indeed the entire cosmos, to be a boundless generative organism. There is a palpable sense of the sacred in this cosmology: for each of the ten thousand things, consciousness among them, seems to be miraculously emerging from a kind of emptiness at its own heart, and emerging at the same time from the very heart of the cosmos itself. As it reflects this cosmology in its empty grammar and pictographic nature, the poetic language is nothing less than a sacred medium. Indeed, the word for poetry, *shih*, is made up of elements meaning "spoken word" and "temple." The left-hand element, meaning "spoken word," portrays sounds coming out of a mouth: 言. And the right-hand element, meaning "temple," portrays a hand below (ancient form: 𦥑) that touches a seedling sprouting from the ground (ancient form: 屮): 寺. Hence: "words spoken at the earth altar": 詩.

Although radically different from the Judeo-Christian worldview that has dominated Western culture, this Taoist cosmology represents a worldview that is remarkably familiar to us in the modern Western world (no doubt part of the reason the poetry feels so contemporary): it is secular, and yet profoundly spiritual; it is thoroughly empirical and basically accords with modern scientific understanding; it is deeply ecological, weaving the human into the "natural world" in the most profound way (indeed, the distinction between human and nature is entirely foreign to it); and it is radically feminist—a primal cosmology oriented around earth's mysterious generative force and probably deriving from Paleolithic spiritual practices centered on a Great Mother who continuously gives birth to all things in an unending cycle of life, death, and rebirth.

By the time the mature written tradition began around 400 C.E., Buddhism had migrated from India to China and was well established. Ch'an, the distinctively Chinese form of Buddhism, was emerging in part as a result of mistranslation of Buddhist texts using Taoist terminology and concepts. Ch'an was essentially a reformulation of the spiritual ecology of early Taoist thought, focusing within that philosophical framework on meditation, which was practiced by virtually all of China's intellectuals. Such meditation allows us to watch the process of *tzu-jan* in the form of thought arising from the emptiness and disappearing back into it. In such meditative practice, we see that we are fundamentally separate from the mental processes with which we normally identify, that we are most essentially the very emptiness that watches thought appear and disappear.

Going deeper into meditative practice, once the restless train of thought falls silent, one simply dwells in that undifferentiated emptiness, that generative realm of absence. Self and its constructions of the world dissolve away, and what remains of us is empty consciousness itself, known in Ch'an terminology as "empty mind" or "no-mind." As absence, empty mind attends to the ten thousand things with mirrorlike clarity, and so the act of perception itself becomes a spiritual act: empty mind mirroring the world, leaving its ten thousand things utterly simple, utterly themselves, and utterly sufficient. This spiritual practice is a constant presence in classical Chinese, in its fundamentally pictographic nature. It is also the very fabric of Chinese poetry, manifest in its texture of imagistic clarity. In a Chinese poem, the simplest word or image resonates with the whole cosmology of *tzu-jan*.

The deep structure of the Taoist/Ch'an cosmology is shared not only by the poetic language but by consciousness as well. Consciousness, too, participates as an organic part of the dynamic processes of the cosmos, for thoughts appear and disappear in exactly the same way as presence's ten thousand things. And the generative emptiness from which thoughts arise is nothing other than absence, the primal source.

Consciousness, cosmos, and language form a unity, and in the remarkably creative act of reading a Chinese poem we participate in this unity, filling in absence with presence, empty mind there at the boundaries of its true, wordless form:

不	覺	初	秋	夜	漸	長
not	aware	beginning	autumn	night	gradually	long

清	風	習	習	重	凄	涼
clear	wind	steadily/ gently	steadily/ gently	double	icy	cold

炎	炎	暑	退	茅	齋	靜
blaze	blaze	summer heat	withdraw	thatch	study	quiet

階	下	叢	莎	看	露	光
stairs	below	clump	grass	see	dew	radiance

The occasion for this poem is a kind of non-occasion: Meng Hao-jan's self-absorbed failure to notice the world around him, which is a kind of exile from the very nature of language and consciousness. It is autumn that attracts Meng's notice, bringing him back to that unity of cosmos, consciousness, and language—the autumnal world dying into winter, season of *wu*, that pregnant emptiness. His "thatch hut grows still," an outer stillness that reflects an inner stillness, an emptiness. This empty self is also alive in the language, for Meng exists in the grammar only as an absent presence, almost indistinguishable from *wu*'s emptiness. He is felt in the first and last lines, where we can infer his presence only because of the convention that such a poem is about the poet's immediate experience. In the last line, we can fill in the grammatical subject to get: *below the stairs, in bunchgrass, [I] see dew shimmer.* But the poet remains more absence than presence. Essentially an act of meditation, the poem ends with a perfectly empty mind mirroring the actual—a person become, in the most profound way, his truest self: *wu*'s enduring emptiness and *tzu-jan*'s ten thousand shimmering things:

AUTUMN BEGINS

Autumn begins unnoticed. Nights slowly lengthen,
and little by little, clear winds turn colder and colder,

summer's blaze giving way. My thatch hut grows still.
At the bottom stair, in bunchgrass, lit dew shimmers.

*

ALTHOUGH IT MEANS ignoring the hundreds of noteworthy poets whose work makes up the evolving texture of China's poetic tradition, and therefore missing much important transitional material, this anthology presents Chinese poetry as a tradition of major poets whose poetics created new possibilities for the art, which is to say, gave new dimensions to the Taoist/Ch'an unity of cosmos, consciousness, and language. In this modern age, vast environmental destruction has been sanctioned by people's assumption that they are spirits residing only temporarily here in a merely physical world created expressly for their use and benefit. This makes the Taoist/Ch'an worldview increasingly compelling as an alternative vision in which humankind belongs wholly to the physical realm of natural process. The range of work gathered in this anthology addresses every aspect of human experience, revealing how it is actually lived from within that alternative perspective—not in a monastery but in the always compromised texture of our daily lives.

Early Collections:
The Oral Tradition

(c. 15th century B.C.E. to 4th century C.E.)

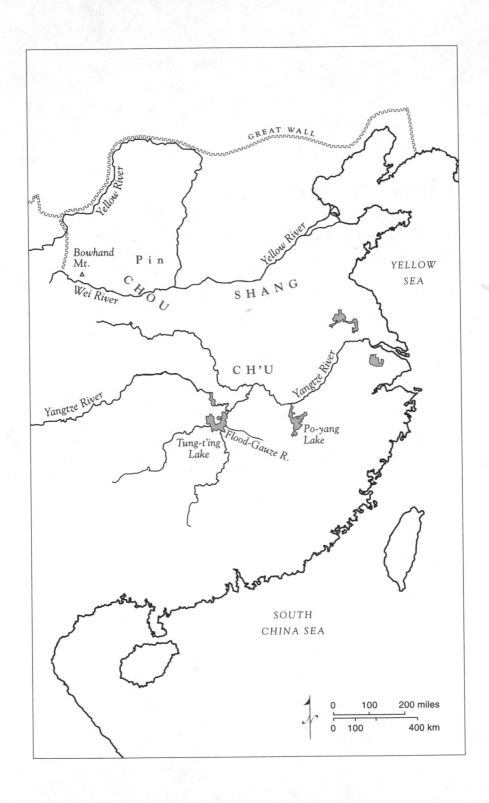

GREAT WALL

Yellow River

Yellow River

Bowhand
Mt.
△

P i n

CHOU

SHANG

Wei River

YELLOW
SEA

CH'U

Yangtze River

Yangtze River

Yangtze River

Po-yang
Lake

Flood-Gauze R.

Tung-t'ing
Lake

SOUTH
CHINA SEA

| 0 | 100 | 200 miles |

| 0 | 100 | 400 km |

ANCIENT CHINESE POETRY survives as a textual tradition written in a literary, as opposed to vernacular, language. Nevertheless, for its first millennium, it was essentially an oral tradition of the nonliterate people. This oral tradition extends back many thousands of years into pre-history, of course, but beginning around the sixth to seventh centuries B.C.E., members of the intellectual class gathered samples of this vast po-etic corpus a number of times, recording a few brief moments from its ongoing evolution. Each of the collections in which the oral literature survives is remarkably unique, focusing on a particular dimension of that literature. The range and diversity of these poetries suggests just how vast China's oral tradition was, as well as how much must have been lost.

In terms of content, the recorded poems are probably quite close to the folk originals, but formally they differ considerably. Spoken Chinese is a very different language from literary Chinese, and to complicate matters, the poems were gathered from many different regions of China, each of which spoke its own distinct dialect. So the poems needed to be translated into the standard literary language not just from spoken Chinese but from various dialects of the spoken language. Additionally, this process of translation no doubt involved substantial amounts of editing and reshaping. But however distant they are from the original material, the written versions represent an impressive body of poetry in their own right, constituting nothing less than the foundation upon which the entire Chinese tradition is built.

THE BOOK OF SONGS

(c. 15th to 6th century B.C.E.)

THE EARLIEST GATHERING from China's oral tradition is *The Book of Songs* (*Shih Ching*), an anthology of 305 poems. This collection was compiled, according to cultural legend, by no less a figure than Confucius (551 to 479 B.C.E.), who selected the poems from a total of about 3,000 that had been gathered from China's various component states, each of which spoke its own dialect. The poems are traditionally dated between the twelfth and sixth centuries B.C.E., but any poem in the oral tradition evolves over time, and the origins of the earliest *Shih Ching* poems no doubt stretch back well beyond the twelfth century. The *Songs* can be seen as an epic of the Chinese people from the origins of China's earliest historical dynasty, the Shang (traditional dates 1766 to 1122 B.C.E.), to the unraveling of the Chou Dynasty (1122 to 221 B.C.E.) in Confucius's age, a span of time during which Chinese culture underwent a fundamental transformation from a spiritualized theocratic society to a secular humanist one.

Religious life in the Shang Dynasty focused on the worship of ancestors, and the Shang emperors ruled by virtue of a family lineage that connected them to Shang Ti, literally "High Lord" or "Celestial Lord," a monotheistic god very like the Judeo-Christian god in that he created the universe and controlled all aspects of its historical process. In the mythological system that dominated Shang culture, the rulers were descended from Shang Ti and so could influence Shang Ti's shaping of events through their spirit-ancestors, thereby controlling all aspects of people's lives: weather, harvest, politics, economics, religion, and so on. Indeed, the Chinese people didn't experience themselves as substantially different from spirits, for the human realm was known as an extension of the spirit realm—a situation very similar to the Judeo-Christian West, where people think of themselves as immortal souls, spirits only temporarily here in a material world before they move on to heaven, their true spirit-home.

Eventually the Shang rulers became cruel and tyrannical, much hated by their people, and they were overthrown by the Chou, a people living on the Shang border who had recently adopted Chinese culture. The Chou conquerors were faced with an obvious problem: if the Shang lineage descended directly from Shang Ti, and so had an absolute claim to rule Chinese society, how could the Chou justify replacing it, and how could they legitimize their rule in the eyes of the Shang people? Their solution was to reinvent Shang Ti in the form of Heaven, an impersonal divine power of the cosmos, thus ending the Shang's claim to legitimacy by lineage. The Chou rulers then proclaimed that the right to rule depended upon a "Mandate of Heaven": once a ruler became unworthy, Heaven withdrew its Mandate and bestowed it on another. This concept was a major event in Chinese society: the first investment of power with an ethical imperative.

The early centuries of the Chou Dynasty appear to have fulfilled that imperative admirably. But the Chou eventually foundered because its rulers became increasingly tyrannical, and they lacked the Shang's absolute metaphysical source of legitimacy: if the Mandate could be transferred to them, it could obviously be transferred again. The rulers of the empire's component states grew increasingly powerful, claiming more and more sovereignty over their lands, until finally they were virtually independent nations. The final result of the Chou's "metaphysical" breakdown was, not surprisingly, all too physical: war. There was relentless fighting among the various states and frequent rebellion within them. This internal situation, so devastating to the people, continued to deteriorate after Confucius compiled the *Shih Ching*, until it finally led to the Chou's collapse two and a half centuries later.

By Confucius's time, the old social order had crumbled entirely, and China's intellectuals began struggling to create a new one. In the ruins of a grand monotheism that had dominated China for over a millennium, a situation not at all unlike that of the modern West, these thinkers created an earthly humanist culture: Confucius and Mencius crafting its political dimensions, Lao Tzu (see p. 36) and Chuang Tzu its spiritual dimensions.

This remarkable cultural transformation is reflected in the *Songs*. Although the situation was complex, with developments evolving differently in different regions and strata of society, the general movement appears to have been from poems of spiritualized power (ritual hymns and historical odes that celebrate the ruling class and its power) to secular folk-songs. The book's older hymns and odes tend to focus on the ruling class and its concerns: the historic and religious framework that legitimized the Shang and Chou rulers, the Chou overthrow of the Shang, and finally the Chou's rule.

Unfortunately, there is only a small group of five poems relating to the Shang Dynasty. They must have originated back in the Shang, eventually evolving into their *Shih Ching* forms, which were performed in a region of the Chou empire that maintained its connection to the Shang. With this one exception, the hymns and odes all relate to the Chou Dynasty. According to legend, a majority of them (nearly seventy) were written by the Duke of Chou, the last of the three revered rulers from the founding of the Chou, and the one credited with expanding and consolidating the Chou empire. He was also widely thought to have composed many of the folk-songs (see Lu Yu's reference on p. 398). This is legend. The concept of a fixed written text composed by a particular individual did not exist at the time, so this attribution must have been invented much later, when that concept did exist. But as with so much of early Chinese culture, this legend became part of the reality upon which the culture was built, so the Duke of Chou might be considered China's first great poet. This remarkable figure is further credited with inventing the concept of the Mandate of Heaven, and so might also be considered the first of China's great philosophers.

It was the Duke of Chou's concept of a Mandate of Heaven that led to the most celebrated and enduring section of *The Book of Songs*: the later folk poetry that makes up nearly two-thirds of the collection. According to Chou ideology, Heaven bestowed its Mandate on a ruler only so long as that ruler successfully furthered the interests of the people, and it was thought that the best indication of the people's well-being was their poetry. So noble rulers would send officials out among the people to gather folk-songs in order to gauge how their policies were succeeding. These songs were translated from regional dialects into the standard literary language by government officials and performed with music at the court. It should, therefore, be remembered that this is not folk poetry itself, but folk poetry that was substantially reshaped by the poet-scholars who edited and translated it.

The organization of the *Songs* reflects China's overall cultural development, though in rough and reverse chronological order, beginning with the more recent folk-songs and ending with the ancient Shang hymns. The selection translated here is arranged chronologically, beginning with hymns and odes that move from Shang origins (pp. 9–10) through the rise of the Chou people and their eventual overthrow of the Shang (pp. 11–17), a period during which all cultural value was focused on the ruling class. It then continues through the troubled Chou, where the increasing value accorded the common people is reflected in the collection of folk-songs, with their quotidian themes and almost complete lack of Shang metaphysics. So at the end of this process, once the spiritualized social framework had been replaced by a secular humanist one, the poetry too had moved from religious hymns and historical odes celebrating the ruling class's interests to a plainspoken poetry of the common people. This latter poetry contains the two fundamental orientations that came to shape the Chinese poetic mainstream: it is a secular poetry having a direct personal voice speaking of immediate and concrete experience, and it is a poetry that functions as a window onto the inner life of a person.

Heaven bade Dark-Enigma bird
descend and give birth to Shang,
our people inhabiting lands boundless and beyond,
then our Celestial Lord bade brave and forceful T'ang
establish boundaries to the far corners of our lands,
bade him then rule these lands,
these nine regions in splendor.
So T'ang, first emperor of Shang,
received the Mandate. Ever safe,
it has passed now to Wu Ting's
sons, to his sons and grandsons,
our emperors brave and forceful,
nothing they will not overcome—
their lords with dragon banners
parading grains to the sacrifice,
their domain thousands of miles
offering the people sure support.
He pushed the boundaries of our land to the four seas,
and now from the four seas comes
homage, such abounding homage.
And our far frontier is the river.
That Shang received the Mandate was due, right and due,
and its hundred blessings continue.

Majestic, O ancestors majestic
ablaze shaping blessings this
bounty on and on stretching
boundless across your lands:
we bring you crystalline wine
and you answer our prayers.
We bring well-seasoned soup,
approach mindful and tranquil
and hushed in silent homage,
leaving all strife far behind,
and you ease our pained brows,
letting old age grow boundless.
Hubs veiled and harness inlaid,
eight phoenix-bells clittering,
we offer sacrifice and homage.
The Mandate we received is vast and mighty.
It's from Heaven—this rich ease,
this life abounding in harvests.
We offer homage, and you accept,
sending boundless good fortune,
honoring autumn and winter
offerings from T'ang's children.

Birth to our people—it was she,
Shepherdess Inception, who
gave birth to our people. How?
She offered sacrifice, prayers
that she not be without child,
wandered the Lord's footprint, quickened
and conceived. She grew round,
dawn-life stirring there within,
she gave birth and she suckled,
and the child—it was Millet God.

And so those months eased by
and the birth—it was effortless.
Free of all rending and tearing,
free of pain and affliction, she
brought forth divine splendor.
The Celestial Lord soothing her,
welcoming sacrifice and prayer,
she bore her son in tranquillity.

And so he was left alone in a narrow lane,
but oxen and sheep nurtured him.
And so he was left alone on a forested plain,
but woodcutters gathered round.
And so he was left alone on a cold ice-field,
but birds wrapped him in wings,
and when the birds took flight,
Millet God began to wail, he
wailed long and wailed loud,
and the sound was deafening.

And so he soon began to crawl,
then stood firm as a mountain.
When he began to feed himself,
he planted broad-beans aplenty,
broad and wind-fluttered beans,
and lush grain ripening in rows,
wheat and hemp thick and rich,
and melons sprawled everywhere.

And so Millet God farmed, understanding
the Way to help things grow.
He cleared away thick grass
and planted yellow treasure.
The seeds swelled and rooted.
Planted well, they grew lovely,
grew tall and lovely in bloom,
they ripened to a fine finish
and bent low with rich plenty.
He built a house there, in T'ai, and settled.

And so he gave to us exquisite
millet: midnight and twin-seed,
red-shafted and white-frosted.
He grew midnight and twin-seed
far and wide, cut acre after acre,
cut red-shafted and white-frosted,
hauled it in, shoulder and back
home to begin offering sacrifice.

And so our offerings—how are they done?
Some thresh and some sweep,
some winnow and some tread;
we wash it clean, whisper-clean,
and steam it misty, misty sweet.
Pondering deeply, thoughts pure,
we offer artemisia soaked in fat,
offer rams to spirits far and wide,
and meat smoke-seared we offer
to bring forth another new year.

We offer bounty in altar bowls,
in altar bowls and holy platters,
and when the fragrance ascends,
fragrance perfect in its season,
our Celestial Lord rests content.
Millet God began these offerings,
and free of trespass always they
continued down to our own time.

Melons sprawl from root.
In Pin riverlands, earth
gave birth to our people.
Our true old father T'ai
made us shelters, kiln-huts,
for houses were unknown.

Then T'ai our true father
went early on his horse,
following the Wei River
west to Bowhand Mountain,
found Lady Shepherdess
and with her shared roof.

Chou plains rich and full,
thistle-weed and bitterroot
like honey-cake, he began
planning. Tortoise shells
said: *This place. This time.*
And soon houses were built.

He comforted and he settled
his people on every side,
laid out bounds and borders,
shaped fields, sent farmers
east and west, everywhere
fashioning his project well.

He called master builders,
master teachers, bade them
build houses, plumb-lines
taut and true, bade them
lash timbers into that regal
temple ancestors would love.

We hauled earth in baskets,
crowds swarming, measuring,
packing it hard *hunk, hunk,*
scraping it clean *ping, ping*:
a hundred walls built so fast
no work-drum could keep up.

Soon outer gates stood firm,
outer gates looming up, lofty,
then inner gates stood firm,
inner gates regal and strong.
And soon the Earth Altar too,
where all our endeavors begin.

True T'ai—his righteous anger never faded,
and he never let his great renown falter.
He cleared oak and thorn-oak
and opened roads far and wide.
And the mud-faced tribes, they
fled in broken-winded panic.

Our neighbors in Yü and Jui pledged peace:
Emperor Wen always kindled native nobility.
And so we call him sovereign near and far,
sovereign we call him over before and after,
sovereign too over those who flee or return
and even over those who ridicule and resist.

Emperor Wen resides on high,
all radiance there in Heaven.
Though it's an ancient nation,
Chou's Mandate is new: Chou
the illustrious, the Celestial
Lord's Mandate well-deserved,
Emperor Wen rising and setting
on the Lord's left, on his right.

It kept on and on, his resolve,
and now his renown lasts: such
bounty granted Chou, granted
Emperor Wen's heirs, his sons and grandsons,
Wen's sons and his grandsons
through a hundred generations.
And Chou officers throughout
future generations illustrious,

through generations illustrious,
their ardent counsels reverent:
O admirable the many officers
who founded our regal nation,
nation they brought into being.
Those pillars supporting Chou,
officers stately and legion, they
brought Emperor Wen repose,

majestic and reverent Wen, O
we stand in the enduring light of his splendor,
pay Heaven's Mandate homage.
Shang sons and grandsons rose,
sons and grandsons of Shang
a hundred thousand and more,
then came our Lord's Mandate
and they succumbed to Chou,

to Chou they quickly succumbed.
Heaven's Mandate is not forever:
Shang officers diligent and pure
offered libations in our capital
then, offered libations wearing
their old caps and hatchet robes.
You ministers pure and devoted,
always remember your ancestor,

always remember your ancestor,
cultivate yourselves his integrity,
and ever worthy of the Mandate
you'll flourish in such prosperity.
Before its armies were torn apart, Shang too
was worthy of the Celestial Lord.
Look at Shang: it's a mirror. Look:
the lofty Mandate's hard to keep,

the Mandate so very hard to keep.
Don't bring ruin upon yourselves:
radiate duty and renown abroad
and ponder all that Heaven visited upon Shang.
The workings of celestial Heaven—
they have no sound and no smell,
but do as Wen did and you'll earn
the trust of ten thousand nations.

SEVENTH MOON

Seventh moon, Fire Star ebbs away,
and ninth, we share out warm robes.
By the eleventh moon, chill winds howl,
and by the twelfth, it's bitter cold, killing
cold, rough-quilt robes a blessing:
they warm us through those months.
Then, by the first moon, we ready plows,
and by the second, we're out in the fields:
I stroll out with my wife and kids,
carry offerings into southern fields,
where the field-foreman is smiling.

Seventh moon, Fire Star ebbs away,
and ninth, we share out warm robes.
Spring days bring the sun's warmth
and orioles full of song, of restless
song, as girls take their fine baskets
and go wandering on subtle paths
in search of tender mulberry leaves.
Spring days lazy and slow, they stroll
along, picking white southernwood
blossoms, a flock of heartsick girls
longing longing for their noble loves to take them home.

Seventh moon, Fire Star ebbs away,
and eighth, we cut reeds for weaving.
Silkworm moon, mulberry branches
tumble—axes and blades swinging
high up and out, they tumble down,
mulberry leaves so lush and tender.
Seventh moon, shrike is full of song,
and eighth, we spin thread again,
spin yellow-earth and azure-heaven
thread, and reds bright as the sun:
cloth to sew my noble love a robe.

Fourth moon, needle-grass ripens,
and fifth, cicadas rise into song.
Eighth moon, we harvest grains,
and tenth, autumn leaves scatter.
By the eleventh moon, we hunt
badgers, shoot foxes and wildcats:
furs to sew my noble love a coat.
Then by the twelfth, we muster
the great hunt, practice for war.
And keeping the young ourselves,
we offer an old boar to our lord.

Fifth moon, grasshoppers stretch legs and leap,
and sixth, locusts are out fluttering their wings.
Seventh moon off in the wildlands
and eighth sheltering under eaves,
ninth moon sunning at the door
and tenth sneaking inside—crickets
hide under beds, and sing and sing.
I seal up all the windows and doors,
plug holes, and smoke out the mice,
then call over to my wife and kids:
Year's end is coming, it's coming—
time we lived our lives inside again.

Sixth moon, we dine on sparrow plum and wild grape,
and seventh, savor steamed mallow greens and beans.
Eighth moon, we pick dates clean,
and tenth, harvest fields of rice,
rice we make into fine spring wine,
long life for age-tangled eyebrows.
Seventh moon, we dine on melons,
and eighth, cut bottle-gourds to dry.
Ninth moon, we gather hemp seed,
thistle-weed, ghost-eye for firewood,
and then feast the field-hands well.

Ninth moon, we turn gardens into threshing-yards,
and tenth, bundle the harvest in from our fields:
summer millet and autumn millet,
rice and hemp, beans and wheat.
Then I call over to the field-hands:
The harvest is bundled up and gathered in,
let's head inside and put the house to rights.
We gather thatch-grass by day
and tie it into sheaves by night,
then hurry it up onto the roof,
for it's soon time to sow the hundred grains again.

By the twelfth moon, we take ice-chisels out, cracking and zinging,
and by the first, we haul it in, blocks of it crowding the icehouse.
By the second moon, we rise early,
offer a lamb sacrificed with leeks.
Ninth moon, we're awed by frost,
and tenth, sweep our threshing-yard,
then we lift winecups two by two,
kill young sheep for a harvest feast,
and parading up to the public hall
raise cups of wild-ox horn for a toast:
Ten thousand lifetimes without limit!

My love's gone off to war,
who knows how long gone
or where O where.
Chickens settle into nests,
an evening sun sinks away,
oxen and sheep wander in—
but my love's gone off to war
and nothing can stop these thoughts of him.

My love's gone off to war,
not for days or even months,
and who survives such things?
Chickens settle onto perches,
an evening sun sinks away,
oxen and sheep wander home—
but my love's gone off to war
if hunger and thirst spared him that long.

NOTHING LEFT

Nothing left, O nothing left,
why not head for home?
Nothing but a lord's whimsy—
why else are we stuck here, warriors drenched in dew?

Nothing left, O nothing left,
why not head for home?
Nothing but a lord's vainglory—
why else are we stuck here, warriors all muck and mud?

IN THE WILDS THERE'S A DEAD DEER

In the wilds there's a dead deer
all wrapped in bleached reeds,
and there's a girl feeling spring
as her fair love brings her on.

In the woods there's thicket oak,
in the wilds there's a dead deer
tangled tight in bleached reeds,
and there's a girl, skin like jade.

Slowly—oh yes, slip it off slowly,
my skirt, oh yes, don't muss it,
and don't start that dog barking.

Gathering thorn-fern, bitter
thorn-fern still green, all we
talk of is home, going home.
Autumn's ending, and there's
no shelter for us, no family,
thanks to those dog-face tribes,
no time to sit, no ease for us
thanks to those dog-face tribes.

Gathering thorn-fern, bitter
thorn-fern still tender, all we
talk of is home, going home,
hearts grief-stricken, hearts
bleak and cold grief-stricken,
hunger dire and thirst worse.
Frontier war drags on and on,
no hope they'll send us home.

Gathering thorn-fern, bitter
thorn-fern now tough, all we
talk of is home, going home.
Winter's begun, and still there's
no pause in the emperor's work,
no time to sit, and no ease for
hearts stricken sick with grief.
When we left, we left for good.

What's all this lavish splendor?
It's a plum flaunting its bloom.
And that, there on the road?
It's our noble lord's war-cart,
war-cart all harnessed up to
four stallions fiery and strong.
How will we ever stop and rest?
Three battles a month we fight,

four stallions all harnessed up,
four eager and strong stallions.
A noble lord driving them on,
we little ones shielding them,
four surging stallions attack,
ivory bow-tips, sealskin quiver.
We keep watch. Those dog-face
tribes—they can strike so fast.

It was long ago when we left.
Fresh willows swayed tenderly.
And now we come back through
driving sleet tangled in snow,
the road long and deathly slow,
hunger dire and thirst worse.
Grief has so slashed our hearts
no one could fathom our cries.

A DOVE

A dove in the mulberry tree,
its young sevenfold, sevenfold.
People fine and noble-minded—
they're at one in their ways,
one in their ways, and constant,
and O their hearts intertwined.

A dove in the mulberry tree,
its young off in winter plums.
People fine and noble-minded—
their robes are made of silk,
made of silk, and quite lovely,
and O their hats of dappled fur.

A dove in the mulberry tree,
its young off in thorn-dates.
People fine and noble-minded—
their ways without any flaw,
without any flaw—they perfect
our nation border to border.

A dove in the mulberry tree,
its young off in brierwoods.
People fine and noble-minded—
perfecting our nation's people,
our nation's people—O this our
future ten thousand years long.

RATS SO FAT

Rats so fat, rats so grand
feasting on our millet—
three years your slaves
and we're nothing to you.
We're dying to leave you,
leave for that joyous land,
that joyous joyous land,
and live out our dreams.

Rats so fat, rats so grand
feasting on our wheat—
three years your slaves
and to us you're heartless.
We're dying to leave you,
leave for that joyous nation,
that joyous joyous nation,
and live out our true way.

Rats so fat, rats so grand
feasting on our sprouts—
three years your slaves
and you give nothing back.
We're dying to leave you,
leave for those joyous fields,
those joyous joyous fields,
and end all this mourning.

In the wilds there's a grass mat
damp with dew, damp and cool,
and there's you, O so beautiful:
eyes crystalline, face exquisite.
We happened upon one another
and O you gave all that I wanted.

In the wilds there's a grass mat
thick with dew, thick and cool,
and there's you, O so beautiful:
face exquisite as crystalline eyes.
We happened upon one another,
and hidden away here, we shine.

He built his hut on the stream,
that stately man so far-seeing,
sleeps alone, wakes and speaks:
a timeless bond not forgotten.

He built his hut on the mountain,
that stately man so lean-eyed,
sleeps alone, wakes and chants:
a timeless bond not surpassed.

He built his hut on the heights,
that stately man so self-possessed,
sleeps alone, wakes and abides:
a timeless bond beyond telling.

Cheereek! cheereek! ospreys cry
ospreys above their riverside nest.
That fine lady, exquisite mystery—
what a match for a worthy man.

The floating-heart's ragged leaves
drift this current here and there.
That fine lady, exquisite mystery—
waking and sleeping I sought her,

sought her but never reached her,
waking and sleeping, all devoted
longing and longing on and on,
tossing and turning side to side.

The floating-heart's ragged leaves,
from every side I gather them in,
and my fine lady, exquisite mystery—
with quiet *ch'in* song I befriend her.

The floating-heart's ragged leaves,
from every side I bring them in,
and my fine lady, exquisite mystery—
with drums and bells I delight her.

I CLIMB A HILLTOP

I climb a rock-strewn hilltop
and gaze, gaze out toward my
father, O father calling: *My child, my child dragged off to war,*
no rest all day and all night.
Take care, take care and be ever
homeward, not stuck out there.

I climb a grass-patch hilltop
and gaze, gaze out toward my
mother, O mother calling: *My little one, my little one dragged off to war,*
no sleep all day and all night.
Take care, take care and be ever
homeward, not lost out there.

I climb some windblown ridge
and gaze, gaze out toward my
brother, O brother calling: *My brother, my brother dragged off to war,*
formation all day and all night.
Take care, take care and be ever
homeward, not dead out there.

CUT AN AXE HANDLE

How do you cut an axe handle?
Without an axe it can't be done.
And how do you marry a wife?
Without a matchmaker you can't.

Cut an axe handle, axe handle—
the pattern's close at hand.
Waiting to meet her, I lay out
offerings in baskets and bowls.

WILLOWS NEAR THE EAST GATE

Willows near the east gate
grow lush and full: at dusk
we were to meet, but now
the morning star's alight.

Willows near the east gate
grow deep and dark: at dusk
we were to meet, but now
the morning star—it burns.

WE CUT GRASSES

We cut grasses, hack brush,
and plow fields so rich, rich,
thousands clearing out roots,
clearing dikes and paddies,
some lords and some elders,
some parents, some children,
some strong and some weak,
all sharing farmland meals,
men adoring beautiful wives
and wives beside their men,
men that hone ploughshares
and till these southern fields.
We sow the hundred grains,
those seeds so quick with life
they sprout in no time at all
and rise up sturdy and tall,
rise sturdy and lush and tall,
weeded over and over again
until we harvest such plenty,
such rich plenty stacked up
a thousand million and more
and more, to make deep wine
we offer lavish to ancestors
according to a hundred rites:
and its scent full of sweetness
brings our homeland splendor,
and its fragrance full of spice
brings our agèd long repose.
This isn't just this one harvest,
and this isn't just this one day:
we live all antiquity in this.

EASTERN MOUNTAINS

Sent off to eastern mountains,
to war unending and no return,
I'm finally back home again,
and the rain drizzles on and on.
Rumors about us heading home
kept me longing for the west,
for the cutting of new clothes
far from our gagged night-raids,
but green caterpillars ravaged
mulberry orchards inside out,
and I spent lonely nights alone
sleeping under those war-carts.

Sent off to eastern mountains,
to war unending and no return,
I'm finally back home again,
and the rain drizzles on and on.
Vines heavy with rife-melons
draped in tangles across eaves,
sowbugs taking over the rooms
and spiderwebs the doorways,
courtyard become a deeryard,
flicker-bugs haunting the night:
nothing so fearful in such things,
but O they bring back memories.

Sent off to eastern mountains,
to war unending and no return,
I'm finally back home again,
and the rain drizzles on and on.
A crane calls from an anthill.
A wife mourns in her rooms.
Plaster, sprinkle, and sweep—
we're back now, we're back!
Bitter melons, bitter melons
sprawling over the woodpile:
it's already been three long
years since I saw them there.

Sent off to eastern mountains,
to war unending and no return,
I'm finally back home again,
and the rain drizzles on and on.
An oriole sets out into flight,
its wings flickering, flickering,
and a lady readies for marriage,
horse dappled sorrel and bay,
her mother tying bridal sashes,
packing wedding gifts aplenty.
Her new marriage looks grand,
but what about the old one she shared with me?

TAO TE CHING

(c. 6th century B.C.E.)

LIKE *The Book of Songs*, the *Tao Te Ching* derives from the oral tradition, but its origins lie in a very different dimension of that tradition. Rather than the folk and political poetries of *The Book of Songs*, the *Tao Te Ching* grew out of an ancient wisdom tradition. The earthly humanist culture that replaced early China's otherworldly theocratic culture was shaped by a spirituality of our immediate empirical experience, and this spirituality was first articulated in the *Tao Te Ching*. The *Tao Te Ching* is generally considered more a book of philosophy than poetry, and the system of thought that it articulates came to shape the conceptual world of China's intellectuals, including poets. Its widespread influence continues today in the West, where new translations appear regularly. Indeed, in terms of the number of people and the amount of cultural production it has influenced, the *Tao Te Ching* may well be the single most influential spiritual text in human history.

According to cultural legend, the *Tao Te Ching* was written by Lao Tzu (c. 6th century B.C.E.), an elder contemporary of Confucius. It is said that they met once, and that after the meeting an awestruck Confucius exclaimed: "A dragon mounting wind and cloud to soar through the heavens—such things are beyond me. And today, meeting Lao Tzu, it was like facing a dragon." But Lao Tzu, whose name simply means "Old Master," was in fact probably constructed out of fragments gleaned from various old sage-masters active in the oral tradition during the centuries prior to the sixth century B.C.E. Perhaps Lao Tzu was the last in that line of sage-masters, and it was he who cobbled the text together. More likely it was a series of sage-editors. Whoever was responsible, they realized that the surprisingly modern sense of fragment and collage was the perfect embodiment of Lao Tzu's mysterious thought, and they managed to weave those fragments into a remarkably personal presence. If we look past the fragmentary text and oracular tone, we find a voice that is consistent and compassionate, unique, and rich with the complexities of personality.

The actual sayings that make up the book may predate Lao Tzu by several centuries, but their origins must go back to the culture's very roots, to a level early enough that a distinctively Chinese culture had yet to emerge, for the philosophy of Tao embodies a cosmology rooted in that most primal and wondrous presence: earth's mysterious generative force. In the Paleolithic period, the mystery of this generative force gave rise to such early forms of human art as vulvae etched into stone and female figures emphasizing fecundity. This art was no doubt associated with the development of humankind's earliest spiritual practices: the various forms of obeisance to a Great Mother who continuously gives birth to all creation and who, like the natural process she represents, also takes life and regenerates it in an unending cycle of life, death, and rebirth. This spiritual system appears to have been ubiquitous among Paleolithic and early Neolithic cultures, where it was integral to gynocentric and egalitarian social structures.

In the *Tao Te Ching*, this venerable generative force appears most explicitly in Lao Tzu's recurring references to the female principle, such as "mother of all beneath heaven," "nurturing mother," "valley spirit," "dark female-enigma." But its dark mystery is everywhere in the *Tao Te Ching*, for it is nothing other than *Tao* itself, the central concept in Lao Tzu's thought. It is a joy to imagine that the earliest of the sage-poets woven into Lao Tzu, those responsible for the core regions of his thought, were in fact women from the culture's proto-Chinese Paleolithic roots.

Lao Tzu's spiritual vision, his philosophical system, is described in the general introduction (pp. xxi–xxiii). But it is interesting to note here how the concept of Heaven evolved in the *Tao Te Ching*, for in it we can see the end result of the historical process of secularization described in the introduction to *The Book of Songs* (p. 5), a process that began only a century or two ago here in the West. The most primitive meaning of *heaven* is simply "sky," a meaning the word continues to have. By extension, it also came to mean "transcendence," for our most primal sense of transcendence must be the simple act of looking up into the sky. By association with the idea of transcendence and that which is beyond us, *heaven* also comes to mean "fate" or "destiny" (this is the Heaven that had been used in the early Chou to replace the personal monotheistic Shang Ti with a more generalized divine force). This complex of ideas was transformed completely when Lao Tzu added "nature" or "natural process" to the weave of meaning (in the translation, this secularization calls for the term to be translated without a capital: *heaven*). And so, *heaven* became an organic sense of destiny: things working out their fates according to their own inborn natures and in interaction with other such destinies. As such, it was almost synonymous with *Tao*. This dramatic transformation infuses the empirical cosmos with sacred dimensions. In it Heaven becomes earth, and earth Heaven. Earth's natural process is itself both our fate in life and our transcendence, for we will soon take on another of earth's fleeting forms, thereby transcending our present selves. And indeed, our truest self is all and none of earth's fleeting forms simultaneously.

The *Tao Te Ching* offers not only a spiritual vision but a social vision as well. Lao Tzu imagined a society in which a benevolent and selfless emperor is all but invisible: he simply establishes a framework within which the people live simple and contented lives as integral parts of *tzu-jan's* perennial burgeoning forth. And Lao Tzu spoke of this society as existing at some time in the distant past, in what we would now call the early Neolithic. It is an idealized version of the simple agrarian culture we see in *The Book of Songs*, and one might almost imagine the more bucolic of those folk-songs emerging from the society Lao Tzu described. But needless to say, the war and injustice that play so large a role in the *Songs* continued into Lao Tzu's time. According to legend, the agèd Lao Tzu was heartbroken by this ongoing situation. In the end, his is not so much a practical political philosophy as a political poetry, a lament that only grows more poignant as stratified societies continue to thrive on social injustice. Overwhelmed by the intractable suffering of the people, and his inability to change the situation, Lao Tzu set out into the western mountains. It is said that we have the *Tao Te Ching* only because a gatekeeper high in a mountain pass convinced Lao Tzu to leave behind his five-thousand-word scroll of wisdom before vanishing beyond the mountains into the dusk–lit mists of the far west.

I

A Way you can call Way isn't the perennial Way.
A name you can name isn't the perennial name:

the named is mother to the ten thousand things,
but the unnamed is origin to all heaven and earth.

In perennial absence you see mystery,
and in perennial presence you see appearance.
Though the two are one and the same,
once they arise, they differ in name.

One and the same they're called *dark-enigma*,
dark-enigma deep within dark-enigma,
gateway of all mystery.

2

All beneath heaven knows beauty is beauty
only because there's ugliness,
and knows good is good
only because there's evil.

Presence and absence give birth to one another,
difficult and easy complete one another,
long and short measure one another,
high and low fill one another,
music and noise harmonize one another,
before and after follow one another:

that's why a sage abides in the realm of nothing's own doing,
living out that wordless teaching.
The ten thousand things arise without beginnings there,
abide without waiting there,
come to perfection without dwelling there.

Without dwelling there: that's the one way
you'll never lose it.

3

Never bestow honors
and people won't quarrel.
Never prize rare treasures
and people won't steal.
Never flaunt alluring things
and people won't be confused.

This is how a sage governs.
Fill bellies and empty minds,
strengthen bones and weaken ambition,

always keep the people from knowing and wanting,
then those who know are those who never presume to act.

If you're nothing doing whatever you do
all things will be governed well.

6

The valley spirit never dies.

It's called *dark female-enigma*,
and the gateway of dark female-enigma
is called *the root of heaven and earth*,

gossamer so unceasing it seems real.
Use it: it's effortless.

7

Heaven goes on forever.
Earth endures forever.

There's a reason heaven and earth go on enduring forever:
their life isn't their own
so their life goes on forever.

Hence, in putting himself last
the sage puts himself first,
and in giving himself up
he preserves himself.

If you aren't free of yourself
how will you ever become yourself?

Can you let your spirit embrace primal unity
without drifting away?

Can you focus *ch'i* into such softness
you're a newborn again?

Can you polish the dark-enigma mirror
to a clarity beyond stain?

Can you make loving the people and ruling the nation
nothing's own doing?

Can you be female
opening and closing heaven's gate?

Can you fathom earth's four distances with radiant wisdom
and know nothing?

Give birth and nurture.
Give birth without possessing
and foster without dominating:

this is called *dark-enigma Integrity*.

13

Honor is a contagion deep as fear,
renown a calamity profound as self.

Why do I call honor a contagion deep as fear?
Honor always dwindles away,
so earning it fills us with fear
and losing it fills us with fear.

And why do I call renown a calamity profound as self?
We only know calamity because we have these selves.
If we didn't have selves
what calamity could touch us?

When all beneath heaven is your self in renown
you trust yourself to all beneath heaven,
and when all beneath heaven is your self in love
you dwell throughout all beneath heaven.

17

The loftiest ruler is barely known among those below.
Next comes a ruler people love and praise.
After that, one they fear,
and then one they despise.

If you don't stand sincere by your words
how sincere can the people be?
Take great care over words, treasure them,

and when the hundredfold people see your work succeed in all they do
they'll say it's just *occurrence appearing of itself*.

20

If you give up learning, troubles end.

How much difference is there
between yes and no?
And is there a difference
between lovely and ugly?

If we can't stop fearing
those things people fear,
it's pure confusion, never-ending confusion.

People all radiate such joy,
happily offering a sacrificial ox
or climbing a tower in spring.
But I go nowhere and reveal nothing
like a newborn child who has yet to smile,
aimless and worn-out
as if the way home were lost.

People all have enough and more.
But I'm abandoned and destitute,
an absolute simpleton, this mind of mine so utterly
muddled and blank.

Others are bright and clear:
I'm dark and murky.
Others are confident and effective:
I'm pensive and withdrawn,

uneasy as boundless seas
or perennial mountain winds.

People all have a purpose in life,
but I'm inept, thoroughly useless and backward.
I'll never be like other people:
I keep to the nurturing mother.

25

There was something all murky shadow,
born before heaven and earth:

O such utter silence, utter emptiness.

Isolate and changeless,
it moves everywhere without fail:

picture the mother of all beneath heaven.

I don't know its name.
I'll call it *Way*,
and if I must name it, name it *Vast*.

Vast means it's passing beyond,
passing beyond means it's gone far away,
and gone far away means it's come back.

Because Way is vast
heaven is vast,
earth is vast,
and the true emperor too is vast.
In this realm, there are four vast things,
and the true emperor is one of them.

Human abides by earth.
Earth abides by heaven.
Heaven abides by Way.
Way abides by occurrence appearing of itself.

35

Holding to the great image
all beneath heaven sets out:
sets out free of risk,
peace tranquil and vast.

Music and savory food
entice travelers to stop,
but the Way uttered forth
isn't even the thinnest of bland flavors.

Look at it: not enough to see.
Listen to it: not enough to hear.
Use it: not enough to use up.

40

Return is the movement of Way,
and yielding the method of Way.

All beneath heaven, the ten thousand things: it's all born of presence,
and presence is born of absence.

43

The weakest in all beneath heaven gallops through the strongest,
and vacant absence slips inside solid presence.

I know by this the value of nothing's own doing.

The teaching without words,
the value of nothing's own doing:
few indeed master such things.

46

When all beneath heaven abides in Way,
fast horses are kept to work the fields.
When all beneath heaven forgets Way,
warhorses are bred among the fertility altars.

What calamity is greater than no contentment,
and what flaw greater than the passion for gain?

The contentment of fathoming contentment—
there lies the contentment that endures.

48

To work at learning brings more each day.
To work at Way brings less each day,

less and still less
until you're nothing's own doing.
And when you're nothing's own doing, there's nothing you don't do.

To grasp all beneath heaven, leave it alone.
Leave it alone, that's all,
and nothing in all beneath heaven will elude you.

52

There's a source all beneath heaven shares:
call it the mother of all beneath heaven.

Once you fathom the mother
you understand the child,
and once you understand the child
you abide in the mother,

self gone, free of danger.

.   .   .

Those who know don't talk,
and those who talk don't know.

Block the senses
and close the mind,
blunt edges,
loosen tangles,
soften glare,
mingle dust:

this is called *dark-enigma union*.

It can't be embraced
and can't be ignored,
can't be enhanced
and can't be harmed,
can't be treasured
and can't be despised,

for it's the treasure of all beneath heaven.

You may govern the nation through principle
and lead armies to victory through craft,
but you win all beneath heaven through indifference.

How can I know this to be so?
Through this.

The more prohibitions rule all beneath heaven
the deeper poverty grows among the people.
The more shrewd leaders there are
the faster dark confusion fills the nation.
The more cleverness people learn
the faster strange things happen.
The faster laws and decrees are issued
the more bandits and thieves appear.

Therefore a sage says:
I do nothing
and the people transform themselves.
I cherish tranquillity
and the people rectify themselves.
I cultivate indifference
and the people enrich themselves.
I desire nothing
and the people return of themselves to uncarved simplicity.

Let nations grow smaller and smaller
and people fewer and fewer,

let weapons become rare
and superfluous,
let people feel death's gravity again
and never wander far from home.
Then boat and carriage will sit unused
and shield and sword lie unnoticed.

Let people knot ropes for notation again
and never need anything more,

let them find pleasure in their food
and beauty in their clothes,
peace in their homes
and joy in their ancestral ways.

Then people in neighboring nations will look across to each other,
their chickens and dogs calling back and forth,

and yet they'll grow old and die
without bothering to exchange visits.

THE SONGS OF CH'U

(c. 3rd century B.C.E.)

The Songs of Ch'u (*Ch'u Tz'u*) is an anthology composed of seventeen mostly large poems and sequences. Unlike *The Book of Songs*, which came from the northern heartland of Chinese civilization, *The Songs of Ch'u* comes from the quite different culture of Ch'u, a large state that occupied central China and the Yangtze valley, the southernmost territory in the Chinese cultural sphere at the time. Ch'u was part of both the Shang and Chou empires, so the intelligentsia of Ch'u was trained in the same tradition as that of the north, but it hadn't lost its connection with local shamanistic traditions that are apparent in the poems: the form of the poems is much more sweeping and energetic than in *The Book of Songs*, with long lines and exclamatory particles, and they often speak of spirit-journeys, fairies, goddesses in the clouds, and so on. This shamanistic dimension made the poems less appealing than the *Shih Ching* poems for the empirical-minded intellectual culture that followed, and no doubt less appealing to us in the modern West for the same reasons.

Authorship of *The Songs of Ch'u* is traditionally ascribed to a master-poet named Ch'ü Yüan (c. 340 to 278 B.C.E.) and several followers writing in his style. However, there are two major texts in *The Songs of Ch'u* that clearly have ancient sources in the oral tradition. The first is "The Question of Heaven," which is altogether different from the other *Ch'u Tz'u* poems.

Its form (four characters per line) is very close to that of the earlier *Shih Ching*, as is its language, and it is otherwise quite reminiscent of the *Tao Te Ching*. Like the *Tao Te Ching*, it derives from a wisdom tradition characterized by brief, enigmatic utterances. And once these utterances were cobbled together into a single text by a later editor-translator (perhaps Ch'ü Yüan himself), it had a collage feel reminiscent of the *Tao Te Ching*.

From our own cultural perspective, "The Question of Heaven" is no doubt the most interesting of the *Ch'u Tz'u* texts because of its fragmentary and enigmatic character. There have been many attempts to explain away these characteristics, as if they were some sort of textual or historical accident. But someone consciously and intentionally gathered these utterances together in this form and called the text a poem, and that makes sense because enigma (that open space in consciousness) is at the heart of Chinese poetry and spirituality. Indeed, its enigmatic and philosophical nature makes "The Question of Heaven" arguably the most deeply influential *Ch'u Tz'u* text for the Chinese tradition.

Mystery pervades every aspect of the poem. The "question" of the title points to the poem's most essential characteristic: it is a list of questions, wonderings about the universe, some of which are unanswerable. The poem's language is itself especially spare and elusive, but this is particularly true of the question words that recur repeatedly, for they are entirely ambiguous. While we must make a choice in English, the Chinese allows any or all of the possibilities: what, why, where, how, as well as various formulations using those words. For example, the first line of section 21 (see p. 62) can be translated in a great number of ways, among them:

> What [door] closes in to bring evening dark?
> How does it [heaven] close, bringing evening dark?
> Where does it close, bringing evening dark?
> Why does it close, bringing evening dark?
> How could it close, bringing evening dark?
> How could its closing bring evening dark?

So a single question might cover the range from an expression of wonder at cosmological phenomena to skepticism at human explanation of those phenomena.

The title does nothing to clarify the poem's mystery. Made up of only two words, *heaven* (*t'ien*) and *question* (*wen*), it can be interpreted to mean a number of things: "questions about heaven," "questioning heaven," "heaven's questions," "heaven asks," and so on. However these two words are read, it should be remembered that, after Lao Tzu's reformulation (see pp. 37–38), heaven meant not only "the heavens," from which follows the poem's cosmological interest, but also "natural process." From this latter meaning comes the title's most profound suggestion—that empirical reality is fundamentally enigmatic, as the T'ang Dynasty poet Tu Fu is suggesting when he speaks of the "question cloud-hidden peaks pose."

"THE NINE SONGS" is the other text originating in an ancient oral tradition. The songs appear to derive from religious festivals and rituals that must have been practiced by the people for millennia. Like the folk-poetry in *The Book of Songs*, these poems would have been collected and translated into a standard Chinese by one or more members of the intellectual class, and again this may have been Ch'ü Yüan. In "The Nine Songs" we see the Ch'u shamanistic elements in their original and fullest manifestation, as the poems render ritual invocations to various nature deities: deities of the great origin, of clouds, rivers, sun, and mountains, as well as a certain Lord of Destiny. Interestingly, the grammatical ambiguity inherent in the Chinese poetic language is exploited here to blur the distinction between shamanesses/ shamans and the deities they are invoking.

IT IS THIS shamanistic world from the folk tradition that Ch'ü Yüan shaped into a personal voice in his long autobiographical lament, "Confronting Grief" ("Li Sao"). This may be considered the moment when self-conscious individual authorship emerged in the Chinese poetic tradition, and even here we see this individual voice being forged from elements of the anonymous oral tradition. From this point on, self-conscious individual poets proliferated in the intellectual class.

Although he is generally considered the first major Chinese poet who can be historically confirmed, little is known about Ch'ü Yüan beyond the legend that he was an adviser of the Ch'u ruler, that he acted with integrity in wisely criticizing the ruler's misguided policies, was exiled, grieved over the damage done to his country by the ruler's actions, and finally drowned himself in the Flood-Gauze (Mi-lo) River as an act of protest. Early legend held that it was during his wandering exile that Ch'ü Yüan wrote *The Question of Heaven* in response to murals he found on temple walls, and "The Nine Songs" in response to rituals and festivals he witnessed in remote villages. In any case, Ch'ü Yüan's life story is the narrative outline of "Confronting Grief." Often considered the most important poem of the collection, "Confronting Grief" is in fact very long and rather tedious (this translation creates a much shortened version of the original). Its influence lay primarily in its basic narrative elements. Helping the emperor care for the people was the only proper place for an intellectual in the Chinese social order, and these intellectuals very often found themselves out of favor and exiled, so they saw in the Ch'ü Yüan story a kind of quasi-mythological archetype for their own cultural situation and their own lives. For these readers, "Confronting Grief" was perhaps less a self-pitying lament than a protest against the government's corrupt incompetence and the tragic impact it had on the people.

THE QUESTION OF HEAVEN

1

From the far origin of all antiquity,
who hands the story down to us?

2

Before heaven and earth take shape,
how do you delve into what's there?

3

When light and dark are still a blur,
who can see through to their source?

4

When it's altogether primal chaos,
how do you see the shape of things?

5

Blazing radiance and utter darkness
and nothing more: how did it happen?

6

And when *yin* and *yang* first gave birth—
what was rooted, and what transformed?

7

Nine celestial compass-points arrayed,
calibrated perfectly and measured out

8

just so—how was heaven ever made,
how, in the beginning, set into motion?

9

How could its vast turning be tethered?
And how was its axle-pole lofted there?

10

How were its eight pillars put in place,
and why is the southeast tilting down?

11

The boundaries of its nine regions—
how could they join, how lead away?

12

And all their meanders back and forth,
who knows how many there might be?

13

What makes heaven entire and whole?
And how is it split into twelve palaces?

14

How are sun and moon joined together?
And how are scattered stars patterned?

15

Rising from the depths of Boiling Abyss,
returning to rest in the Gulf of Obscurity,

16

from morning light on to evening dark:
the sun's journey lasts how many miles?

17

Then night's radiant one—by what power
can it die out and soon come back to life,

18

a bright moon? And what does it gain
from a rabbit inside its belly gazing out?

19

Star Mother never mated—so how is it
she gave birth to nine star-children?

20

Where does great Elder Wind-Star live?
And where do warm *ch'i*-breezes dwell?

21

What closes in to bring evening dark?
What opens out to bring morning light?

22

Before the stars announcing spring rise,
how is Splendor-Spirit sun hidden away?

1 Great-Unity, Sovereign of the East

Auspicious the day,
            the array of stars—
we offer in reverence
            joy to our Sovereign on high.
I hold a long-sword,
            its haft of jade,
surging waist-jewels
            clittering and calling.
At the jeweled mat
            with its jade pins,
let us raise fragrant
            handfuls of flowers,
savory meats laid out
            on beds of orchid,
cinnamon wines
            and pepper broth.
Raise the sticks,
            let the drums sing
and the tranquil chant
            begin, slow and distant,
pipes and strings surging
            swelling into song.
The spirit-one comes,
            all quiet assurance
in graceful gowns, her
            fragrance filling the hall,
the five notes weaving
            together, enthralling,
and our Sovereign delights,
            delights in rich ease.

Bathed in orchid water,
                rinsed in fragrant scents
and dressed in many-colored
                splendor, like blossoms,
the spirit-one meanders,
                twisting and turning,
all radiance ablaze,
                all radiance unceasing,
then she settles to rest
                here in Lifelong Shrine,
her brilliance rivaling
                great sun and moon.
With teams of dragons
                and robes of a god,
she soars up, wandering
                skies far and wide.
Soon our Spirit-Sovereign
                descends in majesty,
whirls back skyward
                and away into clouds,
gazing out across northern
                borders and beyond,
crossing the four seas,
                drifting without bound.
Thinking of our Cloud Lord
                we whisper far-flung sighs,
our hearts full of worry
                and longing, and longing.

7 Lord of the East

Dawn-light flaring
        below the east horizon,
lighting up the threshold,
        the Solar-Perch Tree,
I rouse my team of dragons,
        set them a serene pace,
and night brightens into
        morning's clear brilliance.
Then they mount thunder,
        my chariot sailing behind,
trailing out pennants
        and streamers of cloud,
and whispering a far-flung sigh,
        I begin my slow ascent,
uncertain and hesitant,
        looking back with longing.
Exquisite music and dance
        are delighting people so,
putting them at such ease
        they forget to go home,
and strings are singing
        through drumbeat rhythms,
majestic chime-bells
        shaking the very bell-stands
as flute-song surges
        and cluster-pipes call out.
The spirit-one, wondrous
        guardian so wise and lovely—
she darts and glides
        on kingfisher wingbeats,
offering up song,
        chants gracing her dance.

Echoing calendar-pipes,
> sharing their open rhythm,
that spirit-one—she arrives,
> hiding my sunlight away
behind her azure tunic of cloud,
> her silvered rainbow-skirts.
Then I raise a long arrow,
> shoot down the Wolf Star,
and descend, bow in hand,
> back into the waters of night.
I tip the Northern Dipper,
> pour out cinnamon wine,
and seizing my reins, soar
> on through the darkest
heights of shadowy night,
> sailing back into the east.

9 The Mountain Spirit

A sense of someone there
           in the mountain hollows,
dressed in fig-vine robes
           and sash of wisteria,
her eyes gazing out,
           her smile entrancing:
she longs for me, comes
           all exquisite mystery
astride a crimson leopard
           led by striped cougars,
her magnolia carriage trailing
           pennants of braided cinnamon.
Dressed in rock-orchids
           and sash of asarum flowers,
I pick fragrant wildflowers,
           offer them to her for love.
I live amid bamboo, its recluse
           quiet, never a glimpse of sky,
and the road's full of peril.
           I've come alone, and late,
but she reveals herself
           alone on a mountaintop
summit, up above clouds
           rolling and billowing thick
depths of shadow, dark
           turning broad daylight dark,
bringing a gusty east wind
           and divine spirit-rains.
I linger long with my spirit-
           beauty, all return forgotten,

for once autumn ends,
              who'll clothe me in blossom?
I'll pick triple-bloom
              out among mountain peaks,
among scree-fields of rock,
              vines sprawling everywhere,
thinking of my lost love, all
              sorrow, all return forgotten.
She longs for me,
              but time is so short, so short.
Someone of the mountains,
              that sense of asarum scents
drinking from rocky springs
              shaded by pine and cypress,
she longs for me,
              but holds back, hesitant:
thunder rumbles and roams,
              rain clouds dark and deep;
gibbons wail on and on,
              and cries break out all night
as wind howls and howls,
              and hissing trees moan.
This longing for my lost love:
              nothing comes of it but grief.

Blood descendant of the celestial lord Solaris,
        my departed father's name Elder-Constance,
I was born on the day of Solaris's child, the fire god,
        with Regent's stars in the prime notch of spring,

and judging the portents of my birth, my father
        divined auspicious names and bestowed them:
the familiar name he found was Resolute Exemplar,
        and for my formal name, he chose Divine Balance.

I possessed by birth this many-faceted inner beauty,
        and perfecting it steadily, I cultivated my talents,
dressing myself in river sage and rare angelica,
        then braiding autumn orchids together for a sash,

and hurrying on here and there, before and after,
        I searched into the ways of ancient sage emperors,
but my fragrant lord didn't see my inner thoughts,
        let poisonous words turn him to wild anger instead

I know well that forthright candor is an affliction,
        but I just couldn't bear to cast integrity aside.
I wear the open honesty of ancient sages
        and ignore the tawdry fashions filling this world:

though out of step with people these days, I'm happy
        following the pattern P'eng Hsien handed down.
Sighs and laments on and on, wiping away tears,
        I mourned how much grief the people endure.

Guided by a love for justice and beauty, I offered
        honesty one morning, and by night was exiled,
but still, in exile, I weave a sash of cluster-orchid,
        braid it longer with strands of scent-orchid,

for this is my pure delight of heart and mind,
>   and though I die nine deaths for it, I'll have no regrets.
I kneel on a mat and swear a farewell oath,
>   knowing well my role in this was true and clear,

then harnessing four jade dragons to a rainbow phoenix,
>   I soar away, riding up on wild billows of wind.
I set out one morning from Emperor Shun's ancient tomb,
>   reach K'un-lun Mountain's divine gardens by night,

water my team of dragons at the celestial lake of stars,
>   and for rest, tie their reins to the great Solar-Perch Tree.
I send the moon's charioteer ahead to lead the way,
>   call the wind lord to follow, sweeping us along.

Gale-storms gather together and billow apart,
>   trailing clouds and rainbows that come welcoming us,
seething together and roiling back asunder,
>   swirling up and tumbling away all confusion.

Before the glorious bloom of springtime scatters,
>   I'll go searching for a woman who will share it.
I send the rain lord soaring on the clouds
>   to find the dwelling place of the Lo River goddess,

and offering my sash as allegiance to the words,
>   I send the snake-goddess of marriage to make the offer.
After much seething together and roiling back asunder,
>   she grows capricious and commanding, so sure of herself,

returns to sleep on K'un-lun's Thorough-Stone Peak,
>   mornings rinsing her hair in Flood-Tray Creek,
hiding her beauty away behind arrogant disdain,
>   wandering through her days in wanton pleasure.

Though exquisitely beautiful, she has no sense of ritual,
                      so I forget her, turn away to continue my search:
wanting to roam distances, bereft of destination, I set out
                      drifting and soaring, wandering boundless and free.

If Shao K'ang still hasn't married them,
                      the lord of Yü's two elegant daughters remain,
but the spokesman is weak and the matchmaker dull,
                      and I fear the proposition won't be strong enough,

for this mud-ridden world envies the wise and worthy,
                      delights in obscuring beauty and praising depravity,
so I harness flying dragons, a team of them,
                      to a carriage all swirling constellations of jasper,

for how can minds in opposition be joined together?
                      Setting out into distances far off and free of them,
I veer around on a course for majestic K'un-lun peaks,
                      soaring on and ever on, meandering everywhere,

scattering ranges of rainbow cloud shrouded in shadow,
                      jade phoenix-bells moaning echoes through the sky.
My team of eight dragons writhing and rippling,
                      trailing out pennants and streamers of cloud,

I soar up into the awesome splendor of the heavens.
                      But then, looking down, I see my old homeland.
Suddenly my attendants are grieving, my dragon-team longing,
                      coiling around and gazing back, refusing to go further.

Nothing left! Nothing left!
No one in all the land knows the truth of who I am,
                      so why go on longing for that nation of mine?
With no one to join in building a government of beauty,
                      I'll follow old P'eng Hsien to his watery dwelling-place.

LATER FOLK-SONG COLLECTIONS

(c. 2nd century B.C.E. to 4th century C.E.)

IN SPITE OF Ch'ü Yüan and the beginning of self-conscious individual authorship, the most historically interesting work remained in the oral tradition. Identifiable individual poets proliferated during this period, but none achieved the commanding stature of Ch'ü Yüan and the major poets of the mainstream tradition that would begin five hundred years later. They were generally writing poems imitating the style of Ch'ü Yüan— variations of folk-songs that generally lacked the vitality and energy of the originals or early unconvincing attempts at the personal poetry that came to typify the mainstream tradition.

The oral folk-song tradition first collected in *The Book of Songs* had remained vital, of course, but it was not collected and preserved again for nearly five hundred years. In about 114 B.C.E., Emperor Wu of the Han Dynasty, taking *The Book of Songs* as his model, established a governmental department whose task it was to collect folk-songs from the countryside: the Music Bureau (*Yüeh-fu*). The Music Bureau was in operation until 6 B.C.E. and during that century collected a large number of folk-songs, though most have since been lost. As with *The Book of Songs*, the emperor's intent was to gauge the sentiments of the people in order to rule more effectively.

After the Music Bureau was discontinued, the term *yüeh-fu* continued to be used for any anonymous folk-song, and also for poems in that style by men of the lettered class writing in the voices of common people or of women. Many of the minor poets in these transitional centuries wrote in the *yüeh-fu* mode, and as we will see, there was a major revival of this kind of writing during the T'ang Dynasty, in the work of such poets as Li Po, Tu Fu, and Po Chü-i. One aspect of the transition to self-conscious individual authorship can be seen in the folk-songs of this era, for we see them taking on a regular five-character line and more literary polish, a process that probably originated when translators of folk-songs began to assert their own aesthetic impulses in their translations.

This transitional process culminated in "Nineteen Ancient-Style Poems" (c. 1st to 2nd centuries C.E.), for although the poems are anonymous in authorship and generally continue themes from the folk-song tradition, they lack the intensity of immediate experience that is found in true folk-songs. They also seem more crafted and polished. This literary craftsmanship is especially apparent in the regular five-character line. "Nineteen Ancient-Style Poems" is the first instance of this form (known as *shih*), which became the standard form for the mainstream tradition that began to take shape in the centuries that followed. This represents one more example of how the written tradition grew out of the folk tradition.

THE LADY MIDNIGHT collection is attributed in literary legend to a courtesan named Lady Midnight (Tzu Yeh). Here again we find ourselves in that shadowy realm between the anonymous oral tradition and individual authorship, for in reality this is probably a later gathering from a strain of the anonymous oral tradition that we first saw in *The Book of Songs*: love songs, often of an erotic nature. As such, they introduce the poetic world to which women were generally limited by the misogynistic social structures of Chinese culture. (For an account of women's poetry in ancient China, see p. 451.)

Although still considered *yüeh-fu*, the 117 poems of the Lady Midnight collection are all in the same form: quatrains employing a regular five-character line. This is yet another example of the written tradition growing out of the folk tradition—for in the centuries that followed, this quatrain form (a particular type of *shih* known as *chüeh-chu*) was widely adopted by poets of the intelligentsia. By the T'ang Dynasty, it had developed into a major vehicle of expression for poets who, influenced by Ch'an Buddhism, were drawn to especially distilled forms of poetic expression, Meng Hao-jan (p. 147) and Wang Wei (p. 157) being the first great poets working in this mode.

MUSIC-BUREAU FOLK-SONGS

(c. 2nd to 1st centuries B.C.E.)

EARTH-DRUMMING SONG

When the sun's up we work,
and when it's down we rest.

We dig wells and there's drink,
plow fields and there's food.

An emperor? What's his awesome power to us?

UNTITLED

Give birth to a boy—don't give him a care.
Give birth to a girl—feed her meat dainties.

Haven't you seen, beneath the Great Wall,
all those bleached bones propped together?

THEY DRAGGED ME OFF AT FIFTEEN TO WAR

When brush-fire burns in wild land,
wild ducks set out into depths of sky,

and when young men marry widows,
girls wail with such killing laughter.

Trees on the highest mountain peaks:
loud wind scatters their leaves away,

and leaves a thousand long miles gone,
how will they ever come back home?

They dragged me off at fifteen to war.
Now I'm eighty going back. On the road

I meet someone from my old village, ask
Who's there still, at home? He just says

Look out over there, that's your home:
pine and cypress, swollen gravemounds.

Rabbits come scampering into the house,
pheasants on rafters scatter into flight,

and our courtyard's full of wild grains,
the well lost in wild tangles of mallow.

I thresh some grain and steam it up,
pick mallow and simmer it into broth,

but when grain and broth seem ready
I still don't know who I'll feed with it.

I wander out the gate and stand there,
gazing east, tears staining these robes.

BY HEAVEN ABOVE

By heaven above
I want us together always, heart and mind, my love,
want it destiny on and on, without breach or fail.

Not till mountains have no peaks
and rivers run dry,
not till thunder fills winter days
and summer rains turn to snow,
not till all heaven and earth blur
together, my love, will I part from you.

WE FOUGHT SOUTH OF THE WALL

We fought south of the wall
and died north of the city,
died in wild lands, bodies left unburied, food for crows,

crows—tell them this for us:
We were brave, all of us who
died in wild lands, our bodies just left out there, unburied.
Don't worry. Now our flesh is rotting, we can't avoid your beaks.

Deep waters flow on and on,
rushes and reeds full of shadow.

We owl-riders fought to the death, and now
our horses wander—tired and lost and crying out.

Guardhouses on bridges:
people can't go north
and can't go south.

If no one brings in the millet, how will you eat, great lord?
We wanted to be loyal subjects, but how can we now?

I think of you, my fine subjects,
honestly I do. How could I not think of you—
how you set out for war one morning
and never again returned at night.

GARLIC DEW

Dew on garlic
melts easily away,

melts easily away, dew in morning sun, and falls again another day.
But when you die, it's once and for all, and never again to return.

VILLAGE OF WEEDS

This village of weeds—whose home can it be?
Crowds of spirits thronged with sage and fool alike.

O great Elder-Spirit of the Dead, why hurry us away like this?
It's your destiny: no one pauses, no one lingers a moment.

WATERING HORSES AT A SPRING BENEATH THE GREAT WALL

Riverside grass so lavish and azure-green,
those distant roads, I'm longing in gossamer

skeins unceasing, distant roads I can't bear
longing, longing. He's in midnight dreams,

in dreams, him so close beside me, suddenly
sensing we're away in some strange village,

strange village in a strange far-off place,
then I'm tossing and turning without him.

Dead mulberries understand heaven's wind,
and lakewater understands heaven's cold.

Inside our gate, women were all fussing over
themselves, silent, afraid of talking to me,

then finally a traveler from distant lands
appeared, bringing a treasure, a love-carp.

I called the children, let them open it up,
and inside was a letter-scroll, a foot of silk.

I knelt long, knelt reading that foot of silk,
that treasure—but what could it really say?

It began saying we must eat well, and more,
and ended saying he'll long for us forever.

Sun emerges and sinks away without cease,
living its lifetime of seasons, nothing like humankind:

its spring isn't our spring,
its summer isn't our summer,
its autumn isn't our autumn,
its winter isn't our winter.

Drifting back to rest in its lake of four seas,
gazing everywhere—what shall we call such a blessing?

All our joy is
joy in its six dragons:
their motion moves
hearts the same way.

Why not lead that yellow splendor right down here among us?

EAST GATE

He left their east gate
for war without return,
and then coming back
home tore him apart:

there wasn't a cup of rice in the bin,
and turning he saw the clothes-rack standing empty.
So he set out through the gate again, sword in hand,
wife and kids tugging at his robe, wailing.

Other families long for wealth and renown,
but I'm a simple wife: I just want to share a bowl of rice with you.
It's a blessing out of boundless heaven above
that here below we have these children, these hungry chicks.
You're doing wrong now. You are.

Let me go! I'm leaving,
and you're just slowing me down!
My hair's already white, and I'm not going to live out my life like this!

UNTITLED

I was up gathering lovage. Coming down
off the mountain, I met my old husband.

I bowed deep, then asked: *Your new wife—*
how is she for you, old husband of mine?

My new wife—her words sing, they do,
but she can't match my old wife's grace,

and for beauty, there's no comparison.
There's no comparing loom-work either.

When a new wife came through the gate,
the old one fled from her rooms. Now

my new wife weaves silk double-thread
where the old one wove it plain-cloth:

every day a single strip of double-thread
finery replaces fifty feet of plain-cloth.

Laying double-thread beside plain-cloth,
it's clear the new's nothing like the old.

NINETEEN ANCIENT-STYLE POEMS

(c. 1st to 2nd centuries C.E.)

1

Traveling and traveling on and on,
you opened a lifetime of separation:

ten thousand miles and more apart,
each living out our own edge of sky,

the road long and hard, no knowing
when I'll ever see your face again.

A northern horse in northern winds
and a southern bird in southern trees:

the day we parted is growing distant,
my robe and sash looser every day.

Drifting clouds shroud the bright sun,
you wandering without looking back,

and all this longing has made me old,
year-end moons suddenly gone dark.

I can't tell you how abandoned I feel,
but I'm eating well, building strength.

Far, far off the Ox–Herd star drifts.
And the Star River's radiant lady—

she weaves shadow-and-light finery, ⌐
her shuttle whispering, whispering

all day long. She's never finished.
Her tears fall, scattering like rain.

Star River's a crystalline shallows,
so thin keeping them apart, a mere

wisp of water brimming, brimming.
They gaze and gaze, and say nothing.

Turning the team to begin my long
road vast and distant, I gaze through

four directions boundless and beyond,
wind tearing at the hundred grasses,

everything new and strange. What
can slow the rush of age, the passing

seasons of flourish and perish? Still
here struggling to succeed: it's bitter,

and we're not made of metal or stone:
old age won't last. Suddenly, the great

transformation of things carries us
away, and bright legacy's the jewel.

14

Those who went vanish ever further,
and those to come draw ever nearer.

Leaving the city gate, I gaze ahead,
and it's all mounds and tombs, those

ancient graves now plowed fieldland,
pine and cypress hacked for firewood,

and poplars tangled in wind's grief,
its whispered laments that can kill.

I long to set out for my old village, my
old home, but the road won't go there.

18

A traveler came from far away,
gave me a roll of delicate silk:

ten thousand long miles gone
and my dear one's still in love.

The pattern's all paired ducks.
I piece them into a *revels* quilt,

stuff it with ceaseless longing,
tuck edges and knot them tight.

If you throw glue into varnish,
who can part them ever again?

Lady Midnight Songs of the Four Seasons

(c. 4th century c.e.)

1 Spring

Tunic gathered loose and sash untied,
I put on eyebrows and go to a window.

A gauze skirt's grace is light and airy:
if it slips open, blame a spring breeze.

2

Radiant winds pour through moonrise.
Forests unfurl a brocade of blossoms.

Under a spring moon, we play at love,
trailing gauze sleeves deep in shadow.

3

Spring forests so seductive in bloom,
spring birds such grief, and spring

winds bring all that and yes, much
more breezing my gauze robes open.

4

Tempted by blossoms, a spring moon,
I wander streets and lanes, and smile.

So many I meet ache to get me naked.
Too bad they don't think they should.

5 Summer

How many nights since I put up my hair?
Long and silky, it spills over my shoulders

and sprawls beautifully across his knees.
There's nowhere its sympathies won't go.

6

Thinking of that wild thirst of love,
head over heels, nothing left undone,

I let blinds down again. Who knows
our abandon through thick and thin?

7

Up this high, a bedroom needs no walls.
It welcomes winds from every direction,

tender breezes slipping my gauze robe
wide open, teasing my lips into a smile.

8

Joy fades by early spring. And my sorrow
grows colder still with autumn and winter.

But playing at love these warm and moonlit
summer nights, we tangle so well together.

9

The day's warm, and quiet. Not a breeze.
Summer clouds build. Dusk thins. Here,

under thick leaves, hands lead hands to
a drifting gourd sunk into scarlet plum.

10 *Autumn*

I can't sleep. The night's long and
the bright moon so radiant, radiant.

Thinking I hear his scattered voice,
I call back, answering empty skies.

11

Autumn's chill infuses crystalline wind.
A moon drifts heaven's exquisite depths,

radiant. Lovely women ready winter robes,
ten thousand sticks beating frozen stone.

12

Crystalline dew freezes jade-pure.
Past midnight, an icy wind rises.

Why go home to bed? All love and
allure, I wander radiant moonlight.

13

Wild geese set out for their southlands,
and city-bred swallows wing northward.

If you've lost your way, my far-off love,
just follow the autumn wind back home.

14

Beginnings of spring come to mind,
and I realize autumn's already over.

Chasing after the very heart of joy,
I missed the year's splendor passing.

15

Autumn's cold, the window wide open.
A tilted moon fills the room with light.

It's midnight, and nothing need be said:
just two smiles behind a gauze curtain.

16

Autumn night at the open window
makes bed-curtains float and sway.

I gaze up at the bright moon, send
such love a thousand radiant miles.

17

You left in early spring, and I long
to have you back by autumn's end.

How I hate this river flowing east:
all year, never a care for the west.

18 *Winter*

It's year's end. Skies are ice-cold.
North wind dances snow into flight.

My dream love's here beneath quilts,
and the heat of a long hot summer.

.

19

North wind scattering sleet and rain,
ice on the green lake's lotus shallows:

it's time radiant hands played clear
through a game of *first-snow falling*.

20

Where could such kindred hearts join?
On the west ridge, beneath that cypress,

sheltered by four walls of dazzling light.
There, bitter frost will kill us with cold.

21

White snow drifts along *yin* ridgelines.
Cinnabar blossoms blaze in *yang* forests.

Who needs flute and string? Sounds of
rivers and mountains sing so clear here.

22

Still longing for deep gold-orchid love?
Take a look at forests of pine and cypress,

killing frosts caught up in the treetops.
No other heart in all this year-end cold.

First Masters:
The Mainstream Begins

(4th to 5th centuries C.E.)

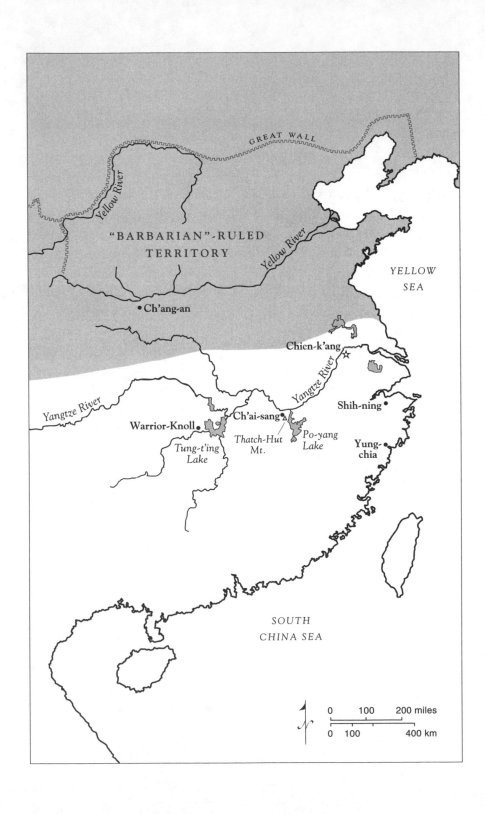

GREAT WALL

Yellow River

Yellow River

"BARBARIAN"-RULED
TERRITORY

• Ch'ang-an

YELLOW
SEA

Chien-k'ang

Yangtze River

Shih-ning •

Yangtze River

Warrior-Knoll •

Ch'ai-sang •

Thatch-Hut
Mt.

Po-yang
Lake

Yung-
chia •

Tung-t'ing
Lake

SOUTH
CHINA SEA

0   100   200 miles

0   100   400 km

N

SLOWLY, AS THE centuries passed, poets of the lettered class moved away from poetry modeled after the two styles that had dominated the oral tradition: folk-songs and shamanistic *Ch'u Tz'u* songs. China's poets began to embrace a poetic world of their own immediate concerns. A number of important poets contributed to this gradual transformation, which culminated in the 4th and 5th centuries C.E. with the appearance of T'ao Ch'ien and Hsieh Ling-yün.

Northern China had recently been lost to foreign invaders, forcing China's artist-intellectuals to immigrate with the government into the southeast. This was the first time their cultural homeland in the north had been overrun, and seeing Chinese culture under siege by the foreigners, the intellectual class felt a historical imperative to cultivate their native tradition and renew it. The resulting artistic accomplishments were revolutionary.

Most of these epoch-making achievements can be seen as part of a new engagement with wilderness that arose among Chinese artist-intellectuals for several reasons: they were enthralled by the new landscape of serenely beautiful mountains; an especially perilous and corrupt political culture drove many of them to retire into the mountains rather than risk the traditional career of public service; a recent revival of Taoist thought had become widely influential, and its transformation of recently imported Indian Buddhism into China's own Ch'an Buddhism was beginning.

The innovations resulting from these influences were wide-ranging. The origins of Chinese landscape (rivers-and-mountains) painting can be traced to this time, probably beginning as illustrations for rivers-and-mountains poetry. Calligraphy was transformed by the organic spontaneity of Wang Hsi-chih, often called the greatest of Chinese calligraphers, and his equally remarkable son, Wang Hsien-chih. And developments in the field of poetry were perhaps even more dramatic, for it is in the work of T'ao Ch'ien and Hsieh Ling-yün that the mainstream tradition really begins.

SU HUI

(4th century C.E.)

REMARKABLY, GIVEN THE misogynistic structures governing the culture, T'ao Ch'ien and Hsieh Ling-yün were preceded by Su Hui, a female poet whose work is so singular that it stands almost outside the tradition. Roughly contemporaneous with the anonymous Lady Midnight collection (p. 89), Su Hui is the earliest major female figure that survives in the written tradition. She is said to have created thousands of literary compositions, but as was typical for women poets in ancient China, they were virtually all lost. Only her *Star Gauge* (*Hsüan-chi Tu*: literally "armillary-sphere map") survived. *Star Gauge* was never included in the canon of great Chinese poetry, no doubt because its creator and its concerns were female, and its form so bizarre. In fact, the text was effectively lost for several centuries and has only recently been reconstructed.

Though the poem itself was generally neglected, the story of its composition is legendary, appearing over the centuries in poems, novels, and plays. Su Hui was married to a major government official, and they were happy together for a time. But then her husband took a concubine, and though it was quite normal for such men to have "second wives," Su Hui was furious. Soon thereafter, he was transferred to a post far away. Su Hui refused to go with him and his lover, so he left with the other woman and broke off all communication with Su Hui. In her grief, she composed *Star*

Gauge to express her love and to lure her husband back. When he read the poem, Su Hui's husband sent the concubine away and rejoined Su Hui, their love deeper than ever.

The pleasures and disappointments of romance dominated women's poetry in the folk tradition, beginning with the *Shih Ching*, and it continued to be the realm allowed women poets in China's sexist literary culture. This was a reflection of the place women occupied in the intellectual culture, that of wives and companions to males who controlled the culture as intellectuals and government officials. Indeed, from within the dominant male literary sphere, women's poetry always remained a kind of "folk-poetry" that was both outside of and inferior to the mainstream tradition.

Although her subject matter was not new, nothing in the tradition before or after suggests such a possibility as Su Hui's altogether unique and extraordinary treatment of that subject matter. The text she composed depends upon the fact that, unlike Western languages, Chinese can be read in any direction, not only because of the nature of Chinese characters but also because characters can operate as any part of speech, depending on context. This fact gave rise to a genre in Chinese poetry of "reversible poems" (*hui-wen shih*), poems that can be read forward (from top right down) or in reverse. Su Hui's text is the grandest example of this genre. It is a grid of twenty-nine characters by twenty-nine characters, which goes far beyond the simple "reversible" poem, for it allows readings in all directions: horizontal, vertical, and diagonal. *Star Gauge* was originally embroidered in five colors, thereby mapping out the poem's complex structure. The colors divide the poem into a number of regions, each of which has a set of rules that tell us how to read the text in that region.

Compounding this formal complexity is the fact that the text itself is often highly ambiguous, making it difficult to decipher a particular meaning from a line. Indeed, Su Hui was proud of the difficulty presented by this immense composition, proud that the poem was all but incomprehensible—and in this complexity is an assertion of her own worth and nobility against the male-dominated social and literary structures that were so oppressive to women. Hence, the poem itself defies the reductive legend of its composition: it is clear that the poem is much more than a woman's plea for her husband's return. It is a complex philosophical statement, as well as an assertion of her own dignity and even superiority to the men who dominated her world.

Star Gauge reads like a vast collage, lines juxtaposed almost randomly, a compositional strategy that would not reappear, even in conventional poetic format, until Li Shang-yin five hundred years later, and not in the West until the twentieth century. The poem is especially striking and original in that it is not only a literary text but a piece of visual art as well, a visual object constructed of text, which is another strategy that has only recently been explored in the West. In this case, the visual object is the very image of obsession. Below is a black-and-white facsimile of the lost original:

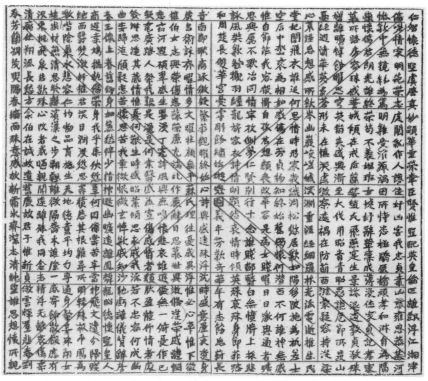

Reconstruction © Michèle Métail

The armature of the poem (between the parallel lines in this reproduction) is made up of seven-character segments, all of which can be read in either direction, and it is the structural feature that relates the poem to the armillary sphere (the *hsüan-chi* of the poem's title), a fairly recent and still exciting invention in Su Hui's time. An instrument used to gauge the movements of the stars, the armillary sphere is made up of a number of concentric rings of metal, and these rings correspond to the important meridians of the celestial sphere. The meridians of the poem's armature correspond to these rings of the armillary sphere. The seven-character segments of the armature can be read in any order, so long as the reader follows the seven-character quatrain form. That is, at the end of each seven-character segment, which corresponds to a poetic line, you encounter a junction of meridians and can choose which direction to go. You can begin anywhere, and the poem ends after four lines have been chosen. This structure generates 2,848 possible poems. Here is another remarkable and very contemporary feature of this poem: the reader creates each poem by choosing where to go at the different junctions.

This feature continues in the other color regions, the text blocks in the squares within the armature that make up the interior of the poem. Each color region is read according to slightly different patterns. The top right corner, for example, is made up of three-character lines, and the poem length is either six or twelve lines. How it is read is limited only by the requirement that applies to all areas of the poem: the second line of every couplet must rhyme. Rhyme words are placed in this six-character-by-six-character grid so that the readings are all completely strange, and indeed very little of *Star Gauge* is read in the traditional Chinese fashion, from the top right down. For instance, one translation of this text block reads from top left horizontally to the right, then drops down a line and reads horizontally to the left, and continues snaking down the grid to end at the bottom right. Another possibility is the exact reverse of that reading. Indeed, this is how Su Hui herself described the text: "It lingers aimlessly, twisting and turning." There are at least 34 possible poems in this one text block. And the entire poem, armature and text blocks, contains something over 3,000 poems!

It is this awesome formal structure itself that is the poem's most immediate and complex statement. The poem opens a kind of meditative space in which thoughts appear out of emptiness and disappear back into that emptiness, and it produces the feel of profound psychological depths by its very form: many thoughts/poems coexisting simultaneously, blurring together as the mind follows its obsessions through their repeating variations. Indeed, this may in the end be the poem's primary subject matter: obsession.

In Taoist cosmology, this relentless transformation reflects the bedrock Taoist principle that change is the fundamental law ruling the cosmos. The source of all change is a pregnant emptiness (*wu*: see general introduction p. xxii) from which all things appear and into which they disappear, and this too is present in the poem: at the center of the grid is the character *hsin* (see Key Terms), meaning both "heart" and "mind," which was apparently left out of many reproductions of the text because, in Taoist and Buddhist thought, *hsin* is most fundamentally empty. *Hsin* also denotes Polaris. The seat of thought and emotion is therefore also the polestar around which the stars move.

By placing our inner psychology within the space of the sky, the poem enacts a different account of the human interior. In this account, the human heart-mind is an integral part of the starry universe, its complex and finally unfathomable movements of thought and feeling swirling through the grand movements of the stars.

The translation of *Star Gauge*, with its simultaneity and graphic layout, cannot be reproduced in traditional book format. A printable version is available in color at fsgbooks.com/classicalchinesepoetry.

T'AO CH'IEN

(365 to 427)

T'AO CH'IEN (T'ao Yüan-ming) was the first writer to make a fully achieved poetry of his natural voice and immediate experience, thereby creating the personal lyricism that became the hallmark of Chinese poetry. So T'ao Ch'ien effectively stands at the head of the great Chinese poetic tradition like a revered grandfather: profoundly wise, self-possessed, quiet, comforting.

Born into the educated aristocracy, T'ao was expected to take his proper place in the Confucian order by serving in the government. Accordingly, he held a number of government positions. But he had little patience for the constraints of official life, and little interest in its superficial rewards, so he finally broke free and returned to the life of a recluse-farmer on the family farm at his ancestral village of Ch'ai-sang (Mulberry-Bramble), just northwest of the famous Thatch-Hut (Lu) Mountain (see note to p. 141). It should be noted, however, that this was not a romantic return to the bucolic but the choice of a life in which the spiritual ecology of *tzu-jan* ("occurrence appearing of itself"; see Key Terms) is the very texture of everyday experience, as he says at the end of the first section in his "Home Again Among Fields and Gardens" (p. 113), one of several poems about quitting his job and returning home.

That outline of T'ao Ch'ien's life became a central myth in the Chinese tradition: artist-intellectuals over millennia admired and imitated the way T'ao lived out his life as a recluse, though it meant enduring considerable poverty and hardship (one poem tells of him going into a village to beg for food). And indeed, T'ao's commitment to the recluse life went so deep that he chose *Ch'ien* ("concealed," "hidden," and so "recluse") as his literary name: Recluse T'ao.

This commitment, so common among China's poets, was the one honorable alternative to government service for the artist-intellectual class. Already an ancient tradition by T'ao Ch'ien's time, it was a complex political and personal gesture. Politically, it represented a criticism of the government in power, a model of authenticity and simplicity for those in government whose vanity and greed were so destructive, and a kind of solidarity with their victims among the common people. Personally, retirement represented a commitment to a more spiritually fulfilling life, in which one inhabited the Taoist/Ch'an wilderness cosmology (see introduction, pp. xxi–xxiii) in the most immediate, day-to-day way. Such a recluse life did not normally mean enduring the spartan existence of an ascetic hermit: it was considered the ideal situation for living a broadly civilized existence and typically included, along with the wonders of mountain wilderness, a relatively comfortable house, a substantial library, family, friends. And finally, this personal fulfillment had its political dimensions, for the wisdom cultivated in such a life was considered essential to sage governing.

The landscape tradition in Chinese poetry is sometimes divided into two branches: fields-and-gardens, which emphasizes the more domestic aspects of landscape, and rivers-and-mountains, which emphasizes the wilder aspects. T'ao Ch'ien is traditionally spoken of as the founder of fields-and-gardens poetry, in contrast to his contemporary Hsieh Ling-yün, founder of rivers-and-mountains poetry. But there is no fundamental distinction between the two: both embody the Taoist cosmology that essentially is the Chinese wilderness, and as rivers-and-mountains is the broader context within which fields-and-gardens operates, it seems more accurate to speak of both modes together as a single rivers-and-mountains poetry. And this rivers-and-mountains framework is at the heart of virtually all poetic thinking in the centuries to follow. The more domestic feel of T'ao Ch'ien's poems is simply a reflection of his profound contentment. Unlike Hsieh Ling-yün, whose poems are animated by the need to establish an enlightened relationship with a grand alpine wilderness, T'ao effortlessly lived everyday life on a mountain farm as an utterly sufficient experience of dwelling.

T'ao's poems initiated the intimate sense of belonging to natural process that shapes the Chinese poetic sensibility. And though this dwelling means confronting death and the existential realities of human experience without delusion, a central preoccupation in T'ao Ch'ien and all Chinese poets, the spiritual ecology of *tzu-jan* provided ample solace. If T'ao's poems seem bland, a quality much admired in them by the Sung Dynasty poets, it's because they are never animated by the struggle for understanding. Instead, they always begin with the deepest wisdom.

HOME AGAIN AMONG FIELDS AND GARDENS

1

Nothing like all the others, even as a child,
rooted in such love for hills and mountains,

I stumbled into their net of dust, that one
departure a blunder lasting thirteen years.

But a tethered bird longs for its old forest,
and a pond fish its deep waters—so now,

my southern outlands cleared, I nurture
simplicity among these fields and gardens,

home again. I've got nearly two acres here,
and four or five rooms in our thatch hut,

elms and willows shading the eaves in back,
and in front, peach and plum spread wide.

Villages lost across mist-and-haze distances,
kitchen smoke drifting wide-open country,

dogs bark deep among back roads out here,
and roosters crow from mulberry treetops.

No confusion within these gates, no dust,
my empty home harbors idleness to spare.

After so long caged in that trap, I've come
back again to occurrence appearing of itself.

2

So little here beyond involves people.
Visitors to my meager lane rare, thorn–

bramble gate closed all day, this empty
home cuts dust-filled thoughts short.

And day after day, coming and going
on overgrown paths, I meet neighbors

without confusion: we only talk about
how the crops are doing, nothing more.

Mine grow taller each day, and I open
more fields, but I can't stop worrying:

come frost or sleet, and it's all tatters
torn down like so much tangled brush.

4

Years never walking mountains and lakes
gone, elated again among forests and fields,

I take our children by the hand and set out
through woods and abandoned farmlands.

Soon, we're walking around aimlessly amid
gravemounds and houses deserted long ago,

their wells and kitchen stoves still standing
among broken-down bamboo and mulberry.

Someone's out gathering firewood, so I ask
where these people, all these people, went.

Turning toward me, he says: *Nothing's left
once you're dead and gone, nothing. Wait*

*a single generation and, court or market,
every last face is new.* It's true, of course.

Life's its own mirage of change. And it ends
returned into all empty absence. What else?

WRITTEN IN THE 12TH MONTH, *KUEI* YEAR OF THE HARE, FOR MY COUSIN HONOR-DISTANCE

At this distant, bramble-weave gate, my
wandering come to rest, the world and I

set each other free. Not a soul in sight.
At dusk, who knows my gate sat closed

all day? This year-end wind bitter cold,
falling snow one thick, daylong flurry,

there's never a trace of sound. I listen,
eyes aching from all this white clarity.

Cold seeping into robes, cups and bowls
rarely agreeing to be set out for meals,

it's all desolation in this empty house,
nothing anywhere to keep my spirits up.

Roaming those thousand-year-old books,
I meet timeless exemplars, but I'll never

reach their lofty principles. About all
I ever mastered is *resolute in privation,*

and there's no chance renown redeems
poverty. Even so, I'm no fool for coming

here. I send findings beyond all words,
a bond shared that no one could fathom.

3

Way's been ruins a thousand years.
People all hoard their hearts away:

so busy scrambling after esteemed
position, they'd never touch wine.

But whatever makes living precious
occurs in this one life, and this life

never lasts. It's startling, sudden as
lightning, a hundred years offering

all abundance. Take it! What more
could you hope to make of yourself?

5

I live here in this busy village without
all that racket horses and carts stir up,

and you wonder how that could ever be.
Wherever the mind dwells apart is itself

a distant place. Picking chrysanthemums
at my east fence, I see South Mountain

far off: air lovely at dusk, birds in flight
going home. All this means something,

something absolute: whenever I start
to explain it, I forget words altogether.

7

Color infusing autumn chrysanthemums
exquisite, I gather dew-drenched petals,

float them on that forget-your-cares stuff.
Soon, even my passion for living apart

grows distant. I'm alone here, and still
the winejar soon fills cups without me.

Everything at rest, dusk: a bird calls out,
returning to its forest home. Chanting,

I settle into my breath. Somehow, on this
east veranda, I've found my life again.

15

Old, too poor to hire help, we watch wild
tangles of brush take over, our house

bitter silence, birds drifting clear skies
and isolate silence, no sign of others.

Time and space go on forever, but who
lives even to a hundred? Months and

years tighten, bustling each other away,
and my hair had gone white long ago.

If we don't give up failure and success,
that promise we hold just turns to regret.

UNTITLED

I couldn't want another life. Tending
fields and mulberries—it's my true

calling. I've never failed it, and still,
against hunger and cold, there's only

hull and chaff. I never wanted more
than a full stomach. All I've asked is

a little rice, heavy clothes for winter
and open-weaves for summer heat.

But I haven't even managed that. O,
all this grief cuts deep. And character

is fate. If you're simpleminded, life's
ways elude you. It's the inner pattern:

no one's likely to change it. But then,
I delight in even a single cup of wine.

Spending an idle 9/9 at home, I think fondly of how the day's name sounds like it's saying *ever and ever*. Autumn chrysanthemums fill the dooryard. But without wine, their blossoms promising *ever*lasting life are useless, so I trust my feelings to words.

Life too short for so many lasting desires,
people adore immortality. When the months

return to this day of promise, everyone
fondly hears *ever and ever* in its name.

Warm winds have ended. Dew ice-cold,
stars blaze in crystalline skies. And now

swallows have taken their shadows south,
arriving geese keep calling and calling.

Wine eases worry, and chrysanthemums
keep us from the ruins of age, but if you

live in a bramble hut, helplessly watching
these turning seasons crumble—what then?

My empty winejar shamed by a dusty cup,
this cold splendor of blossoms opens for itself

alone. I tighten my robe and sing to myself,
idle, overwhelmed by each memory. So many

joys to fill a short stay. I'll take my time
here. It is whole. How could it be any less?

CHA FESTIVAL DAY

Seeing off the year's final day, windblown
snow can't slow this warm weather. Already,

at our gate planted with plum and willow,
there's a branch flaunting lovely blossoms.

If I chant, words come clear. And in wine
I touch countless distances. So much still

eludes me here. Who knows how much with
all this unearthly Manifest Mountain song?

During the Great-Origin years of the Chin Dynasty, there was a man at Warrior-Knoll who caught fish for a living. One day he went up a stream, and soon didn't know how far he'd gone. Suddenly, he came upon a peach orchard in full bloom. For hundreds of feet, there was nothing but peach trees crowding in over the banks. And in the confusion of fallen petals, there were lovely, scented flowers. The fisherman was amazed. Wanting to see how far the orchard went, he continued on.

The trees ended at the foot of a mountain, where a spring fed the stream from a small cave. It seemed as if there might be a light inside, so the fisherman left his boat and stepped in. At first, the cave was so narrow he could barely squeeze through. But he kept going and, after a few dozen feet, it opened out into broad daylight. There, on a plain stretching away, austere houses were graced with fine fields and lovely ponds. Dikes and paths crossed here and there among mulberries and bamboo. Roosters and dogs called back and forth. Coming and going in the midst of all this, there were men and women tending the fields. Their clothes were just like those worn by people outside. And whether they were old with white hair or children in pigtails, they were all happy and of themselves content.

When they saw the fisherman, they were terribly surprised and asked where he had come from. Once he had answered all their questions, they insisted on taking him back home, and soon they had set out wine and killed chickens for dinner. When the others in the village heard about this man, they all came to ask about him. They told him how, long ago, to escape those years of turmoil during the Ch'in Dynasty [221 to 206 B.C.E.], the village ancestors gathered their wives and children, and with their neighbors came to this distant place. They'd kept themselves cut off from the people outside ever since. So now they wondered what dynasty it was. They'd never heard of the Han, let alone Wei or Chin. As the fisherman carefully told them everything he knew, they all sighed in sad amazement. Each of the village families in turn invited him to their house, where they also served wine and food.

After staying for some days, the fisherman prepared to leave these people. As he was going, they said, *There's no need to tell the people outside.*

He returned to his boat and started back, careful to remember each place along the way.

When he got back home, he went to tell the prefect what had happened. The prefect sent some men to retrace the route, but they were soon lost and finally gave up the search.

Liu Tzu-chi, who lived in Nan-yang, was a recluse of great honor and esteem. When he heard about this place, he joyfully prepared to go there. But before he could, he got sick and passed away. Since then, no one's asked the way.

Days and months never take their time.
The four seasons keep bustling each other

away. Cold winds churn lifeless branches.
Fallen leaves cover long paths. We're frail,

crumbling more with each turning year.
Our temples turn white early, and once

your hair flaunts that bleached streamer,
the road ahead starts closing steadily in.

This house is an inn awaiting travelers,
and I yet another guest leaving. All this

leaving and leaving—where will I ever
end up? My old home's on South Mountain.

2

I never had wine to drink, and now
my empty cup's all depths of spring

wine crowned with ant-fluff foam,
but how will I ever taste it again?

Delicacies crowd altars before me,
and at my side, those I love grieve.

I try to look—it's eyes of darkness.
I try to speak—a mouth of silence.

I once slept beneath high ceilings,
but a waste village of weeds is next:

leaving my gate behind, I'll set out
and never again find my way back.

3

Boundless—across boundless, weed-ridden
wastes, white poplars moan in long winds.

In bitter ninth-month frost, come to this
distant place, they bid me farewell. Empty

directions, not a house in sight, nothing
but looming gravemounds humped up and

isolate wind moaning to itself in branches,
horses rearing up, crying out to heaven.

Once they close me inside this dark house,
day won't dawn again in a thousand years.

Day won't dawn again in a thousand years,
and what can all our wisdom do about it?

Those who were just here saying farewell—
they'll all go back home again, and though

my own family may grieve on, the others
will soon be full of such song. Once you're

dead and gone, what then? Trust yourself
to the mountain's flank. It will take you in.

HSIEH LING-YÜN

(385 to 433)

As a PATRIARCH in one of China's wealthiest and most powerful fami-
lies, Hsieh Ling-yün was deeply involved at the highest levels in the tur-
bulent political world for decades, but he was a mountain recluse at heart.
When he was eventually exiled, finding himself in a period of quiet reflec-
tion at Yung-chia (Prosper-Perpetual), a beautiful site on the mountain-
ous seacoast in southeast China, he underwent a Buddhist awakening
(pp. 130–31). As a result, he abandoned politics and retired to his family
home high in the mountains at Shih-ning (Origin-Serene)—a move that
he speaks of, like T'ao Ch'ien in his "Home Again Among Fields and Gar-
dens" (p. 113), as a return to *tzu-jan* (see Key Terms) when he speaks of
"choosing the sacred beauty in occurrence appearing of itself" (p. 133).
There he created a revolutionary body of work that marked the beginning
of the rivers-and-mountains tradition in Chinese poetry, in contrast to
T'ao Ch'ien's more domestic fields-and-gardens poetry.

The influx of Buddhist thought from India had started nearly two cen-
turies earlier, and by Hsieh's time it had begun intermingling with Taoist
thought, a process that eventually gave rise to Ch'an (Zen) Buddhism. At
the time of his awakening, Hsieh wrote an essay that is considered the ear-
liest surviving Ch'an text in China, and its ideas provide a framework for
his poetry, and for much of the rivers-and-mountains poetry to follow. It

describes enlightenment as becoming the emptiness of absence (*wu*: see Key Terms) and, as such, mirroring presence (*yu*: see Key Terms) as it unfolds according to the *inner pattern* (*li*), a key concept that recurs often in Hsieh's poetry and throughout the wilderness tradition. The philosophical meaning of *li*, which originally referred to the veins and markings in a precious piece of jade, is something akin to what we call natural law. It is the system of principles according to which the ten thousand things burgeon forth spontaneously from the generative void. For Hsieh, one comes to a deep understanding of *li* through *adoration* (*shang*), another recurring concept in the poems (pp. 132, 140). *Adoration* denotes an aesthetic experience of the wild mountain realm as a single overwhelming whole. It is this aesthetic experience that Hsieh's poems try to evoke in the reader, this sense of inhabiting that wilderness cosmology in the most profound way.

As with China's great landscape paintings, Hsieh's mountain landscapes enact "absence mirroring the whole" (Hsieh's description of empty mind mirroring the whole), rendering a world that is profoundly spiritual and, at the same time, resolutely realistic. Here lies the difficulty Hsieh's work presents to a reader. It is an austere poetry, nearly devoid of the human stories and poetic strategies that normally make poems engaging. You would never know from the poetry that Hsieh led a rebellion against the central government and was finally exiled to the far south, the very outskirts of the Chinese cultural sphere, where he was eventually put to death for his continuing criticism of the government. In the poetry, Hsieh's central personal "story" is the identification of enlightenment with wilderness, and this is precisely why he has been so admired in China.

Rendering the day-to-day adventure of a person inhabiting the universe at great depth, Hsieh's poems tend more to the descriptive and philosophical, locating human consciousness in its primal relation to the cosmos. In so doing, they replace narrow human concerns with a mirror-still mind that sees its truest self in the vast and complex dimensions of mountain wilderness. But as there was no fundamental distinction between mind and heart in ancient China (see Key Terms: *hsin*), this was a profound emotional experience as well, and it remains so for us today. With their grandiose language, headlong movement, and shifting perspective, Hsieh's poems were celebrated for possessing an elemental power that captures the dynamic spirit and inner rhythms which infuse the numinous

realm of rivers and mountains, and reading them requires that we partici-
pate in his mirror-still dwelling. Hsieh's poems may seem flat at first, and
very much alike—but in that dwelling, each day is another form of en-
lightenment, and each walk another walk at the very heart of the cosmos
itself.

Quiet mystery of lone dragons alluring,
calls of migrant geese echoing distances,

I meet sky, unable to soar among clouds,
face a river, all those depths beyond me.

Too simpleminded to perfect Integrity
and too feeble to plow fields in seclusion,

I followed a salary here to the sea's edge
and lay watching forests bare and empty.

That sickbed kept me blind to the seasons,
but opening the house up, I'm suddenly

looking out, listening to surf on a beach
and gazing up into high mountain peaks.

A warm sun is unraveling winter winds,
new *yang* swelling, transforming old *yin*.

Lakeshores newborn into spring grasses
and garden willows become caroling birds:

in them the ancient songs haunt me with
flocks and flocks and *full lush and green.*

Isolate dwelling so easily becomes forever.
It's hard settling the mind this far apart,

but not something ancients alone master:
that serenity is everywhere apparent here.

CLIMBING GREEN-CLIFF MOUNTAIN IN YUNG-CHIA

Taking a little food, a light walking-stick,
I wander up to my home in quiet mystery,

the path along streams winding far away
onto ridgetops, no end to this wonder at

slow waters silent in their frozen beauty
and bamboo glistening at heart with frost,

cascades scattering a confusion of spray
and broad forests crowding distant cliffs.

Thinking it's moonrise I see in the west
and sunset I'm watching blaze in the east,

I hike on until dark, then linger out night
sheltered away in deep expanses of shadow.

Immune to high importance: that's renown.
Walk humbly and it's all promise in beauty,

for in quiet mystery the way runs smooth,
ascending remote heights beyond compare.

Utter tranquillity, the distinction between
yes this and *no that* lost, I embrace primal

unity, thought and silence woven together,
that deep healing where we venture forth.

I'VE PUT IN GARDENS SOUTH OF THE FIELDS, OPENED UP A STREAM AND PLANTED TREES

Woodcutter and recluse—they inhabit
these mountains for different reasons,

and there are other forms of difference.
You can heal here among these gardens,

sheltered from rank vapors of turmoil,
wilderness clarity calling distant winds.

I *ch'i*-sited my house on a northern hill,
doors opening out onto a southern river,

ended trips to the well with a new stream
and planted hibiscus in terraced banks.

Now there are flocks of trees at my door
and crowds of mountains at my window,

and I wander thin trails down to fields
or gaze into a distance of towering peaks,

wanting little, never wearing myself out.
It's rare luck to make yourself such a life,

though like ancient recluse paths, mine
bring longing for the footsteps of friends:

how could I forget them in this exquisite
adoration kindred spirits alone can share?

4

Embracing the seasons of heaven through bright insight,
the impulse turning them, and the inner pattern's solitude,

my grandfather came to this retreat in the dusk of old age,
leaving behind his renown engraved in memorial hymns.

He thought Ch'ü Yüan a fool for drowning himself in exile,
admired Yüeh Yi for leaving his country. And he himself—

choosing the sacred beauty in occurrence appearing of itself,
he made the composure of these mountain peaks his own.

5

Looking up to the example that old sage handed down,
and considering what comes easily to my own nature,

I offered myself to this tranquil repose of dwelling,
and now nurture my lifework in the drift of idleness.

Master Pan's early awakening always humbled me,
and I was shamed by Master Shang's old-age insight,

so with years and sickness both closing in upon me
I devoted myself to simplicity and returned to it all,

left that workaday life for this wisdom of wandering,
for this wilderness of rivers-and-mountains clarity.

6

Here where I live,
lakes on the left, rivers on the right,
you leave islands, follow shores back

to mountains out front, ridges behind.
Looming east and toppling aside west,

they harbor ebb and flow of breath,
arch across and snake beyond, devious

churning and roiling into distances,
cliff-top ridgelines hewn flat and true.

7

Nearby in the east are
Risen-Fieldland and Downcast-Lake,
Western-Gorge and Southern-Valley,

Stone-Plowshares and Stone-Rapids,
Forlorn-Millstone and Yellow-Bamboo.

There are waters tumbling a thousand feet in flight
and forests curtained high over countless canyons,

endless streams flowing far away into distant rivers
and cascades branching deeper into nearby creeks.

12

Far off to the south are
peaks like Pine-Needle and Nest-Hen,
Halcyon-Knoll and Brimmed-Stone,

Harrow and Spire Ridges faced together,
Elder and Eye-Loft cleaving summits.

When you go deep, following a winding river to its source,
you're soon bewildered, wandering a place beyond knowing:

cragged peaks towering above stay lost in confusions of mist,
and depths sunken away far below surge and swell in a blur.

24

There are fish like
snake-fish and trout, perch and tench,
red-eye and yellow-gill, dace and carp,

bream, sturgeon, skate, mandarin-fish,
flying-fish, bass, mullet, and wax-fish:

a rainbow confusion of colors blurred,
glistening brocade, cloud-fresh schools

nibbling duckweed, frolicking in waves,
drifting among ghost-eye, flowing deep.

Some drumming their gills and leaping through whitewater,
others beating their tails and struggling back beneath swells,

shad and salmon, each in their season, stream up into creeks and shallows,
sunfish and knife-fish follow rapids further, emerge in mountain springs.

26

On mountaintops live
gibbon, jackal, wildcat and badger,
fox and wolf, cougar and bobcat,

and in mountain valleys
black and brown bear, coyote, tiger,
bighorn and deer, antelope and elk.

Things gambol among branches soaring out over cliffs
and leap across rifts of empty sky within deep gorges,

lurk down through valleys, howls and roars perpetual,
while others climb, calling and wailing among treetops.

33

As for my
homes perched north and south,
inaccessible except across water:

gaze deep into wind and cloud
and you know this realm utterly.

36

Tracing the way back home here,
I might round North Mountain

on roads hung along cliff-walls,
timbers rising in switchbacks,

or I could take the watercourse
way winding and circling back,

level lakes broad and brimming,
crystalline depths clear and deep

beyond shorelines all lone grace
and long islands of lush brocade.

Gazing on and on in reverence
across realms so boundless away,

I come to the twin rivers that flow through together.
Two springs sharing one source,

they follow gorges and canyons
to merge at mountain headlands

and cascade on, scouring sand out and mounding dunes
below peaks that loom over islands swelling into hills,

whitewater carrying cliffs away in a tumble of rocks,
a marshy tangle of fallen trees glistening in the waves.

Following along the south bank that crosses out front,
the snaking north cliff that looms behind, I'm soon

lost in thick forests, the nature of dusk and dawn in full view,
and for bearings, I trust myself to the star-filled night skies.

ON STONE-GATE MOUNTAIN'S HIGHEST PEAK

I started thinking of impossible cliffs at dawn
and by evening was settled on a mountaintop,

scarcely a peak high enough to face this hut
looking out on mountains veined with streams,

forests stretching away beyond its open gate,
a tumble of talus boulders ending at the stairs.

Mountains crowd around, blocking out roads,
and trails wander bamboo confusions, leaving

guests to stray on clever new paths coming up
or doubt old ways leading people back home.

Hissing cascades murmuring through dusk,
the wail of gibbons howling away the night,

I keep to the inner pattern, deep in meditation,
and nurturing this Way, never wander amiss.

Mind now a twin to stark late autumn trees
while eyes delight in the flowering of spring,

I inhabit the constant and wait out the end,
content to dwell at ease in all change and loss,

in this regret there's no kindred spirit here
to climb this ladder of azure clouds with me.

OVERNIGHT AT STONE-GATE CLIFFS

I spent the morning digging out orchids,
afraid frost would soon leave them dead,

passed the night among fringes of cloud,
savoring a moon up beyond all this rock,

chortles telling me birds have settled in,
falling leaves giving away fresh winds.

Sounds weave together in the ear, strange
unearthly echoes all crystalline distance,

though there's no one to share wonders
or the joys in wine's fragrant clarities.

We'll never meet again now. I sit beside
a stream, sun drying my hair for nothing.

FOLLOWING AXE-BAMBOO STREAM, I CROSS OVER A RIDGE AND HIKE ON ALONG THE RIVER

Though the cry of gibbons means sunrise,
its radiance hasn't touched this valley all

quiet mystery. Clouds gather below cliffs,
and there's still dew glistening on blossoms

when I set out along a wandering stream,
climbing into narrow canyons far and high.

Ignoring my robe to wade through creeks,
I scale cliff-ladders and cross distant ridges

to the river beyond. It snakes and twists,
but I follow it, happy just meandering along

past pepperwort and duckweed drifting deep,
rushes and wild rice in crystalline shallows.

Reaching tiptoe to ladle sips from waterfalls
and picking still unfurled leaves in forests,

I can almost see that lovely mountain spirit
in a robe of fig leaves and sash of wisteria.

Gathering orchids brings no dear friends
and picking hemp-flower no open warmth,

but the heart finds its beauty in adoration,
and you can't talk out such shadowy things:

in the eye's depths you're past worry here,
awakened into things all wandering away.

ON THATCH-HUT MOUNTAIN

.　.　.

Above jumbled canyons opening suddenly
out and away, level roads all breaking off,

these thronging peaks nestle up together.
People come and go without a trace here,

sun and moon hidden all day and night,
frost and snow falling summer and winter.

.　.　.

scale cliff-walls to gaze into dragon pools
and climb trees to peer into nursery dens.

.　.　.

no imagining mountain visits. And now
I can't get enough, just walk on and on,

and even a single dusk and dawn up here
shows you the way through empty and full.

.　.　.

T'ang Dynasty I:
The Great Renaissance

(c. 700 to 800)

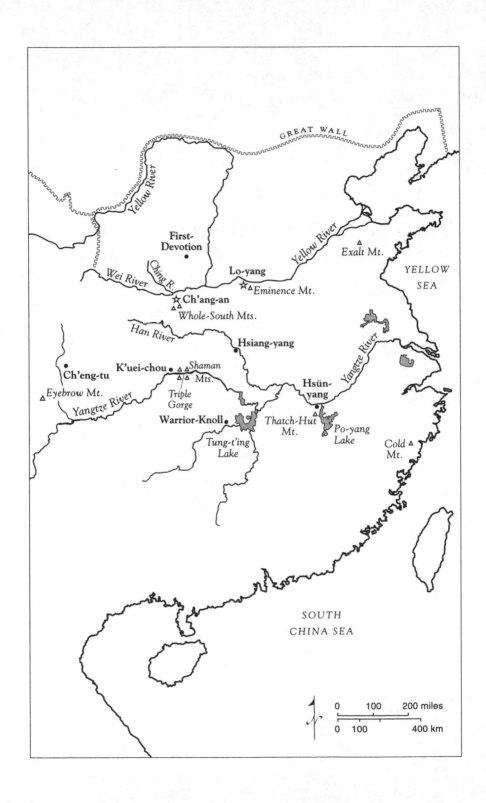

GREAT WALL

Yellow River

First-
Devotion

Lo-yang

Yellow River

Exalt Mt.

YELLOW
SEA

Wei River

Ch'ing R.

☆△ Eminence Mt.

☆ Ch'ang-an
△△
Whole-South Mts.

Han River

Hsiang-yang

Ch'eng-tu

K'uei-chou

△ △ Shaman
△ △ Mts.

Hsün-
yang

Yangtze River

Eyebrow Mt.

Yangtze River

Triple
Gorge

Warrior-Knoll

Thatch-Hut
Mt.

Po-yang
Lake

Cold △
Mt.

Tung-t'ing
Lake

SOUTH
CHINA SEA

0   100   200 miles

0   100   400 km

CHINA REMAINED FRAGMENTED in the centuries following T'ao
Ch'ien and Hsieh Ling-yün, controlled by a welter of shifting and com-
peting regional states. It was not until the short-lived Sui Dynasty (581 to
618), and its successor, the T'ang (618 to 907), that China was again uni-
fied. This political history is reflected in the poetic tradition. After T'ao
Ch'ien and Hsieh Ling-yün, Chinese poetry was generally mired in life-
less convention, producing no truly major figures until the golden age of
the T'ang Dynasty three centuries later, when it blossomed into its first
full splendor. The eighth century produced a spectacular constellation of
poets, each of whom is so singular that generalizations about the poetry of
the period are difficult, but underlying the diversity is a commitment to
T'ao Ch'ien's personal authenticity, as opposed to the mere technical fa-
cility that typified poetry in the centuries preceding the T'ang. And in-
deed, the "discovery" of the long-neglected T'ao Ch'ien was a central
catalyst in the T'ang renaissance. This was part of a more general move-
ment from poetry practiced as a social skill of the lettered class to poetry
practiced as high art with a serious purpose.

The T'ang is generally considered the pinnacle of Chinese civilization:
the government was admirable and the country at peace, the capital was the
largest and most cosmopolitan city in the world, the common people pros-

pered, and the most dramatic cultural renaissance in Chinese history was under way. *Pinnacle* is a tragically apt word to describe this period, however, for it didn't last long. The T'ang didn't really achieve its legendary status until around 700, and in 755 a catastrophic civil war broke out. Known as the An Lu-shan Rebellion, after the infamous leader of the rebel forces, it devastated the country and left two-thirds of the people either dead or cast adrift as homeless refugees. Although the arts remained dynamic for another century or so, they were deeply haunted, and the dynasty never recovered from the chronic militarism spawned by the civil war.

MENG HAO-JAN

(689 to 740)

UNLIKE T'AO CH'IEN and Hsieh Ling-yün, who settled into their re-
cluse ways later in life, Meng Hao-jan never left his native region to fol-
low a government career. Rather than subject himself to the strictures of
a conventional life, Meng cultivated the independence of a simple life in
his home mountains. He traveled extensively, making all China his neigh-
borhood landscape, but his home remained always in Hsiang-yang, a re-
gion known for its lovely mountains rising over the Han River. Meng
explored the area extensively, often hiking its mountains and valleys, pad-
dling its rivers and lakes. And indeed, his character seems to have been
shaped by this intimacy: he became legendary for possessing the protean
freedom of Hsiang-yang's rivers and mountains. There, far from the cul-
tural centers of the time, his poetry developed outside prevailing literary
taste and in direct response to the mountain landscape.

Meng Hao-jan was the first of the great T'ang poets who looked to
T'ao Ch'ien and Hsieh Ling-yün as his poetic masters. From Hsieh Ling-
yün he inherited the practice of expansive rambling among China's rivers
and mountains, a practice replete with the spontaneity and freedom of
those rivers and mountains themselves. And from T'ao Ch'ien, the model
of recluse integrity, came a plainspoken voice that embodied deep wis-
dom: rather than straining for dramatic effect, T'ao's was a relaxed lan-

guage that moved with ease and spontaneity, and so was the language of dwelling as an organic part of the wilderness cosmology. But Meng added new elements to the poetics of Hsieh and T'ao, and his highly original amalgam forms a bridge leading from Hsieh and T'ao to the great T'ang poets who followed.

During the three-century hiatus that preceded Meng Hao-jan and the T'ang renaissance, Ch'an (Zen) Buddhism (see general introduction, pp. xxiii–xxiv) came to maturity, and in the T'ang it was widely practiced by the intelligentsia of China—among them Meng, who was clearly a very serious practitioner. In poetry, Ch'an gave rise to a much more distilled language, especially in its concise imagism. This imagism fulfills in poetic practice Hsieh Ling-yün's Ch'an idea that one should become the emptiness of absence (*wu*: see Key Terms) and mirror presence's ten thousand things (*yu*: see Key Terms). It is a poetics that weaves consciousness into the wilderness cosmology, making this weave the very texture of poetic experience.

Although later poets developed this new aesthetic further, there is a sense in which Meng remained its most radical exemplar. While this focus on emptiness and imagistic concision dramatically opened the poem to silence, Meng went further. It is said that Meng's practice was to destroy poems after writing them because they inevitably failed to render experience at the absolute level that lies beyond words.

AUTUMN BEGINS

Autumn begins unnoticed. Nights slowly lengthen,
and little by little, clear winds turn colder and colder,

summer's blaze giving way. My thatch hut grows still.
At the bottom stair, in bunchgrass, lit dew shimmers.

GATHERING FIREWOOD

Gathering firewood I enter mountain depths,
mountain depths rising creek beyond creek

choked with the timbers of bridges in ruins.
Vines tumble low, tangled over cragged paths,

and at dusk, scarce people grow scarcer still.
Mountain wind sweeping through simple robes,

my chant steady, I shoulder a light bundle,
watch smoke drift across open country home.

LISTENING TO CHENG YIN PLAY HIS *CH'IN*

Another Juan Chi ripening wine's renown
in bamboo forests full of crystalline wind,

you sit half drunk, let down flowing sleeves
and sweep your dragon-rimmed *ch'in* clean.

Then it's a fresh tune for each cup of wine,
dusk's blaze sinking away unnoticed. Soon,

thoughts deep among rivers and mountains,
I hear this mind my former lives all share.

ON REACHING THE JU RIVER DIKES, SENT TO MY FRIEND LU

Road-weary, giving the horse a break,
I find myself gazing at Ju River dikes.

The Lo River is open now, free of snow.
Eminence Peak's twilight clouds linger,

trailed halfway across empty skies, lit
colors surging elemental and swelling.

I'm sending here this moment of itself—
how it just keeps unfurling, unfurling.

CLIMBING LONG-VIEW MOUNTAIN'S HIGHEST PEAK

Rivers and mountains beyond the form seen:
Hsiang-yang's beauty brings them in reach,

and Long-View has the highest peak around.
Somehow I'd never climbed its cragged heights,

its rocky cliffs like walls hacked and scraped
and towering over mountains crowded near,

but today, skies so bright and clear, I set out.
Soon the far end of sight's all boundless away,

Cloud-Dream southlands a trifle in the palm,
Warrior-Knoll lost in that realm of blossoms.

And back on my horse, riding home at dusk,
a vine-sifted moon keeps the stream lit deep.

OVERNIGHT ON ABIDING-INTEGRITY RIVER

I guide the boat in, anchor off island mist.
It's dusk, time a traveler's loneliness returns.

Heaven settles far and wide into the trees,
and on this clear river, a moon drifts near.

LOOKING FOR MEI, SAGE MASTER OF THE WAY

T'ao Ch'ien's five recluse willows are here,
and the geese of North-Slope's sage master.

Come following all I adore up to countless
summer clouds, I leave my walking-stick,

and echoing the joy seen in drifting fish,
set out on the song of a drumming paddle.

The regal path of high peaks never falters:
a thousand years bowing into clear waters.

SENT TO CH'AO, THE PALACE REVISER

You polish words in rue-scented libraries,
and I live in bamboo-leaf gardens, a recluse

wandering each day the same winding path
home to rest in the quiet, no noise anywhere.

A bird soaring the heights chooses its tree,
but the hedge soon tangles impetuous goats.

Today, things seen becoming thoughts felt:
this is where you start forgetting the words.

SEARCHING INCENSE MOUNTAIN FOR THE MONK CLARITY-DEEP

Leaving for mountains of renown at sunrise,
mountains empty kingfisher-green distances,

I wander a hundred miles of nurturing mist
until finally, as the sun sinks low, I arrive.

At the canyon's mouth, I hear a bell call out.
Where forests begin, I breathe incense sky,

and leaving my horse free to graze, I set out,
walking-stick in hand, to find my old friend.

I pass stone-gate peaks into a cragged ravine,
bamboo paths meandering depths of shadow,

and there, all joy, I meet him: a dharma-mate
so kindred our crystalline talk lasts all night.

I've cultivated true seclusion for a lifetime,
probing all this sacred wonder day by day:

farmers returning to mists and fields at dawn,
and mountain monks to monasteries at dusk,

crystalline voices of pine cascades countless,
moss-covered cliffs thick with ancient truths.

It's my one wish: given to mountains, human
realms far away, this old self abandoned too.

AT LUMEN–EMPTY MONASTERY, VISITING THE HERMITAGE OF MASTER JUNG, MY DEPARTED FRIEND

The blue-lotus roof standing beside a pond,
White-Horse Creek tumbling through forests,

and my old friend some strange thing now.
A lingering visitor, alone and grief-stricken

after graveside rites among pines, I return,
looking for your sitting-mat spread on rock.

Bamboo that seems always my own thoughts:
it keeps fluttering here at your thatch hut.

ADRIFT AT WARRIOR–KNOLL

Warrior-Knoll's river thin, my long-ago
boat glides on into peach-blossom forests

where headwaters harbored such quiet
mystery: immortal families so deep away.

Water meanders, blurs into blue cliffs,
darkens green beneath a crossing cloud.

I sit listening. Idle gibbons cry out, mind
sudden clarity far beyond a world of dust.

ANCHORED OFF HSÜN-YANG IN EVENING LIGHT, I GAZE AT THATCH-HUT MOUNTAIN'S INCENSE-BURNER PEAK

Our sail up full, thousands of miles pass
without meeting mountains of renown,

then anchored beside Hsün-yang's wall,
I'm suddenly gazing up at Incense-Burner.

I've read the teachings: of Prajñā-Distance,
followed his pure path beyond the dust,

and now his East-Forest home is so near.
It is dusk. A bell sounds, and it's empty.

RETURNING HOME TO DEER-GATE MOUNTAIN AT NIGHT

As day fades into dusk, the bell at a mountain temple sounds.
Fish-Bridge Island is loud with people clamoring at the ferry,

and others follow sandy shores toward their river village.
But returning home to Deer-Gate, I paddle my own little boat,

Deer-Gate's incandescent moonlight opening misty forests,
until suddenly I've entered old Master P'ang's isolate realm.

Cliffs the gate, pines the path—it's forever still and silent,
just this one recluse, this mystery coming and going of itself.

ON A JOURNEY TO THOUGHT-ESSENCE MONASTERY, INSCRIBED ON A WALL AT THE ABBOT'S MOUNTAIN HUT

Happening into realms peach-blossom pure,
I begin to feel the depths of a bamboo path,

and soon come to know a master's timeless
dwelling. It's far beyond things people seek.

Cranes dancing over steps all stone idleness,
gibbons in flight howling amid thick forests,

I slowly fathom dark-enigma's inner pattern,
and sitting at such depths, forget mind itself.

SPRING DAWN

In spring sleep, dawn arrives unnoticed.
Suddenly, all around, I hear birds in song.

A loud night. Wind and rain came, tearing
blossoms down. Who knows few or many?

WANG WEI

(701 to 761)

WANG WEI IS the great condensery of Chinese poetry. He distills expe-
rience to its most basic elements: consciousness, landscape, emptiness.
Many of his best poems are incredibly concise, composed of only twenty
words, and they often turn on the sparest of images: a bird's cry, a splinter
of light on moss, an egret's wingbeat. Such poems have made Wang Wei
one of China's most immediately appealing and revered poets, and this
achievement has inevitably been connected to his accomplishment as a
painter. Wang is traditionally considered the first to paint the inner spirit
of landscape, rather than its realistic image, and since that became the
essence of Chinese landscape painting as it blossomed in the following
centuries, he must be counted as one of landscape painting's seminal fig-
ures. This ability to capture a kind of inexpressible inner spirit is also the
essence of Wang's poetry.

   For the ancient Chinese, the most majestic and complete manifestation
of Taoism's wilderness cosmology was the realm of rivers and mountains.
It is there in countless paintings from the Chinese landscape tradition, such
as those by Wang Wei himself: the pregnant emptiness, in the form of
blank rivers and lakes, empty mist and space; and the mountain landscape
as it emerges from that emptiness and hovers, peopled sparsely, seemingly
on the verge of vanishing back into the emptiness. The Way of a Chinese

sage was to dwell as an organic part of this cosmological process, most commonly as a mountain recluse, and Wang Wei was a consummate master of this dwelling.

Wang enjoyed a long and successful career in the government, virtually all of it in Ch'ang-an (Enduring Peace), the capital, but it is clear that he found his truest self in mountain solitude. In his middle years, Wang acquired his famous Wheel-Rim River (see p. 162) retreat in the Whole-South Mountains, which rise to a height of three thousand meters just south of Ch'ang-an. For the rest of his life, he spent as much time as he could at his house among those peaks, and when he died he was buried there.

It was at Wheel-Rim River that Wang perfected a tranquil landscape poem that dramatically extends Meng Hao-jan's imagist poetics. As with Meng Hao-jan, this poetics can be traced to his assiduous practice of Ch'an (Zen) Buddhism. Wang's brief poems resound with the mirrored depths of no-mind, manifest in their texture of imagistic clarity, and in them the simplest image resonates with the whole cosmology of *tzu-jan*. Wang takes the poem beyond words on the page, as he returns consciousness to its most elemental dimensions of emptiness and landscape. The result is a breathtaking poetry, one that renders the ten thousand things in such a way that they empty the self as they shimmer with the clarity of their own self-sufficient identity.

MOURNING MENG HAO-JAN

My dear friend nowhere in sight,
this Han River keeps flowing east.

Now, if I look for old masters here,
I find empty rivers and mountains.

UNTITLED

You just came from my old village
so you know all about village affairs.

When you left, outside my window,
was it in bloom—that winter plum?

BIRD-CRY CREEK

In our idleness, cinnamon blossoms fall.
In night quiet, spring mountains stand

empty. Moonrise startles mountain birds:
here and there, cries in a spring gorge.

IN THE MOUNTAINS, SENT TO *CH'AN* BROTHERS AND SISTERS

Dharma-companions filling mountains,
a *sangha* forms of itself: chanting, sitting

ch'an stillness. Looking out from distant
city walls, people see only white clouds.

MOURNING YIN YAO

Giving you back to Stone-Tower Mountain, we bid farewell
among ash-green pine and cypress, then return home.

Of your bones now buried white cloud, this much remains
forever: streams cascading empty toward human realms.

IN REPLY TO P'EI TI

The cold river spreads boundless away.
Autumn rains darken azure-deep skies.

You ask about Whole-South Mountain:
mind knows far beyond white clouds.

1 Elder-Cliff Cove

At the mouth of Elder-Cliff, a rebuilt house
among old trees, broken remnants of willow.

Those to come: who will they be, their grief
over someone's long-ago life here empty.

2 Master-Flourish Ridge

Birds in flight go on leaving and leaving.
And autumn colors mountain distances again:

crossing Master-Flourish Ridge and beyond,
is there no limit to all this grief and sorrow?

3 *Apricot-Grain Cottage*

Roofbeams cut from deep-grained apricot,
fragrant reeds braided into thatched eaves:

no one knows clouds beneath these rafters
drifting off to bring that human realm rain.

4 *Bamboo-Clarity Mountains*

Tall bamboo blaze in meandering emptiness:
kingfisher-greens rippling streamwater blue.

On Autumn-Pitch Mountain paths, they flaunt
darkness, woodcutters there beyond knowing.

5 Deer Park

No one seen. Among empty mountains,
hints of drifting voice, faint, no more.

Entering these deep woods, late sunlight
flares on green moss again, and rises.

6 Magnolia Park

Autumn mountains gathering last light,
one bird follows another in flight away.

Shifting kingfisher-greens flash radiant
scatters. Evening mists: nowhere they are.

8 Scholar-Tree Path

On the side path shaded by scholar-trees,
green moss fills recluse shadow. We still

keep it swept, our welcome at the gate,
knowing a mountain monk may stop by.

10 South Point

I leave South Point, boat light, water
so vast who could reach North Point?

Far shores: I see villagers there beyond
knowing in all this distance, distance.

11 *Vagary Lake*

Flute-song carries beyond furthest shores.
In dusk light, I bid you a sage's farewell.

Across this lake, in the turn of a head,
mountain greens furl into white cloud.

13 *Golden-Rain Rapids*

Wind buffets and blows autumn rain.
Water cascading thin across rocks,

waves lash at each other. An egret
startles up, white, then settles back.

15 *White-Rock Shallows*

White-Rock Shallows open and clear,
green reeds past prime for harvest:

families come down east and west,
rinse thin silk radiant in moonlight.

16 *North Point*

At North Point north of these lakewaters,
railings flash red through tangled trees.

Here, meandering azure-forest horizons,
South River shimmers in and out of view.

17 Bamboo-Midst Cottage

Sitting alone in silent bamboo dark,
I play a *ch'in,* settle into breath chants.

In these forest depths no one knows
this moon come bathing me in light.

18 Magnolia Slope

Lotus blossoms adrift out across treetops
flaunt crimson calyxes among mountains.

At home beside this stream, quiet, no one
here. Scattered. Scattered open and falling.

IN THE MOUNTAINS

Bramble stream, white rocks jutting out.
Heaven cold, red leaves scarce. No rain

up here where the mountain road ends,
sky stains robes empty kingfisher-blue.

AUTUMN NIGHT, SITTING ALONE

Lamenting this hair of mine, I sit alone
in empty rooms, the second watch close.

Mountain fruit falls out there in the rain,
and here in lamplight, field crickets sing.

No one's ever changed white hair back:
might as well try conjuring yellow gold.

If you want to elude the old-age disease,
there's only one way: study unborn life.

Autumn color so full of moving beauty:
it's fuller still in this lakeside idleness.

Below western forests, distances vast, we
see ourselves in mountains at the gate:

darkness bleeds across a thousand miles,
scattered peaks breaking through cloud,

and ridgelines scrawl across Ch'in lands,
or bunch up, hiding Thorn-Bramble Pass.

Amid remnant rain, slant light's radiant.
Birds take flight, return to evening mist.

Same as ever. Nothing much changed, old
friend. Why grieve over a timeworn face?

IN REPLY TO VICE-MAGISTRATE CHANG

In these twilight years, I love tranquillity
alone. Mind free of all ten thousand affairs,

self-regard free of all those grand schemes,
I return to my old forest, knowing empty.

Soon mountain moonlight plays my *ch'in*,
and pine winds loosen my robe. Explain this

inner pattern behind failure and success?
Fishing song carries into shoreline depths.

OFFHAND POEM

I'm ancient, lazy about making poems.
There's no company here but old age.

I no doubt painted in some former life,
roamed the delusion of words in another,

and habits linger. Unable to get free,
I somehow became known in the world,

but my most fundamental name remains
this mind still here beyond all knowing.

LI PO

(701 to 762)

THERE IS A set-phrase in Chinese referring to the phenomenon of Li Po: "Winds of the immortals, bones of the Tao." He is called the Banished Immortal, an exiled spirit moving through this world with an unearthly ease and freedom from attachment. But at the same time, he belongs to earth in the most profound way, for he was also free of attachments to self, and that freedom allowed him to blend easily into that spontaneous burgeoning forth of the ten thousand things. Li Po's work is suffused with the wonder of being part of this process, and he also enacted it, making it visible in the self-dramatized spontaneity of his life and work. To live as part of the earth's process of change is to live one's most authentic self: rather than acting with self-conscious intention, one acts with the same selfless spontaneity as flowing water, mountain winds, or a wild summer thunderstorm. This spontaneity is *wu-wei* (see Key Terms), and it is an important part of Taoist and Ch'an (Zen) Buddhist practice, the way to experience one's life as an organic part of *tzu-jan* (see Key Terms). *Wu-wei* was a widely held ideal during the T'ang, appearing most famously in the "wildgrass" calligraphy of Chang Hsü and Huai Su, friends of Li Po who would get drunk and, in a sudden flurry, create flowing landscapes of virtually indecipherable characters; in the antics of Ch'an masters; and in Li Po himself.

Li Po's life was characterized by whimsical travel, wild drinking, and a gleeful disdain for decorum and authority. This spontaneity is also central to his experience of the natural world. He was primarily engaged by the natural world in its wild, rather than domestic, forms. Not only does the wild evoke wonder but it is also where the spontaneous energy of *tzu-jan* is most clearly visible, energy with which Li Po identified. And the spontaneous movement of a Li Po poem literally enacts this identification, this belonging to earth in the fundamental sense of belonging to its processes. This selfless spontaneity also allowed him to speak out of all aspects of the Chinese tradition with an effortless virtuosity: folk-poetry (*yüeh-fu*), in which he speaks in other voices; shamanistic poetry; the romantic poetry typical of the feminine tradition; wild rivers-and-mountains poetry; quiet Buddhist poetry; poems of social protest.

Only T'ao Ch'ien is as closely identified with the "sage in the cup" as Li Po, and Li Po put wine to his own unique use. Usually in Chinese poetry, the practice of wine involves drinking just enough so the ego fades and perception is clarified. T'ao Ch'ien called this state "idleness" (see Key Terms: *hsien*): *wu-wei* as stillness. But although Li Po certainly cultivated such stillness, he usually ended up thoroughly drunk, a state in which he was released fully into his most authentic and enlightened self: *wu-wei* as spontaneity.

Li Po's spontaneous energy is finally nothing other than the unfolding of presence (*yu*: see Key Terms), which is rooted in the profound stillness of absence (*wu*: see Key Terms), a stillness often found in his more meditative poems. And according to legend, when the phenomenon of Li Po returned in the end to that stillness of absence, it too was an event replete with that same spontaneity: out drunk in a boat, he fell into a river and drowned trying to embrace the moon.

ON YELLOW-CRANE TOWER, FAREWELL TO MENG HAO-JAN, WHO'S LEAVING FOR YANG-CHOU

From Yellow-Crane Tower, my old friend leaves the west.
Downstream to Yang-chou, late spring a haze of blossoms,

distant glints of lone sail vanish into emerald-green air:
nothing left but a river flowing on the borders of heaven.

WANDERING UP AMPLE-GAUZE CREEK ON A SPRING DAY

At the canyon's mouth, I'm singing. Soon
the path ends. People don't go any higher.

I scramble up cliffs into impossible valleys,
and follow the creek back toward its source.

Up where newborn clouds rise over open rock,
a guest come into wildflower confusions,

I'm still lingering on, my climb unfinished,
as the sun sinks away west of peaks galore.

THOUGHTS OF YOU UNENDING

Thoughts of you unending
here in Ch'ang-an,

crickets where the well mirrors year-end golds cry out
autumn, and under a thin frost, mats look cold, ice-cold.

My lone lamp dark, thoughts thickening, I raise blinds
and gaze at the moon. It renders the deepest lament

empty. But you're lovely as a blossom born of cloud,

skies opening away all bottomless azure above, clear
water all billows and swelling waves below. Skies endless

for a spirit in sad flight, the road over hard passes
sheer distance, I'll never reach you, even in dreams,

my ruins of the heart,
thoughts of you unending.

NIGHT THOUGHTS AT EAST-FOREST MONASTERY ON THATCH-HUT MOUNTAIN

Alone, searching for blue-lotus roofs,
I set out from city gates. Soon, frost

clear, East-Forest temple bells call out,
Tiger Creek's moon bright in pale water.

Heaven's fragrance everywhere pure
emptiness, heaven's music endless,

I sit silent. It's still, the entire Buddha-
realm in a hairsbreadth, mind-depths

all bottomless clarity, in which vast
kalpas begin and end out of nowhere.

INSCRIBED ON A WALL AT SUMMIT-TOP TEMPLE

Staying the night at Summit-Top Temple,
you can reach out and touch the stars.

I venture no more than a low whisper,
afraid I'll wake the people of heaven.

These bangs not yet reaching my eyes,
I played at our gate, picking flowers,

and you came on your horse of bamboo,
circling the well, tossing green plums.

We lived together here in Steady-Shield,
two little people without any suspicion.

At fourteen, when I became your wife,
so timid and betrayed I never smiled,

I faced wall and shadow, eyes downcast.
A thousand pleas: I ignored them all.

At fifteen, my scowl began to soften.
I wanted us mingled as dust and ash,

and you always stood fast here for me,
no tower vigils awaiting your return.

At sixteen, you sailed far off to distant
Billow-Ease in Fear-Wall Gorge, fierce

June waters impossible, and howling
gibbons calling out into the heavens.

At our gate, where you lingered long,
moss buried your tracks one by one,

deep green moss I can't sweep away.
And autumn's come early. Leaves fall.

It's September now. Butterflies appear
in the west garden. They fly in pairs,

and it hurts. I sit all heart-stricken
at the bloom of youth in my old face.

Before you start back from out beyond
all those gorges, send a letter home.

I'm not saying I'd go far to meet you,
no further than Steady-Wind Sands.

MOUNTAIN DIALOGUE

You ask why I've settled in these emerald mountains:
I smile, mind of itself perfectly idle, and say nothing.

Peach blossoms drift streamwater away deep in mystery
here, another heaven and earth, nowhere people know.

DRINKING ALONE BENEATH THE MOON

1

Among the blossoms, a single jar of wine.
No one else here, I ladle it out myself.

Raising my cup, I toast the bright moon,
and facing my shadow makes friends three,

though moon has never understood wine,
and shadow only trails along behind me.

Kindred a moment with moon and shadow,
I've found a joy that must infuse spring:

I sing, and moon rocks back and forth;
I dance, and shadow tumbles into pieces.

Sober, we're together and happy. Drunk,
we scatter away into our own directions:

intimates forever, we'll wander carefree
and meet again in Star River distances.

2

Surely, if heaven didn't treasure wine,
there would be no Wine Star in heaven,

and if earth didn't treasure wine, surely
there would be no Wine Spring on earth.

Heaven and earth have always loved wine,
so how could loving wine shame heaven?

I hear clear wine called enlightenment,
and they say murky wine is like wisdom:

once you drink enlightenment and wisdom,
why go searching for gods and immortals?

Three cups and I've plumbed the great Way,
a jarful and I've merged with occurrence

appearing of itself. Wine's view is lived:
you can't preach doctrine to the sober.

SPRING THOUGHTS

When grasses in Yen ripple like emerald silk
and lush mulberry branches sag in Ch'in,

he'll still dream of coming home one day,
and I'll still be waiting, brokenhearted.

We're strangers, spring wind and I. Why is it
here, slipping inside my gauze bed-curtains?

Carrying a *ch'in* cased in green silk, a monk
descended from Eyebrow Mountain in the west.

When he plays, even in a few first notes,
I hear the pines of ten thousand valleys,

and streams rinse my wanderer's heart clean.
Echoes linger among temple frost-fall bells,

night coming unnoticed in emerald mountains,
autumn clouds banked up, gone dark and deep.

Sun rises over its eastern harbor
as if coming from some underworld,
and crossing heaven, returns again to western seas,
nowhere its six sun-dragons could ever find rest.
It's kept up this daily beginning and ending forever,
but we're not made of such
ancestral *ch'i*, so how long can we wander with it here?

Flowers bloom in spring wind. They never refuse.
And trees never resent leaf-fall in autumn skies.
No one could whip the turning seasons along so fast:
the ten thousand things rise and fall of themselves.

Hsi Ho, O great
Sun Mother, Sun Guide—how could you drown
                              in those wild sea-swells of abandon?
And Lu Yang, by what power
halted evening's setting sun?
It defies Way, offends heaven—
all fake and never-ending sham.
I'll toss this Mighty Mudball earth into a bag
and break free into that boundless birthchamber of it all!

7

A woman alone east of Thresher-Knoll
while you stay among Han River islands,

I look out across bright blossoms all day:
a lit path of white stretching between us.

We made clouds-and-rain love our farewell,
then nothing but autumn grasses remained,

autumn grasses and autumn moths rising,
and thoughts of you all twilight sorrow.

Will I ever see you again, ever darken
this lamp as you loosen my gauze robes?

9

Short and tall, spring grasses lavish
our gate with green, as if passion-driven,

everything returned from death to life.
My burr-weed heart—it alone is bitter.

You'll know that in these things I see
you here again, planting our gardens

behind the house, and us lazily gathering
what we've grown. It's no small thing.

9/9, OUT DRINKING ON DRAGON MOUNTAIN

9/9, out drinking on Dragon Mountain,
I'm an exile among yellow blossoms smiling.

Soon drunk, I watch my cap tumble in wind,
dance in love—a guest the moon invites.

UNTITLED

Waking in the gallery
at dawn, and told it's snowing,

I raise the blinds and gaze into pure good fortune.
Courtyard steps a bright mirage of distance,

kitchen smoke trails light through flurried skies,
and the cold hangs jewels among whitened grasses.

Must be heaven's immortals in a drunken frenzy,
grabbing cloud and grinding it into white dust.

Delirium, battlefields all dark and delirium,
convulsions of men swarm like armies of ants.

A red wheel in thickened air, the sun hangs
above bramble and weed blood's dyed purple,

and crows, their beaks clutching warrior guts,
struggle at flight, grief-glutted, earthbound.

Those on guard atop the Great Wall yesterday
became ghosts in its shadow today. And still,

flags bright everywhere like scattered stars,
the slaughter keeps on. War-drums throbbing:

my husband, my sons—you'll find them all
there, out where war-drums throb and throb.

REVERENCE-PAVILION MOUNTAIN, SITTING ALONE

Birds have vanished into deep skies.
A last cloud drifts away, all idleness.

Inexhaustible, this mountain and I
gaze at each other, it alone remaining.

JADE-STAIRCASE GRIEVANCE

Night long on the jade staircase, white
dew appears, soaks through gauze stockings.

She lets down crystalline blinds, gazes out
through jewel lacework at the autumn moon.

5

Autumn River's white gibbons seem countless,
a dancing flurry of leaps, snowflakes flying:

Coaxing kids out of the branches, they descend,
and in a frolic, drink at the moon in water.

14

Smelter fires light up heaven and earth,
red stars swirling through purple smoke.

In the moonlit night, men's faces flushed,
work-song echoes out over the cold river.

AT GOLDEN-RIDGE

Golden-Ridge City tucked into the earth,
the river curving past, flowing away:

there were once a million homes here,
and crimson towers along narrow lanes.

A vanished country all spring grasses,
the palace buried in ancient hills, this

moon remains, facing timeless islands
across Thereafter Lake waters, empty.

THOUGHTS IN NIGHT QUIET

Seeing moonlight here at my bed
and thinking it's frost on the ground,

I look up, gaze at the mountain moon,
then back, dreaming of my old home.

TU FU

(712 to 770)

TU FU IS generally described as the greatest of China's poets. Although he is much admired for the erudition and formal virtuosity of his poetry, neither of which translate well, Tu Fu's most important achievements lie elsewhere, and fortunately they do translate. Aside from the immediate impact of his work, Tu Fu's renown derives most fundamentally from a realism that opened poetry to all aspects of human experience, from the intimate and concrete to the political and abstract, as well as new depths of subjective experience. Indeed, these different dimensions are often combined in a single poem, a poetic method that was itself a substantial innovation. And although the innovative nature of his poetry denied him recognition during his own lifetime, Tu Fu soon began awing poets, his work inspiring such dissimilar poetics as Po Chü-i's plainspoken social realism and Meng Chiao's black, quasi-surreal introspection.

Tu Fu was forty-four when the civil war that devastated China broke out in 755, and the dire social situation is a constant presence in his major poems, nearly all of which were written during these war years. Although there was a long tradition of certain established political themes in *yüeh-fu* poetry, Tu Fu was the first poet to write extensively about real, immediate social concerns, and as a result he is often referred to as the "poet-historian." After rebel armies overran the capital, Tu Fu was caught in the city, where he hid in monasteries (p. 198). After somehow escaping, he tried to do his share in the government's campaign to rescue the country, but after much frustration and little success, he resigned in the hope of establishing a more reclusive life devoted to his art. Tu Fu succeeded spectacularly as an artist, but his was not to be a settled life of tranquil dwelling far from human affairs. He never stopped agonizing over his country's struggles, which are a constant presence in his poems. And though the fighting had appeared to be nearly over when he resigned, it was not. Tu Fu did manage to settle his family several times, but they were always driven on—either by the incessant fighting that kept flaring up all around the country or by his longing to return to his home in the capital and assist the government in its struggle to salvage the situation.

Tu Fu spent these years wandering the outer fringes of the Chinese cultural sphere: the far west (pp. 202–205) and Ch'eng-tu in the southwest (pp. 205–206); then K'uei-chou, perched above the Yangtze's spectacular Triple Gorge, in territory populated by non-Chinese aboriginal people (pp. 207–11); and beyond into the south (p. 212), where he finally died in a boat on Tung-t'ing Lake. It was this exile wandering that provided him with his unique perspective. Though he responded poetically at the level of immediate experience, Tu Fu achieved in his late poems a panoramic view of the human drama: he saw it as part of China's vast landscape of natural process. Poised between black despair and exquisite beauty, his was a geologic perspective, a vision of the human cast against the elemental sweep of the universe.

GAZING AT THE SACRED PEAK

What's this ancestor Exalt Mountain like?
An unending green of north and south,

ethereal beauty Change-Maker distills
where *yin* and *yang* split dusk and dawn.

It breathes out banks of cloud. Birds clear
my eyes vanishing home. One day soon,

at the top, those other peaks will be small
enough to hold, all in a single glance.

INSCRIBED ON A WALL AT CHANG'S RECLUSE HOME

In spring mountains, alone, I set out to find you.
Axe strokes crack—crack and quit. Silence doubles.

I pass snow and ice lingering along cold streams,
then, at Stone Gate in late light, enter these woods.

You harm nothing: deer roam here each morning;
want nothing: auras gold and silver grace nights.

Facing you on a whim in bottomless dark, the way
here lost—I feel it drifting, this whole empty boat.

SONG OF THE WAR-CARTS

War-carts clatter and creak,
horses stomp and splutter:
each wearing quiver and bow, the war-bound men pass.

Mothers and fathers, wives and children—they all flock
alongside, farewell dust so thick you can't see All-Solar,

grief's bridge. They get everywhere in the way, crying
cries to break against heaven, tugging at war clothes.

On the roadside, when a passerby asks war-bound men,
war-bound men say simply: *Our lots are so often drawn.*

*Taken north at fifteen, we guard Yellow River shorelines,
and taken west at forty, we man frontier battle camps.*

*Village elders tied our headcloths then. And here we
return, hair white, only to leave again for borderlands,*

*lands swollen with seas of blood. And our fine emperor's
imperial dreams of conquest never end, they never end.*

*Haven't you heard that
east of the mountains, in our homeland, ten hundred towns
and ten thousand villages are overrun by thorned weeds,*

*that even though strong wives keep hoeing and plowing,
you can't tell where crops are and aren't? It's worst for*

*mighty Ch'in warriors: the more bitter war they outlive,
the more they're herded around like chickens and dogs.*

Though you're kind to ask, sir,
how could we complain? Imagine

this winter in Ch'in. Their men
still haven't returned, and those

clerks are out demanding taxes.
Taxes! How could they pay taxes?

A son's birth means tragedy now.
People prefer a daughter's birth,

a daughter's birth might at least end in marriage nearby,
but a son's birth ends in an open grave who knows where.

Haven't you seen how
bones from ancient times
lie, bleached and unclaimed, scattered along shores of

Sky-Blue Seas—how the bitter weeping of old ghosts is
joined by new voices, the gray sky by chittering rain.

from FIRST-DEVOTION RETURN CHANT

.   .   .

The hundred grasses in tatters, high wind-
scoured ridges and stars—it is year's end

on the imperial highway. Mountain shadow
towering in the heart of night, I set out.

Soon I can't tie my loose coat-sash closed,
fingers frostbitten among bitter morning

peaks. Our emperor's sound asleep here
on Black-Horse Mountain, demon banners

trailed skyward in this cold canyon passing
armies have polished smooth. Steam billows

over his jasper-green pools. Constellations
chafe and jar against his imperial lances.

Regal ministers were up late taking their
fine pleasure here. Music swelling through

gnarled canyons, not a poor man in sight,
they were bathed by their choice women,

women pampered with silks painstakingly
woven out by shivering farm wives, their

husbands horsewhipped by tax collectors
come demanding tributes for the palace,

and our sage king, wishing his people well,
sends baskets stuffed with heartfelt gifts.

With trusted ministers so blind to inner
pattern, why squander all those supplies?

The number of august men dawn brings to
court frightens any decent man. And I hear

the emperor's own gold tableware has been
divvied out among blue-blooded families.

Dancing goddesses grace the hall, jade-white
bodies furling incense mists. And grieving

flutes echoing *ch'in* song's pure clarity,
sables warm, guests savor camel-hoof soup,

frost-whipped kumquats, fragrant coolie
oranges . . . The imperial-red gate: rank

wine and meat dumped inside, frozen bones
dead by the road outside. All and nothing

here but a key and half-step different. How
could such misery endured ever be retold?

I turn north to the rivers Wei and Ching.
At the flooded ferry-landing, I turn again.

A sea of water pouring from the west looms
and summits to the end of sight and beyond

to Empty-Alike Mountain peaks, and I fear
it may wreck the pillars holding up heaven.

One bridge still spans the river, its welcome
trestlework a creaking howl and whisper

in wind, and we travelers help each other
across the current raging broad and wild.

My dear wife in a strange place, sheltering
our family from wind and snow—how could I

leave them so long alone? Thinking we'll
at least be together again going without,

I come home to sounds of weeping, wailing
cries for a child stone-dead now of hunger.

Neighbors sob in the street. And who am I
to master my grief like some sage, ashamed

even to be a father   I whose son has died
for simple lack of food? After full autumn

harvests, how could I have known, how
imagined the poor so desperate with want?

Son of an untaxed family, never dragged off
to make someone's war, I have lived a life

charmed, and still too sad. O, but the poor
grieve like vast winds across ravaged trees.

Those who've lost all for war, those on far
frontiers dead: they wander dark thoughts,

and elusive engines of grief still loom like
all South Mountain, heave and swing loose.

MOONLIT NIGHT

Tonight at Fu-chou, this moon she watches
alone in our room. And those little, far-off

kids, too young to understand what keeps me
away, or even remember Ch'ang-an. By now

her hair will be mist-scented, her jade-pure
arms chilled in its crystalline light. O when

will it find us together again, drapes drawn
open, light traced where it dries our tears?

SPRING LANDSCAPE

The country in ruins, rivers and mountains
continue. The city's grown lush with spring.

Blossoms scatter tears for us, and all these
separations in a bird's cry startle the heart.

Beacon-fires three months ablaze: by now
a simple letter's worth ten thousand in gold,

and worry's thinned my hair into such white
confusion I can't even keep this hairpin in.

Death at least gives separation repose.
Without death, its grief only sharpens.

You drift malarial southlands beyond
Yangtze distances, and I hear nothing,

exiled friend. Knowing I think of you
always now, you visit my dreams, my

heart frightened it is no living spirit
I dream. Fathomless miles—you come

so far from bright azure-green maples
night shrouds passes when you return,

and tangled as you are in nets of law,
with what bird's wings could you fly?

Flooding my room to the last roofbeam,
the moon sinks. You linger in its light,

but the waters deepen into long swells,
dark dragons: take good care, old friend.

It was late, but he was out in the village
night when I arrived, rounding up men.

Her worn-out old husband slipped away
over the wall, and she went to the gate.

The officer cursed loud and long, lost in
his rage. And lost in grief, an old woman

palsied with grief and tears, she offered
regrets: *My three sons left to guard Yeh,*

then finally, from one, a letter arrived
full of news: two killed in battle. Living

a stolen life, my last son can't last long,
and if you're dead you're forever dead

and gone. We've no men left—only my
baby grandson still at his mom's breast.

Coming and going, hardly half a ragged
skirt to put on, she can't leave him yet.

I'm old and weak, but I could hurry to
River-Brights with you tonight. Listen—

if you'd let me, I could be there in time,
cook an early meal for our brave boys.

Later, deep in long night, voices fade.
I almost hear crying hush—silence . . .

And morning, taking the road out front,
I find no one but the old-timer to leave.

THE NEW MOON

Thin slice of ascending light, arc tipped
aside all its bellied dark—the new moon

appears and, scarcely risen beyond ancient
frontier passes, edges behind clouds. Silver,

changeless—the Star River spreads across
empty mountains scoured with cold. White

dew dusts the courtyard, chrysanthemum
blossoms clotted there with swollen dark.

1

A wanderer—O all year this wanderer that I am,
white hair a shoulder-length confusion, gathering

acorns all year, like the monkey sage. Under cold
skies, the sun sets in this mountain valley. No word

arrives from the central plain, and for my failing
skin and bone, ice-parched hands and feet, no return

no return there Song, my first song
                    sung, O song already sad enough,
winds come from the furthest sky grieving my grief.

2

Sturdy hoe, O long sturdy hoe, my white-timbered
fortune—now I'm depending on you, on you alone

for life, there isn't a wild yam shoot to dig. Snow
fills the mountains. I tug at a coat never covering

my shins. And when we come home empty-handed
again—children's cries are deafening, four walls

harboring quiet Song, my second song
                    sung, O song beginning to carry,
this village is peopled with the faces of my sorrow.

3

Brothers of mine, my brothers in far-off places, O
three thin brothers all frail and weak, and these

scattered lives we wander never meet, Mongol dust
smothering sky, roads between us going on forever.

Cranes flock eastward, following geese. But cranes—
how could cranes carry me there, to a life beside

my brothers Song, my third song
                              sung, O song sung three times over,
who knows where they'll come to gather my bones?

4

Sister of mine, my sister off in Love-Apart—husband
dead young, orphan children unhinged, O my sister,

the long Huai is all deep swells, all flood-dragon fury:
how will you come now? And after ten years, how

will I find you in my little boat? Arrows fill my eyes,
and southlands riddled with war banners and flags

harbor another dark Song, my fourth song
                              sung, O song rehearsed four times through,
gibbons haunt midday forest light wailing my wails.

5

Four mountains all windswept, headlong streams and
rain—O the cold rain falling through bare trees falls,

and clouds hang low. Among brown weeds and ancient
city walls—white foxes prowl, brown foxes keep still.

This life of mine—how can I live out this life in some
starveling valley? I sit up in the night, ten thousand

worries gathering Song, my fifth song
                    sung, O song already long enough
calling my spirit, my lost spirit gone to my lost home.

6

Dragon—O a dragon in southern mountains, cragged
trees tangling their ancient branches above its pool:

when yellowed leaves fall, it sinks into hibernation,
and from the east come vipers prowling the waters.

A traveler amazed they would dare show themselves,
I slice them apart with my sword, and once I finish I

begin to rest here Song, my sixth song
                    sung, O song wearing your thoughts thin,
spring's gracing streams and valleys again with me,

a man
every distinction has eluded, a man grown old only
to wander three hungry years on mountain roads.

How long for Ch'ang-an ministers? Honor, wealth—
they all devote themselves early. Wise men I knew

long ago live in these mountains. Our talk is all old
times gone by, nothing more—old friends harboring

wounded memories Song, my seventh song
                              sung, O uneasy silence ending my tune,
white sun empties majestic sky with headlong flight.

THE RIVER VILLAGE

In one curve, cradling our village, the clear river
flows past. On long summer days, the business of

solitude fills this river village. Swallows in rafters
come and go carelessly. On the water, tender gulls

nestle together. My wife draws a paper chessboard,
and tapping at needles, the kids contrive fishhooks.

Often sick, I need drugs and herbs—but what more,
come to all this, what more could a simple man ask?

LEAVING THE CITY

It's frost-bitter cold, and late, and falling
dew muffles my gaze into bottomless skies.

Smoke trails out over distant salt mines.
Snow-covered peaks angle shadows east.

Armies haunt my homeland still, and war-
drums throb in this other place. A guest

here in this river city tonight, I return
again to shrieking crows, my old friends.

BRIMMED WHOLE

A river moon only feet away, storm-lanterns
alight late in the second watch . . . Serene

flock of fists on sand—egrets asleep when
a fish leaps in the boat's wake, shivering, cry.

NIGHT AT THE TOWER

Yin and *yang* cut brief autumn days short. Frost and snow
clear, leaving a cold night open at the edge of heaven.

Marking the fifth watch, grieving drums and horns erupt.
The Star River, shadows trembling, floats in Triple Gorge.

Pastoral weeping, war's sound now in how many homes,
and tribal songs drifting from woodcutters and fishermen . . .

Slumber-Dragon, Leap-Stallion: all brown earth in the end.
And the story of our lives just opens away—vacant, silent.

THATCH HOUSE

Our thatch house perched where land ends,
we leave the brushwood gate always open.

Dragons and fish settle into evening waters.
Moon and stars drifting above autumn peaks,

dew gathers clarity, then thaws. High clouds
thin away—none return. Women man wind-

tossed boats anchored here: young, ashamed,
that river life battering their warm beauty.

8TH MOON, 17TH NIGHT: FACING THE MOON

The autumn moon rose full again tonight.
In this river village, a lone old wanderer

hoisting blinds, I return to its radiance.
As I struggle along with a cane, it follows,

and bright enough to rouse hidden dragons,
it scatters roosting birds back and forth.

All around my thatched study, orange groves
shine: clear dew aching with fresh light.

DAWN LANDSCAPE

The last watch has sounded in K'uei-chou.
Color opening above Solar-Terrace Mountain,

a cold sun clears high peaks. Clouds linger,
blotting out canyons below tangled ridges,

and deep Yangtze banks keep sails hidden.
Beneath clear skies: clatter of falling leaves.

And these deer at my bramble gate: so close
here, we touch our own kind in each other.

THOUGHTS

I sit on our south porch in deep night,
moonlight incandescent on my knees,

gusty winds tumbling Star River over
until morning sun clears the rooftops.

Things wild sleep alone. Then waking,
they set out in herds and flocks. And I

too hurry kids along, scratch out our
living with the same stingy industry.

Passersby grow rare under cold, year-
end skies. Days and months slip away.

Caught in the scramble for glory, we
people made bedlam lice of ourselves.

Before emperors, people ate their fill
and were content, then someone began

knotting ropes, and now we're mired
in the glue and varnish of government.

It all started with Sui, inventor of fire,
and Tung's fine histories made it utter

disaster. If you light candles and lamps,
you know moths will gather in swarms.

Search out through all eight horizons:
you find nothing anywhere but isolate

emptiness, departure and return one
movement, one ageless way of absence.

RIVERSIDE MOON AND STARS

The sudden storm's left a clear, autumnal
night and Jade-String stars radiant in gold

waves. Star River white with all beginning,
its clarity claims Yangtze shallows anew.

Strung-Pearls snaps, scattering shimmering
reflections. A mirror lofts into blank space

of origins. Of last light a waterclock hides,
what remains with frost seizing blossoms?

NIGHT

1

Flutes mourn on the city wall. It is dusk:
the last birds cross our village graveyard,

and after decades of battle, their war-tax
taken, people return in deepening night.

Trees darken against cliffs. Leaves fall.
The river of stars faintly skirting beyond

frontier passes, I gaze at a tilting Dipper,
the moon thin, magpies done with flight.

2

A sliver of moon lulls through clear night.
Half abandoned to sleep, lampwicks char.

Deep wander, uneasy among howling peaks,
and forests of falling leaves startle cicadas.

I remember mince treats east of the river,
think of our boat adrift in falling snow . . .

Tribal songs rise, rifling the stars. Here,
at the edge of heaven, I inhabit my absence.

LEAVING EQUAL-PEACE AT DAWN

In town to the north, a watchman's final clapper
falls silent again. Venus slipping away in the east,

neighborhood roosters mourn, same as yesterday.
How long can life's own sights and sounds endure?

My oar-strokes hushed, I leave for rivers and lakes,
distances without promise. I step out the gate, look

away—and all trace has vanished. These drug-cakes
shoring this old life up—they alone stay with me.

OVERNIGHT AT WHITE-SAND POST-STATION

Another night on the water: last light,
cook-smoke, thatched post-station. Here

beyond the lake, against ancient white
sand: fresh green reeds. Ten thousand

forms of spring *ch'i*—among all this,
my lone raft is another Wandering Star:

carried by waves, moon's light limitless,
I shade into pellucid Southern Darkness.

COLD MOUNTAIN (HAN SHAN)

(c. 7th to 9th centuries)

LIKE GOVERNMENT OFFICIALS, monks in ancient China were part of the intelligentsia, so virtually all of them wrote poetry. For the most part, however, theirs was doctrinal Buddhist verse with little lasting literary value. The greatest of these poet-monks is, in fact, an anti-monk who lived on Cold Mountain in southeast China and took that mountain's name as his own.

Almost nothing is known about Cold Mountain the poet: he exists more as legend than as historical fact. It is said that he often visited a nearby Ch'an (Zen) monastery, where a like-minded friend in the kitchen shared leftovers with him, and the resident monks thought him quite insane. There are stories of his antics there, bantering with his friend and ridiculing the monks for their devout pursuit of an enlightenment they already possessed as part of their inherent nature. But mostly he roamed the mountains alone, a wild Ch'an sage writing poems on rocks and trees. These poems were gathered by the local prefect who, recognizing Cold Mountain's genius, assembled them into a collection that has been preserved. This collection now has about 310 untitled poems, a number that makes one suspect it was shaped with an eye to giving it the status of a classic by associating it with *The Book of Songs*, which has 305 poems (probably a few poems were added to the Cold Mountain collection in later years). Indeed, it appears likely that the collection is, in fact, the work of two primary poets, and perhaps others. In any case, the Cold Mountain poems came to be widely admired in the literary and Ch'an communities of China. This admiration spread to Korea and Japan, and recently to the West, where Gary Snyder's influential translations re-created Cold Mountain as a contemporary American poet.

Cold Mountain is remembered as a Ch'an poet, and as such he identifies the empty mind of Ch'an enlightenment with the mountain itself. And he is no less a Taoist poet, sage-master of belonging utterly to the cosmology, the dynamic spiritual ecology that mountain realm manifests so dramatically. Indeed, Cold Mountain emptied out the distinction between Cold Mountain the poet and Cold Mountain the mountain. This is the essence of the Cold Mountain poems. And according to the legend, Cold Mountain the poet was last seen when, slipping into a crevice that closed behind him, he vanished into the mountain. Only poems remained, scrawled on rocks and trees: the record of a mountain working further and further into its own voice, its own singular language.

9

People ask for the Cold Mountain Way.
Cold Mountain Road gives out where

confusions of ice outlast summer heat
and sun can't thin mists of blindness.

So how did someone like me get here?
My mind's just not the same as yours:

if that mind of yours were like mine,
you'd be right here in the midst of it.

2 8

If you're climbing the Cold Mountain Way,
Cold Mountain Road grows inexhaustible:

long canyons opening across fields of talus,
broad creeks tumbling down mists of grass.

Moss is impossibly slick even without rain,
but this far up, pines need no wind to sing.

Who can leave the world's tangles behind
and sit with me among these white clouds?

67

The cold in these mountains is ferocious,
has been every year since the beginning.

Crowded peaks locked in perennial snows,
recluse-dark forests breathing out mists,

grasses never sprout before the solstice
and leaves start falling in early August.

This confusion includes a lost guest now,
searching, searching—no sky to be seen.

81

Springs flowing pure clarity in emerald streams,
moonlight's radiant white bathes Cold Mountain.

Leave wisdom dark: spirit's enlightened of itself.
Empty your gaze and this world's beyond silence.

163

I've lived out tens of thousands of years
on Cold Mountain. Given to the seasons,

I vanished among forests and cascades,
gazed into things so utterly themselves.

No one ventures up into all these cliffs
hidden forever in white mist and cloud.

It's just me, thin grass my sleeping mat
and azure heaven my comforting quilt:

happily pillowed on stone, I'm given to
heaven and earth changing on and on.

199

Under vast arrays of stars, dazzling depths of night,
I light a lone lamp among cliffs. The moon hasn't set.

It's the unpolished jewel. Incandescence round and full,
it hangs there in blackest-azure skies, my very mind.

205

The cloud road's choked with deep mist. No one gets here that way,
but these Heaven-Terrace Mountains have always been my home:

a place to vanish among five-thousand-foot cliffs and pinnacles,
ten thousand creeks and gorges all boulder towers and terraces.

I follow streams in birch-bark cap, wooden sandals, tattered robes,
and clutching a goosefoot walking-stick, circle back around peaks.

Once you realize this floating life is the perfect mirage of change,
it's breathtaking—this wild joy at wandering boundless and free.

220

Everyone who glimpses Cold Mountain
starts complaining about insane winds,

about a look human eyes can't endure
and a shape nothing but tattered robes.

They can't fathom these words of mine.
Theirs I won't even mention. I just tell

all those busy people bustling around:
Come face Cold Mountain for a change.

226

I delight in the everyday Way, myself
among mist and vine, rock and cave,

wildlands feeling so boundlessly free,
white clouds companions in idleness.

Roads don't reach those human realms.
You only climb this high in no-mind:

I sit here on open rock: a lone night,
a full moon drifting up Cold Mountain.

282

Amid ten thousand streams up among
thousands of clouds, a man all idleness

wanders blue mountains all day long,
returns at night to sleep below cliffs.

In the whirl of springs and autumns,
to inhabit this calm, no tangles of dust:

it's sheer joy, depending on nothing,
still as an autumn river's quiet water.

People take the Cold
Mountain Way, never

arrive. Whoever does
is a tenfold Buddha.

Cicadas are singing,
raucous crows quiet.

Yellow leaves tumble.
White clouds sweep

across fields of talus,
peaks hidden deep.

Dwelling this alone,
I'm the perfect guide.

Look, look all around
here: any sign of me?

306

No one knows this
mountain I inhabit:

deep in white clouds,
forever empty, silent.

309

Sage Cold Mountain
is forever like this:

dwells alone and free,
not alive, not dead.

WEI YING-WU

(c. 737 to 792)

LIKE HSIEH LING-YÜN, Wei Ying-wu was born into one of the
wealthiest and most powerful families in the empire. But the family's for-
tunes were in decline, and when Wei was about twenty, the An Lu-shan
Rebellion ravaged the country, leaving the Wei family in ruins. The loss of
his aristocratic life was a kind of awakening for Wei: he soon moved to
Mind-Jewel Monastery (see p. 231), where he stayed for several years. This
marked the beginning of a life centered in quiet contemplation and po-
etry. He was by nature a recluse, but like Wang Wei, he never left govern-
ment service completely: he needed the salary to survive, and he was also
very concerned with the desperate plight of common people in an age of
widespread poverty and devastation. He held a number of positions, both
in the capital and in distant provinces. But it seems Wei was never really
comfortable in these appointments, though some were quite important,
and he generally ended up leaving them. He preferred the simplicity of a
recluse life at a mountain monastery or farm, in spite of the hardship it
sometimes entailed.

Wei Ying-wu's poetry is historically noteworthy because it heralds the
transition into the second phase of T'ang Dynasty poetry, which is charac-
terized by more introspective and experimental work, for his poems often
make elusive leaps that operate outside traditional poetic logic. But in

Wei's case, rather than the hermetic disorientations produced by the experimental poetries to come, those introspective leaps often identify self and landscape in a way that reflects a profound Ch'an (Zen) balance, revealing deep insights that go beyond logical thought structures. This poetics reflects the social situation of the time. Wei lived in the ruins of what was perhaps China's greatest moment of cultural splendor, and his poems are often suffused with an ineffable sense of absence. Here lies the uneasy magic of Wei's poems: in them, loss and absence often seem indistinguishable from the emptiness of an enlightened mind.

AT WEST CREEK IN CH'U-CHOU

Alone, I savor wildflowers tucked in along the creek,
and there's a yellow oriole singing in treetop depths.

Spring floods come rain-swollen and wild at twilight.
No one here at the ferry, a boat drifts across of itself.

AT TRUTH-EXPANSE MONASTERY, IN THE DHARMA-MASTER'S WEST LIBRARY

At a thatch hut above riverside cliffs,
rapids far below: crystalline chimes

in vast rivers-and-mountains solitude.
Climbing into such views means pure

confusion. I straggled up First-Origin,
then followed Well-Creek Trail back to

temple trees hissing in endless winds,
this river lit with regret turning dark.

AUTUMN NIGHT, SENT TO CH'IU TAN

This autumn night become thoughts of you,
I wander along, offer cold heaven a chant.

In mountain emptiness, a pinecone falls.
My recluse friend must not be asleep either.

SENT TO A MASTER OF THE WAY IN
THE UTTER-PEAK MOUNTAINS

In my office library, the morning cold,
I suddenly think of a mountain guest

searching creeks for bramble kindling
and returning to cook white-stone soup.

I long to bring you a gourd full of wine,
soften endless nights of wind and rain,

but fallen leaves fill empty mountains,
all trace of your coming and going gone.

Sun sinks away. Dark distances deepen,
tangles of sorrow I'll never open out.

A meager quilt isn't warm enough now
sleet's smeared white over white frost,

the year's dusk ending dawn's resolve.
It startles geese—such depths of grief,

depths of grief come who knows how.
Her peach-and-plum beauty suddenly

scattered. Inner curtains sway, empty:
no return from a tomb of dark silence.

We shared a lifetime of love, but now
she's gone, entrusted so utterly to dust.

Embracing that ache my girls endure
and quite lost to the insight of masters,

I shake out robes and get up. Midnight.
Star River too drifts on: restless, aimless.

NEW YEAR'S

Memories ache on, same as yesterday,
and the last winter moon's gone dark.

It startles me, the year suddenly new
and I alone, bitter about growing old.

The lake's turning green, ice melting.
White plum and willow sway. Exquisite

light returns morning after morning
and lasts, impossible to think through.

MOONLIT NIGHT

A brilliant moon wanders the spring city,
thick dew luminous among fragrant grasses.

I sit, longing. Empty, this window of gauze
torn and fluttering in crystalline radiance,

crystalline radiance where it ends like this:
torn more and more, a person growing old.

IN IDLENESS, FACING RAIN

All dark mystery, I embrace it replete,
alone, night thinning into morning.

In this empty library, I face tall trees,
sparse rain soaking through rustling

leaves. Nesting swallows flutter, wet.
Orchid petals blur across stone steps.

It's quiet. Memories come, and grief
suddenly caught and buffeted in wind.

LAMENT OVER A MIRROR

Cast at Distance-Ridge, water-chestnut
blossom wide-open there in its little

coffin, this mirror was devoted to her
always. She's dead now, but it remains:

a frozen disk, implement of sheer ice,
flawless talisman of purest white jade.

Her form and reflection gaze no more,
but it shines on and on. Before lament

over our lifetime of wise words begins,
autumn moon drifts branches of pine.

AUTUMN NIGHT

1

It's autumn again. Courtyard trees rustle.
Deep in shadow, insects grieve on and on.

Alone, facing the upper library, I doze,
listening to cold rain clatter in the dark,

window-lattice now and then in the wind
trembling, lamp left failing on the wall.

Grief and sorrow, a lifetime remembered
this far away—all abandoned to the night.

2

Frost and dew spread away—thick, cold.
Star River swings back around, radiant.

Come a thousand miles, north wind rises
past midnight, startling geese. Branches

whisper. Icy leaves fall. And such clarity
in isolate depths of quiet, fulling-stones

grieve. I gaze out through empty space,
tangles of the heart all cold scattered ash.

EVENING VIEW

Already at South Tower: evening stillness.
In the darkness, a few forest birds astir.

The bustling city-wall sinks into shadow—
deeper, deeper. Just four mountain peaks.

AT CLOUD-WISDOM MONASTERY, IN THE CH'AN MASTER'S COURTYARD

Exalted with age, you never leave here:
the gate-path is overgrown with grass.

But summer rains have come, bringing
fruits and herbs into such bright beauty,

so we stroll down into forests of shadow,
sharing what recluse birds feel at dusk,

freed even of our names. And this much
alone, we wander the countryside back.

OUTSIDE MY OFFICE, WANDERING IN MOONLIGHT

Outside the office, night such luminous depths,
the lovely moon's a delight wandering with me.

Descending across the river, it comes halfway
adrift on dew-tinged air, then suddenly startles

autumn, scattering color through open forests,
scrawling its disk on the current's utter clarity.

And reaching mind, it bestows boundless light
all silver-pure azure eluding us to perfection.

CLIMBING ABOVE MIND-JEWEL MONASTERY, WHERE I LIVED LONG AGO

Incense terraces and kingfisher-green ridgelines tower into sky.
Misty trees and ten thousand homes fill the river's sunlit water.

The monks live nearby, but they would be such strangers by now.
I sit all stillness, listening to a faint bell record these lost years.

T'ang Dynasty II: Experimental Alternatives

(c. 800 to 875)

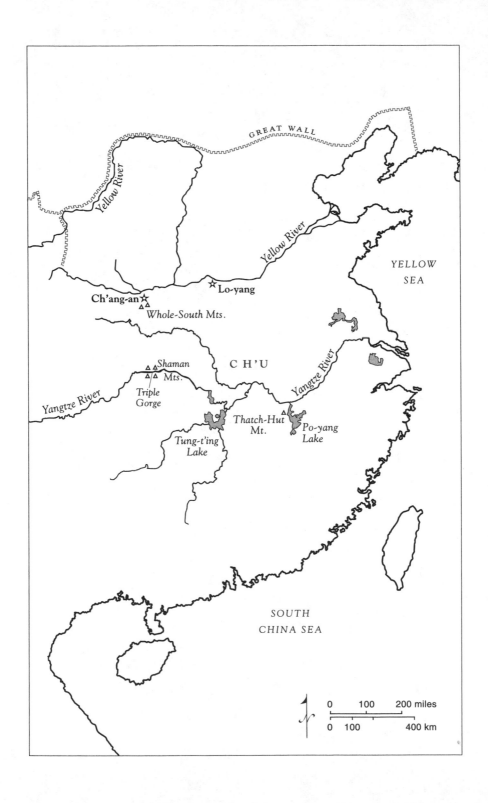

GREAT WALL

Yellow River

Yellow River

YELLOW
SEA

☆ Lo-yang

Ch'ang-an ☆
△△ Whole-South Mts.

CH'U

△△ Shaman
△△ Mts.
Triple
Gorge

Yangtze River

Yangtze River

Thatch-Hut
Mt.
△
Po-yang
Lake

Tung-t'ing
Lake

SOUTH
CHINA SEA

0   100   200 miles

0   100   400 km

THE CIVIL WAR launched in 755 by An Lu-shan created widespread so-
cial chaos and chronic militarism that haunted China until the T'ang Dy-
nasty finally fell a century and a half later, in 906, replaced by the Sung
Dynasty. This situation inspired a new and quite different kind of poetry.
The transition was prefigured in the dark work of late Tu Fu and the enig-
matic poems of Wei Ying-wu, and then began in earnest with the work
of Meng Chiao. Although major poetry continued to be written in the
mainstream (most notably by Po Chü-i, probably the greatest poet of this
period), Meng Chiao initiated an alternative tradition of experimental po-
etry that made the late T'ang years a period that opened a whole new
range of poetic diversity.

Traditionally, Chinese poets rendered immediate experience and their
responses to it, but the late T'ang experimentalists reversed that equation:
their focus was on imagining poems and, in so doing, creating new ex-
perience. The essence of this poetry is the attempt to create worlds of
imagination and intense interiority, and it employed strikingly modern
techniques to achieve these effects: surrealism, symbolism, collage, nonlog-
ical juxtapositions and imagistic fragmentation, hermetic ambiguity. That
this approach, so dominant and taken for granted in the modern West,

would be considered experimental is eloquent testimony to the fierce bond that connected Chinese poets to the landscape of empirical reality.

From the perspective of the modern West, where similar experimental strategies have largely defined innovation for over a century, it is interesting to consider how short-lived this alternative tradition was. In creating the poetic revival that made their dynasty the second great age of Chinese poetry, Sung poets saw in this experimental poetry a kind of decadence, a withdrawal from the social chaos ravaging the country into dreamy private realms. While their often bleak and disorienting strategies are no doubt the artistic embodiment of the chaotic social situation, the Sung poets felt this poetry was merely expressing that chaos, rather than standing against it, with a voice of clear-eyed empiricism, social responsibility, and spiritual insight. Still, those Sung critics admired the imaginative virtuosity of the late T'ang experimentalists and the new psychological depths their work opened.

MENG CHIAO

(751 to 814)

MENG CHIAO LIVED for many years as a poet-recluse associated with Ch'an (Zen) poet-monks in south China, but his mind and poetic practice were too restless for such a life. At the age of forty, he went north, eventually settling as an unemployed and impoverished poet in Lo-yang, the eastern capital. There, he became a leader of the experimental movement that made late T'ang poetry unlike anything else in the tradition. Meng developed a new poetics of startling disorientations. It was a poetry of virtuosic beauty that anticipated landmark developments in the modern Western tradition by a millennium. Reflecting the T'ang Dynasty's catastrophic social situation, Meng's later work employs quasi-surreal and symbolist techniques, extending the dark extremities of Tu Fu's late work into a radically new poetry of bleak introspection. And the dimensions of Meng's late poetry are also striking: in a tradition typified by the short lyric poem, Meng's major work almost exclusively takes the shape of large poetic sequences, a strategy that enabled Meng to layer his poetic world with complexity.

There is a black side to the profound sense of dwelling that grounds Chinese culture, and Meng Chiao is perhaps its consummate poetic master. Our belonging to earth's natural processes has always been the primary source of spiritual affirmation in China's Taoist/Ch'an intellectual culture, but it also means belonging to the consuming forces that drive those processes. In an intellectual culture that found a meditative serenity in the emptiness of absence (*wu*: see Key Terms), Meng was a dissenting voice. At its limits, as in "Laments of the Gorges" (pp. 245–48), his quasi-surreal and symbolist techniques are capable of articulating absence as a murderous furnace at the heart of change. But quite unlike his counterparts in our modern Western tradition, Meng Chiao employs these "avant-garde" techniques to explore the experience of being an integral part of the organic universe, and that sense of integration gives his fearful vision a kind of balance and deeper truth.

COLD CREEK

1

Frost rinsing water free of color, delicate
scales appear in Cold Creek. Come to this

hollow mirror of emptiness with delight,
I find a spent and sullen body shining back

there. Unable to hide itself now, something
prowling at bottom reappears—new again,

shimmering. Clear and open as the noblest
affections, this stream's a trap set for us.

Grown bright again, simple and shallow,
its heart frozen by night already flows full

this morning. And one handful, all emerald
clarity, rinses dust of a thousand worries

far away. Once footsteps muddy this water,
it's nothing like a pure mountain stream.

The Way flowing along these Lo-yang
shores is a creek fronting my ancestral

village. Pale ice passing boats shatter
clatters like blue agate. Green water

freezes into green jasper, whitewater
blossoming into emblems of white jade.

Setting this priceless mirror ablaze,
heaven's light evens all things out:

climbing down to its snaking menace,
clutching dead wood, I hear widows

crying. Frost too, leaving spring scents
faint, evens out these frozen reaches.

Losing the path, I sit like some fool,
just watching and listening. Children

work, hoe brambles along the shore,
talk sorrow, sorrow and more sorrow.

3

I sip wine at dawn, then cross the snow
out to this clear creek. Frozen into knife-

blades, rapids have sliced ducks open,
hacked geese apart. Stopping overnight

here left their feathers scattered, their
blood gurgling down into mud and sand.

I stand alone, dazed, words giving way
to that acrid clamor of the heart. Frozen

blood mustn't beget spring. If it begets
spring, newborn life's never evened out,

and if frozen blood breaks into blossom,
widow-tears begin. What isolate beauty:

a village all thorns and brambles, fields
all frozen and dead no one could plow.

4

Men pole boats, banking jade stars aside,
trailing out scattered fireflies. And cold

north plunging icy lament deep, starved
hunters chant invocations to hidden fish.

Frozen teeth gnaw and grind at themselves.
Windchimes clatter in sour wind. All this

immaculate grief—it's inescapable. It
rinses hearing clean of the least sound.

The current of rippling emerald is gone,
and colorful floss fallen, flight-tattered.

Ground glare ice, branches splintered,
things can't walk, can't roost. Wounded,

they squawk and shriek, yelp and howl,
accusing heaven: *will things ever rest?*

7

Bitter cold, the old man of the creek
weeps, frozen tears falling, a tinkling

clatter. Taking the form of birds dead,
beasts dead, snow slices a flurried heart.

Once frozen, a sword's edge won't cut,
and no one pulls bowstrings back now.

They say the valiant never eat heaven's
slaughter. Chopping down into jade,

I bury meat and bones, grief-stricken
sight itself a lament for all that beauty.

8

Windblown, last ice shudders on the creek,
creek holding the land's bright spring.

Blossoms drip and drip and drip. Jade melts,
setting the newborn dragon loose, scales

glittering into rippling curves clear. Spring
thaw begun, I bathe in these scented waters,

distant, a thousand miles of ice split open,
kindhearted warmth in every ladleful.

Frozen spirits rinsing each other clean,
trickles struggle into life and flow anew.

Suddenly, as if all sword wounds were over,
the body of a hundred battles begins rising.

3

Triple Gorge one thread of heaven over
ten thousand cascading thongs of water,

slivers of sun and moon sheering away
above, and wild swells walled-in below,

splintered spirits glisten, a few glints
frozen how many hundred years in dark

gorges midday light never finds, gorges
hungry froth fills with peril. Rotting

coffins locked into tree roots, isolate
bones twist and sway, dangling free,

and grieving frost roosts in branches,
keeping lament's dark, distant harmony

fresh. Exile, tattered heart all scattered
away, you'll simmer in seething flame

here, your life like finespun thread,
its road a trace of string traveled away.

Offer tears to mourn the water-ghosts,
and water-ghosts take them, glimmering.

4

Young clear-voiced dragons in these
gorges howl. Fresh scales born of rock,

they spew froth of fetid rain, breath
heaving, churning up black sinkholes.

Strange new lights glint, and hungry
swords await. This venerable old maw

still hasn't eaten its fill. Ageless teeth
cry a fury of cliffs, cascades gnawing

through these three gorges, gorges
full of jostling and snarling, snarling.

9

Water swords and spears raging in gorges,
boats drift across heaving thunder. Here

in the hands of these serpents and snakes,
you face everyday frenzies of wind and rain,

and how many fleeing exiles travel these
gorges, gorges rank inhabitants people?

You won't find a heart beneath this sheen,
this flood that's stored away aftermath

forever. Arid froth raising boundless mist,
froth all ablaze and snarling, snarling—

what of that thirst for wisdom when you're
suddenly here, dead center in these waters?

10

Death-owls call in human voices. Dragons
wolf down heaving mountain waters. Here

in broad daylight, with all the enticing
serenity of a clear and breezy sky, they

beggar wisdom, snarling everything alive
in fetid gatherings of vine-covered depths.

Want filling fanged cascades bottomless,
sawtooth froth swells everywhere. Nesting

birds can't settle in trees tilted so askew,
trees gibbons leaping and swinging fill.

Who can welcome laments of the gorges,
gorges saying *What will come will come.*

AUTUMN THOUGHTS

1

Lonely bones can't sleep nights. Singing
insects keep calling them, calling them.

And the old have no tears. When they sob,
autumn weeps dewdrops. Strength failing

all at once, as if cut loose, and ravages
everywhere, like weaving unraveled,

I touch thread-ends. No new feelings.
Memories crowding thickening sorrow,

how could I bear southbound sails, how
wander rivers and mountains of the past?

2

Under this autumn moon's face of frozen
beauty, the spirit driving an old wanderer

thins away. Cold dewdrops fall shattering
dreams. Biting winds comb cold through

bones. The sleeping-mat stamped with my
seal of sickness, whorled grief twisting,

there's nothing to depend on against fears.
Empty, sounds beginning nowhere, I listen.

Wu-t'ung trees, bare and majestic, sing
sound and echo clear as a *ch'in*'s lament.

5

Bamboo ticking in wind speaks. In dark
isolate rooms, I listen. Demons and gods

fill my frail ears, so blurred and faint I
can't tell them apart. Year-end leaves,

dry rain falling, scatter. Autumn clothes
thin cloud, my sick bones slice through

things clean. Though my bitter chant
still makes a poem, I'm withering autumn

ruin, strength following twilight away.
Trailed out, this fluttering thread of life:

no use saying it's tethered to the very
source of earth's life-bringing change.

HAN YÜ

(768 to 824)

HAN YÜ IS remembered as a crusader against the pervasive influence of institutionalized Buddhist and Taoist religions, though this antipathy did not extend to Ch'an (Zen) and philosophical Taoism (that of Lao Tzu and Chuang Tzu), which he saw as philosophical practices and alternatives to the reigning religious institutions. He saw these institutions of superstitious belief as perverting clarity in political thinking, and so contributing greatly to the country's ongoing crisis (especially insofar as the emperor and court were influenced by them). He also saw them distorting social priorities: people's energies had turned to religion rather than social well-being, most blatantly in the huge amount of wealth that was being given to the religious institutions. This had become a major problem for the government because those institutions had come to control vast amounts of wealth and land, all of which was exempt from taxation, thereby starving the struggling government of resources. Han famously advocated a return to secular and practical Confucian principles, and his forthright advocacy of these principles in defense of common people and against the religious institutions aroused considerable hostility and resulted in two exiles.

The literary dimension of Han's politics was to abandon the more precious and formalistic writing that had become commonplace, and replace it with a language based on ancient ideals of clarity and utility. He put these ideas into practice most clearly and prominently in prose, but they are also reflected in his poetry, which is characterized by a rejection of the distilled imagistic lyric that had been perfected earlier in the T'ang Dynasty. Instead, Han favored narrative structure and prosaic language. His poems tended to be long, with extended descriptive passages and great attention to detail. And in general, he advocated a poetry of ideas rather than the personal sentiment typical of the short lyric.

Under the influence of his close friend Meng Chiao, Han Yü turned for a time to a wildly imaginative poetry that flaunted the bizarre and strange. Indeed, with Meng he led the tightly knit circle of experimental poets that made this era so unique, among them Li Ho and Chia Tao. Nevertheless, this was clearly not the kind of poetry that came naturally to Han Yü: his work in this mode tended to be gratuitous and merely hyperbolic, and nowhere near as successful as the work of Meng Chiao, or that of the younger Li Ho, which it prefigures. Han Yü came to see it as exaggerated posturing and so soon returned to the deeper practice of a more straightforward mainstream poetry. In this, Han reflected the overall movement of the poetic tradition itself: after working through various alternative strategies, he returned to the balanced wisdom of an engagement with the immediacy of things at hand.

Great poetry is never the expression of literary or political dogma. Although Han Yü did write such poems, he was generally open to whatever directions his poetic intelligence happened to go, allowing himself a wide range of sometimes contradictory poetic possibilities. Han bridged the two strands of late T'ang poetry. He wrote poems of highly imaginative experimentation, and he also wrote poems in the mainstream tradition that continued through the late T'ang years, most notably in the work of Po Chü-i. But the best of his work combines both of these tendencies into a particularly unique poetry.

A GIRL FROM SPLENDOR-BLOOM MOUNTAIN

Along streets east and west, Buddhists preach sutra truths,
a racket of bells and shell-horns rattling palace courtyards:

it's *sin* and *blessing* far and wide, enticing threats and lies,
and thick as duckweed adrift, crowds push and shove to hear.

Yellow-robed masters of Tao are out preaching truths too,
but crowds are sparse below their seats, sparse as dawn stars.

A girl from Splendor-Bloom Mountain, Taoist family, longed
to drive the foreign faith out, restore the divine immortals,

so she washed away her makeup, and donned cap and cloak.
Neck white and cheeks red, azure-black eyebrows O so long,

she came to ascend the high seat and expound true mysteries.
Temple gates are consecrated, but someone swung them open,

and someone, I can't imagine who, quietly spread the news.
Suddenly things broke loose, crashing like a thunderstorm,

and the Buddhist temples were swept clean, footprints gone.
Regal horses and carriages come too, clogging the streets.

Soon the temple yard's so crowded people have to sit outside,
and if you're late, there's nowhere left: you miss the show.

People pull out hairpins, strip off bracelets and waist-jewels:
piles of jade and gold offered up, sparkling under azure skies,

and from the gates of heaven, luminaries bring a summons:
six palaces wish acquaintance with the master's countenance.

The Jade Emperor nods his approval. He permits her return,
and she rides a dragon-drawn crane into azure depths of sky.

Fine sons of those great families—what do they know of Tao?
They come a hundred deep, mill around, restless, imagining

cloudy windows, misty bedrooms—affairs vague and obscure
behind kingfisher-green bed-curtains, depths of gold screens.

Stairs to immortality hard, weighed down by flesh and blood,
they spare no expense, send tender regards via azure birds.

LOSING TEETH

Last year a lone molar tumbled out,
and this year, an incisor vanished,

then all at once, six or seven tipped
away, and it's not over yet, oh no:

every tooth I have's a rickety mess.
This won't end till they're all gone.

When the first one went, I just felt
a bit embarrassed about it, that hole,

but then, after two or three more,
I began to think death was at hand,

and every time another threatened,
terror quaked straight through me

as it teetered there. I couldn't chew
for fear, or even rinse it with water,

and breaking loose, abandoning me,
it seemed like a mountain collapsing.

Lately, though, I've gotten used to it.
Now, seeing one go is pure emptiness,

and I still have a couple dozen left.
I know they'll topple out one by one,

but if they take their time, fall maybe
one per year, they'll last two decades,

and if they tumble all at once, all that
emptiness—the end result's the same.

People say once your teeth start to go,
you may as well forget about long life,

but I say every life has its own limits,
and long life or short, death is death.

People say tooth-holes glaring out
spook anyone looking you in the face,

but I say Chuang Tzu's right: singing
geese, junk trees: either way, life's joy.

Besides, better dark silence than lies,
and soft food's fine without any teeth,

like this poem sung: quite a shocker,
I'm sure, for my sweet wife and kids.

.   .   ..

I often climbed onto a hilltop to gaze out,
and fold upon fold, saw them crowded up:

edges and corners beneath brilliant skies
flashed, lit threads of tattered embroidery,

or mist blurred them all together, outside
and inside billowing through each other,

whirled on and winnowed without wind
away, settled wet on leaves, warmed forests.

Cloud stretched across them, frozen layers
where summits appeared, tiny peak by peak,

or they floated, elegant eyebrow traced clear
across sky, freshly drawn in lavish greens,

or lone crest cragged: that vast P'eng bird,
plumes awash in seas, beak raised skyward.

Spring *yang* under sodden ground sprouts
floral depths bathed shimmering in light,

and summits, though hacked and chiseled,
seem languid, as if drunk on pristine wine.

In summer heat the hundred trees flourish,
leaves thicken, burying slopes in shadow,

while divine spirits breathe day-mists out
into cloud, *ch'i* struggling form and shape.

Etched and polished as autumn frosts frolic,
tearing them open, they stand emaciate and

majestic, ragged ridge layered above ridge,
steely radiance spanning all time and space.

Though winter brings ink-black darkness,
they're cut and polished by snow and ice,

radiant in fresh sunlight, impossible peaks
towering up, spread a thousand miles away.

They're ceaseless dawn to dusk: appearance
all transformation moment by lit moment.

       .   .   .

Skies cleared yesterday, blues crystalline,
so following my old dream, I set out today,

delight in climbing up among scampering
weasels and squirrels to the highest peak,

and see it all spreading broken away below:
a brimful shimmer of wrinkles heaped up,

strung together as if parading on through,
or crouched as if fighting among themselves,

settled down as if bowing deep and quiet,
or soaring like startled pheasants shrieking,

strewn about like loose roof-tiles smashed,
or unswerving like wheel-spokes leading in,

fluttering to and fro like boats under way,
or breaking out like horses into a gallop,

turned away as if consumed by such hate,
or facing each other as if kind and caring,

tangled in confusion like sprouting bamboo,
or heaped like moxa burning wounds clean,

pretend and pretense as if painted on silk,
or twists and turns traced like seal script,

gauzy open-weave like the patterns of stars,
or rife profusion like clouds loafing around,

surging and adrift like billows and waves,
or all broken up like well-hoed fieldland,

like the time Pen and Yü, mighty warriors,
bravely tried their luck for that triumph,

victors rising high above, coursing power,
vanquished blunted and muttering in rage,

like the most venerable of sage emperors,
the poor and the young filling their courts,

intimate but never familiar or irreverent,
distant but never estranged or rebellious,

like looking over a well-laid banquet table,
wondering at the opulent array of dishes,

and like some graveyard cortege carrying
boxes and coffins past mounds and tombs,

heaped around like earthen pots and bowls,
or standing high like sacrificial stem-urns

humped up like turtles basking in the sun,
or sprawled like wild animals fallen asleep,

writhing and rippling like hidden dragons,
or spread like wings of hovering condors,

standing shoulder to shoulder like friends,
or filing along like leaders and followers,

wandering away like drifting vagabonds,
or looking back as if lingering overnight,

hostile and malevolent like bitter enemies,
or tender and intimate like man and wife,

grave and stately like advisers in tall hats,
or fluttering like the sleeves of dancers,

commanding heights like battle formations,
or trapped and harried like hunted prey,

flowing slowly and steadily into the east,
or laid out in death, head toward the north,

like fires lighting the radiance of stars,
like steam simmering dumplings and rice,

traveling on and on with never a pause,
giving away and away and never gathering,

tipped askew without anything to lean on,
unstrung bows that are never used again,

bare-skinned like a crowd of bald pates,
or smoking like brushwood pyres in flame,

like diviner's cracks tracing tortoise shells,
like interpretations of *I Ching* hexagrams.

      .   .   .

All vast majesty between heaven and earth,
skin patterns all woven vein and wrinkle,

how is it they began opening out into form?
Who could push something like that ahead,

conjuring rough essentials and fine detail,
many joining forces to manage such a task,

and who succeed without hatchet and axe,
without mastering spells and incantations?

Stories from that age of primal chaos lost,
this magisterial feat was never celebrated,

but priests at the shrine say the mountain
spirit comes, accepting fragrant sacrifice,

so I write this poem well-adorned, offer it
chanted in admiring praise and gratitude.

POND IN A BOWL

1

This old-timer's like a sage monk, simple as a child:
draw water, bury a bowl—suddenly I've got a pond!

Green frogs call all night, straight through till dawn
and those good old days, lazy fishing at Square-Gape!

2

Don't say you can't really make a pond in a bowl.
Those lotus roots I planted are growing already!

From now on, when it rains, you can hurry over:
we'll listen to its windblown patter on the leaves.

3

In my porcelain pool, water's pure clarity at dawn.
Tiny insects, who knows what kind or how many,

scatter suddenly away, not a trace of them anywhere.
Just baby fish, in a school, darting here and there.

4

Muddy bowl, tiny, shallow—how could it be a pond?
Green frogs at midnight, sage masters, they know:

hearing a croak, they bring their friends—all that
squabbling male and female. Don't mind the racket.

5

Alight, my pond mirrors sky, azure into azure.
I just pour in a few jars of water, fill it brimful,

then wait. Evening deepens and the moon sets,
and look, swimming down there: all those stars!

AUTUMN THOUGHTS

Falling leaves twist and turn earthward,
follow wind across the terrace out front,

their clatter saying something, it seems,
as they chase each other tumbling away.

Dusk light goes dark in the empty room.
Not a single word: I sit alone, all stillness,

all deep silence. From outside, my child
enters, lights the lamp there before me.

He asks how I'm feeling: I don't answer.
He offers a tasty bowl of food: I don't eat.

So he drifts off to the west wall and sits
there with a book, chants a few poems.

I'm not the man I was when I wrote them.
He's gone, a thousand sudden years gone,

and those words, they somehow cut deep,
return me to bitter confusion and grief.

I turn toward my son, and say: *Little one,
put the book away and go, sleep in peace.*

*Old fathers like me, our thoughts go back:
it's a calling no amount of years will end.*

PO CHÜ-I

(772 to 846)

PO CHÜ-I WAS born into the lower levels of the educated class, and his youth was lived in poverty. But he nevertheless managed to pass the governmental examinations and then so distinguish himself as an official that, at thirty-six, he became a personal adviser to the emperor. By then, he was also a wildly popular poet. Po was more active and forceful in influencing national policy during these years than at any other time in his life, and he clearly had not forgotten the experience of his youth, for he was adamant and outspoken in his defense of the long-suffering common people, whose situation had become desperate as a result of inept governance and the chronic militarism that followed the An Lu-shan Rebellion. Finding his official efforts hampered by conservative elements that controlled the central administration, Po decided to use his widely circulated poetry to further his cause.

Declaring poetry's highest purpose to be the instigation of social change, he attempted to revive the ancient tradition of *yüeh-fu* (see p. 72), poems that criticized social conditions and the government. Although *yüeh-fu* had been composed by numerous poets in the written tradition (see pp. 186, 193, 200), Po Chü-i's many poems in this mode (pp. 268–74 are a sampling from about eighty such poems) were the most programmatic and historically influential. They were a systematic attempt to return poetry to the moral dimensions of *The Book of Songs*, and they had a very real political impact. Po's protest poetry influenced the emperor and his advisers directly, and as it was read and sung throughout the land, it also stirred up popular indignation and broad support for reforms. This made his poems a double affront to conservative elements in the administration, and before long Po found himself exiled. The dangers of his political stance were now apparent, and Po abandoned it for a more detached and reclusive existence. Although he remained in the government for the rest of his life, holding a number of important positions, he tended to avoid controversy, focusing instead on poetry and spiritual cultivation. Indeed, it is the subtle insight of Po's quiet recluse poetry that established him as one of China's very greatest poets.

The Chinese poetic tradition consistently values clarity and depth of wisdom, rather than mere complexity and virtuosity. In this, Po Chü-i is the quintessential Chinese poet, and quite out of step with the experimental poetry of his time. He was a devoted student of Ch'an (Zen) Buddhism, and it was Ch'an that gave much of that clarity and depth to both his life and his work. This is immediately apparent in his voice and subject matter, but Ch'an is perhaps more fundamentally felt in the poetics shaping Po's work. In Ch'an practice, the self and its constructions of the world dissolve away until nothing remains but empty mind mirroring the world, leaving its ten thousand things utterly simple, utterly themselves, and utterly sufficient. This suggests one possible Ch'an poetry: a poetry of egolessness, such as Wang Wei's.

But there is another possibility for Ch'an poetry: the poetry of an egoless ego. The quiet response of even Wang Wei's emptiest poem is still a construction. Po knew this well, but he came to see that the self is also one of those ten thousand things, as are its various constructions. This insight resulted in a poetics quite different from Wang Wei's. Rather than Wang's strategy of emptying the mind, this poetics opens the poem to the various movements of the mind, weaving self into the fabric of *tzu-jan*'s unfolding, and Po Chü-i was a master of its subtle ways. As such, he perfected a major strand in Chinese poetic thinking: an interiorization of *tzu-jan* that first appeared in T'ao Ch'ien and came to be the most distinctive trait of Sung Dynasty poetry.

PEONY BLOSSOMS—SENT TO THE SAGE MONK UNITY-EXACT

Today, in front of the steps, these peonies out in such full red bloom:
how many of their blossoms are old now, and how many still young?

As they open, I can't think of comparisons to describe their color,
and as they fall, I'm just beginning to see we're the shapes of mirage

when they scatter through the Empty Gate into how many distances.
I wanted to gather a few withered petals, ask some sage about them.

AUTUMN THOUGHTS, SENT FAR AWAY

We share all these disappointments of failing
autumn a thousand miles apart. This is where

autumn wind easily plunders courtyard trees,
but the sorrows of distance never scatter away.

Swallow shadows shake out homeward wings.
Orchid scents thin, drifting from old thickets.

These lovely seasons and fragrant years falling
lonely away—we share such emptiness here.

267

9 The Old Broken-Armed Man from Prosper-Anew

A frail and ancient man from Prosper-Anew, eighty-eight years
old, hair and eyebrows white as fresh snow: he makes his way

toward the inn's front gate, leaning on a great-great-grandson,
his left arm over the boy's shoulder, his right broken at his side.

If you ask this old man how many years his arm's been broken,
if you ask how it happened, an arm broken like that, he'll say:

When I was born at our village in the district of Prosper-Anew,
it was an age of sage rule, never a hint of wartime campaigns,

so I grew up listening to the flutes and songs of the Pear Garden,
knowing nothing at all about spears and flags, bows and arrows.

Suddenly, in the Heaven-Jewel reign, they began building armies,
and for every three men in every household, one was taken away,

taken and hurried away. And can you guess where they all went?
To Cloud-South, a march five months and ten thousand miles long,

a march everyone kept talking about: how you face the Black River
and malarial mists that rise and drift when pepper blossoms fall,

how great armies struggle to cross the river's seething floodwaters,
and before they make it across, two or three in ten are drowned.

North of home, south of home, wailing filled villages everywhere,
sons torn from fathers and mothers, husbands torn from wives,

for people knew what it meant to make war on southern tribes:
ten million soldiers are sent away, and not one comes back alive.

It was all so long ago. I was hardly even twenty-four back then,
but my name was listed on those rolls at the Department of War,

so in the depths of night, careful to keep my plan well-hidden,
I stole away, found a big rock, and hacked my arm till it broke.

Too lame to draw a bow or lift banners and flags into the wind,
I escaped: they didn't send me off to their war in Cloud-South.

It was far from painless, the bone shattered and muscles torn,
but I'd found a way to go back and settle quietly in my village.

Now sixty years have come and gone since I broke this arm:
I gave up a limb, it's true, but I'm still alive, still in one piece,

though even now, on cold dark nights full of wind and rain,
I'm sleepless all night long with pain and still awake at dawn.

Sleepless with pain
but free of regrets,
for I'm the only man in my district who lived to enjoy old age.

If I hadn't done it, I'd have ended where the Black River begins,
a dead body, my spirit adrift and my bones abandoned there,

just one of ten thousand ghosts drifting above southern graves,
gazing toward their home, all grief-torn and bleating, bleating.

When such elders speak
how can we ignore them?

Haven't you heard
about Sung K'ai-fu, prime minister during the Open-Origin reign,
how he nurtured peace by refusing to reward frontier victories?

Haven't you heard
about Yang Kuo-chung, prime minister during the Heaven-Jewel,
how he launched frontier campaigns to flatter that emperor,

how the people were wild with anger before he won anything?
Just ask that old man from Prosper-Anew with a broken arm.
Just ask him, ask the old broken-armed man from Prosper-Anew.

29 Crimson-Weave Carpet

Crimson-weave carpet,
silk reeled off select cocoons and boiled in clear water,
sun-bleached and steeped in dyes of crimdigo flower,

dyes turning thread crimson, indigo depths of crimson,
then woven to grace the Hall of Widespread Fragrance.

The Hall of Widespread Fragrance is a hundred feet long,
and the carpet's crimson weave will stretch end to end,

its iridescence soft and deep, its fragrance everywhere,
plush weave and mirage blossoms beyond all compare,

awaiting beautiful women who come to sing and dance,
gauze stockings and embroidered slippers sinking deep.

Even those carpets from T'ai-yüan seem stiff and rough,
and Ch'eng-tu rugs thin, their embroidered flowers cold:

they'll never compare to these, so warm and sumptuous
and sent each year from Hsüan-chou in the tenth month.

Hsüan-chou's grand prefect orders a new pattern woven,
saying they'll spare no effort on the emperor's behalf,

and then a hundred reverent men haul it into the palace,
the weave so thick and silk so lavish it can't be rolled up.

Can you fathom what it means, O prefect of Hsüan-chou:
for ten feet of carpet
a thousand taels of silk?

Floors don't feel the cold—people do. People need warmth.
No more floors dressed in clothes stolen from the people.

An old charcoal seller
cuts firewood and sears it to charcoal below South Mountain,

his face smeared with dust and ash the color of woodsmoke,
his hair gone grizzled and gray, his ten fingers utter black,

and yet daring such hopes for the profits he'll take home
once the charcoal's all sold: warm robes to wear, food to eat.

His clothes are worn so miserably thin, and yet he worries
charcoal's selling too cheap, so he hopes for colder weather,

then one night an inch of snow falls in the city's foothills
and at dawn he takes his cart crackling through ruts of ice.

A tired ox and hungry man: the sun is already high when
they pause to rest in marketplace mud outside the south gate

and two riders no one knows appear in a dashing flourish:
one an envoy dressed in yellow, the other a servant in white.

The envoy carries an imperial warrant, and after citing it,
he chases the ox away, turns the cart and takes it off north.

A cart like that easily carries a thousand pounds of charcoal,
but a palace envoy hurries it away without a second thought:

half a length of crimson lace and a few yards of fine damask
draped over the old ox's neck: isn't that a fair enough price?

7 Light and Sleek

Riding proud in the streets, parading
horses that glisten, lighting the dust . . .

When I ask who such figures could be,
people say they're imperial favorites:

vermilion sashes—they're ministers;
and purple ribbons—maybe generals.

On horses passing like drifting clouds
they swagger their way to an army feast,

to those nine wines filling cup and jar
and eight dainties of water and land.

After sweet Tung-t'ing Lake oranges
and mince-fish from a lake of heaven,

they've eaten to their hearts' content,
and happily drunk, their spirits swell.

There's drought south of the Yangtze:
in Ch'ü-chou, people are eating people.

10 Buying Flowers

Late spring in this emperor's city,
horses and carts clattering past:

it's peony season on the avenues
and the people stream out to buy.

They won't be this cheap for long.
At these prices, anyone can buy.

Showing five delicate whites amid
hundreds of huge luminous reds,

they rig canopies to shelter them
and bamboo screens to shield them,

sprinkle them, stand them in mud,
keeping their color rich and fresh.

Families come back day after day:
people just can't shake their spell.

Happening by the flower markets,
an old man from a farm somewhere

gazes down and sighs to himself,
a sigh no one here could fathom:

a single clutch of bottomless color
sells for taxes on ten village farms.

CH'IN SONG IN CLEAR NIGHT

The moon's risen. Birds have settled in.
Now, sitting in these empty woods, silent

mind sounding the borders of idleness,
I can tune the *ch'in*'s utter simplicities:

from the wood's nature, a cold clarity,
from a person's mind, a blank repose.

When mind's gathered clear calm *ch'i*,
wood can make such sudden song of it,

and after lingering echoes die away,
song fading into depths of autumn night,

you suddenly hear the source of change,
all heaven and earth such depths of clarity.

WINTER NIGHT

Those I love scattered away, poor
and far too sick for friendly visits,

I'm shut up inside, no one in sight.
Lying in this village study alone,

the wick cold and lamp-flame dark,
wide-open drapes torn and tattered,

I listen as the snow begins to fall
again, that hiss outside the window.

Older now, sleeping less and less,
I get up in the night and sit intent,

mind utterly forgotten. How else
can I get past such isolate silence?

Body visiting this world steadfast,
mind abandoned to change limitless:

it's been like this four years now,
one thousand three hundred nights.

SETTING A MIGRANT GOOSE FREE

Snows heavy at Nine-Rivers this tenth-year winter,
riverwater spawns ice, tree branches break and fall,

and hungry birds flock east and west by the hundred,
a migrant goose crying starvation loudest among them.

Pecking through snow for grass, sleeping nights on ice,
its cold wings lumber slower and slower up into flight,

and soon it's tangled in a river-boy's net, carried away
snug in his arms, and put for sale alive in the market.

Once a man of the north, I'm accused and exiled here.
Man and bird: though different, we're both visitors,

and it hurts a visiting man to see a visiting bird's pain,
so I pay the ransom and set you free. Goose, O soaring

goose rising into the clouds—where will you fly now?
Don't fly northwest: that's the last place you should go.

There in Water-Gale, rebels still loose, there's no peace,
just a million armored soldiers long massed for battle:

imperial and rebel armies grown old facing each other.
Starved and exhausted—they'd love to get hold of you,

those tough soldiers. They'd shoot you and have a feast,
then pluck your wings clean to feather their arrows.

AFTER LUNCH

After eating lunch, I feel so sleepy.
Waking later, I sip two bowls of tea,

then notice shadows aslant, the sun
already low in the southwest again.

Joyful people resent fleeting days.
Sad ones can't bear the slow years.

It's those with no joy and no sorrow—
they trust whatever this life brings.

EARLY AUTUMN

Two gray hairs appear in the lit mirror,
a single leaf tumbling into the courtyard.

Old age slips away, nothing to do with me,
and when grief comes, who does it find?

Idle months and years emptying away,
loved ones from long ago lost to sight,

I'll play with my girl here, my little girl:
we keep coaxing smiles from each other.

IN THE MOUNTAINS, ASKING THE MOON

It's the same Ch'ang-an moon when I ask
which doctrine remains with us always.

It flew with me when I fled those streets,
and now shines clear in these mountains,

carrying me through autumn desolations,
waiting as I sleep away long slow nights.

If I return to my old homeland one day,
it will welcome me like family. And here,

it's a friend for strolling beneath pines
or sitting together on canyon ridgetops.

A thousand cliffs, ten thousand canyons—
it's with me everywhere, abiding always.

LI THE MOUNTAIN RECLUSE STAYS
THE NIGHT ON OUR BOAT

It's dusk, my boat such tranquil silence,
mist rising over waters deep and still,

and to welcome a guest for the night,
there's evening wine, an autumn *ch'in*.

A master at the gate of Way, my visitor
arrives from exalted mountain peaks,

lofty cloudswept face raised all delight,
heart all sage clarity spacious and free.

Our thoughts begin where words end.
Refining dark-enigma depths, we gaze

quiet mystery into each other and smile,
sharing the mind that's forgotten mind.

ENJOYING PINE AND BAMBOO

I treasure what front eaves face
and all that north windows frame.

Bamboo winds lavish out windows,
pine colors exquisite beyond eaves,

I gather it all into isolate mystery,
thoughts fading into their source.

Others may feel nothing in all this,
but it's perfectly open to me now:

such kindred natures need share
neither root nor form nor gesture.

MOURNING LITTLE SUMMIT-PEAK

A three-year-old son, lone pearl treasured so in the hand.
A sixty-year-old father, hair a thousand streaks of snow,

I can't think through it—you become some strange thing,
and sorrow endless now you'll never grow into a person.

There's no swordstroke clarity when grief rips the heart,
and tears darkening my eyes aren't rinsing red dust away,

but I'm still nurturing emptiness—emptiness of heaven's
black black, this childless life stretching away before me.

WAVES SIFTING SAND

1

One anchorage of sand appears as another dissolves away,
and one fold of wave ends as another rises. Wave and sand

mingling together day after day, sifting through each other
without cease: they level up mountains and seas in no time.

2

White waves swell through wide-open seas, boundless and beyond,
and level sands stretch into the four directions all endless depths:

evenings they dissolve and mornings reappear, sifting ever away,
their seasons transforming eastern seas into a field of mulberries.

3

Ten thousand miles across a lake where the grass never fades,
a lone traveler, you find yourself in rain among yellow plums,

gazing grief-stricken toward an anchorage of sand. Dark waves
wind keeps churned up: the sound of them slapping at the boat.

5

A day will no doubt come when dust flies at the bottom of seas,
and how can mountaintops avoid the transformation to gravel?

Young lovers may part, a man leaving, setting out on some boat,
but who could say they'll never come together again one day?

A magisterial rock windswept and pure
and a few bamboo so lavish and green:

facing me, they seem full of sincerity.
I gaze into them and can't get enough,

and there's more at the north window
and along the path beside West Pond:

wind sowing bamboo clarities aplenty,
rain gracing the subtle greens of moss.

My wife's still here, frail and old as me,
but no one else: the children are gone.

Leave the window open. If you close it,
who'll keep us company for the night?

IDLE SONG

In moonlight, I envied vistas of clarity,
and in pine sleep adored green shadow.

I wrote grief-torn poems when young,
plumbed the depths of feeling when old.

Now I sit up all night practicing *ch'an*,
and autumn can still bring a sudden sigh,

but that's it. Two last ties. Beyond them,
nothing anywhere holds this mind back.

AT HOME GIVING UP HOME

There's plenty of food and clothes. My children are married.
Now that I'm free and clear of all those duties to the family,

I fall asleep at night with the body of a bird reaching forests
and eat at dawn with the mind of a monk who begs for meals.

A scatter of crystalline voices calls: cranes beneath pines.
A single fleck of cold light burns: a lamp in among bamboo.

On a sitting cushion, I'm all *ch'an* stillness deep in the night.
A daughter calls, a wife hoots: no answer, no answer at all.

LI HO

(790 to 816)

IT IS SAID that Li Ho's strange poetry grew out of the conditions of his life. A branch of the imperial house in serious decline, Li Ho's family clung to a world of splendor in which they imagined their ancestors to have lived. Although Li had proven himself quite brilliant and had renowned sponsors such as Han Yü, he was prevented from taking the governmental exam that would have guaranteed him a secure career on a technicality: those who passed the exam were called *chin-shih*, but the name of Li's father was also pronounced *chin*, and using the name of one's father was taboo. Finally, Li was sickly his entire life, dying at the young age of twenty-seven. But such considerations can only begin to explain his altogether singular work.

Li Ho was known as the "ghostly genius." When he wrote of his own experience, it was usually transformed by the ghostly or demonic. But his most representative work moves in a wholly imagined realm, a phantasmagoric poetry representing an extreme point in the tradition. He was nurtured by Han Yü from an early age, knew and was heavily influenced by Meng Chiao; he in turn deeply influenced the two major figures to follow in this alternative tradition: Tu Mu, who wrote the preface to Li's collected poems; and Li Shang-yin, who wrote his biography. And Li Ho found his other major sources in the most atypical and otherworldly moments of the tradition: the shamanistic world of *The Songs of Ch'u* and the virtuosic and startling spontaneity of Li Po.

The surprising leap or juxtaposition had come to be used occasionally by poets such as Wei Ying-wu as a way of opening deeper insights into our immediate experience of the world. But Li Ho made such discontinuities the very texture of his poems. Between the fantastical nature of Li's lines and their discontinuous assemblage, his poems have all but lost their connection with the ever-changing empirical world—enduring source of insight and balance in mainstream Chinese poetry—posing against it the timeless realm of our mythmaking psyche.

Li cultivated the interior, imaginal realm in the most consuming way. He completed the inversion begun in Meng Chiao: rather than rendering immediate experience and his response to it, Li's work creates a kind of quasi-symbolist, even abstract, world that exists only in the poem itself. At their most extreme, his poems conjure an almost hallucinogenic interiority of passions rendered in a language seductive in its sensuality. These imaginal and otherworldly tendencies almost seem to have more in common with Western literary practice than with that of ancient China. And indeed, Li is perhaps the most problematic of poets for a tradition that so values deep empirical clarity and wisdom, although his virtuosic genius has remained undeniable.

In addition to describing the conditions out of which Li Ho's particular poetry may have grown, Li Shang-yin's biography also describes Li Ho's working habits, and they reveal much about his poetry. According to Li Shang-yin, Li Ho spent his days wandering on the back of a donkey, and when a line came to him, he would scribble it down and toss it into a bag. Back home at the end of the day, he would take out the lines he had written and assemble them into a poem. Li's mother watched this with despair, saying that in his poems her son was "vomiting out his heart." And the legend Li Shang-yin tells about the end of this imaginal life also summarizes both Li Ho himself and his problematic place in the tradition: altogether unlike T'ao Ch'ien, the archetypal poet of Taoist/Ch'an wisdom who saw death and burial as a return to his mountain home (pp. 124, 126), Li was carried away to the Emperor of Heaven by a spirit in crimson robes riding a scarlet dragon.

Among lacquer ash, bone dust, cinnabar river-stone,
ancient bitter-ice blood spawning bronze blossoms,

rain dissolved white feathers and thin gilt bamboo:
nothing left but a battered old three-spine wolf fang.

I took two horses, scoured a battleground, flat rocky
fields east of a post-station, below weed-choked hills,

sun cut short. Wind blew on and on, stars moaning,
black cloud-banners hung drenched in empty night,

spirits and ghosts everywhere, emaciate, crying out.
I offered sacrificial cream, a jarful, and roast lamb.

Insects silent, geese sick, spring reeds red. Tangled
gusts bid a traveler farewell, feeding shadow-flames.

I searched antiquity in tears, and found a loose barb,
tip broken, cracked red. It sliced through flesh once,

and in South Lane at the east wall, a boy on horseback
wanted my bit of metal, offered me a bamboo basket.

DAWN AT SHIH-CH'ENG

A late moon out across the long dike sets,
and crows on battlements startle away,

delicate dew soaking scarlet bulbs, chill
scents thinning the night's wine away.

Weaver-Girl and Ox-Herd crossed their
Star River, willow mist taking city walls,

but now he rises, leaving her a love-tassel.
She knits moth-eyebrows smudged green.

Spring bed-curtains in the thinnest cicada-wing gauze,
spread cushions embossed in gold faint-blossom patterns,

and outside the bed-curtains, crane-feather catkins adrift.
The passion of spring: it's not something words will tell.

SKY DREAM

A moon's old rabbit and cold toad weeping colors of sky,
lucent walls slant across through half-open cloud towers.

A jade-pure wheel squeezes dew into bulbs of wet light.
Phoenix waist-jewels meet on cinnamon-scented paths.

Transformations of a thousand years gallop by like horses,
yellow dust soon seawater below changeless island peaks,

and all China seen so far off: it's just nine wisps of mist,
and the ocean's vast clarity a mere cup of spilled water.

CH'IN SPIRIT SONG

Sun sunk into western mountains, eastern mountains go dark.
Whirlwinds whip up horses, hooves pounding across clouds.

Painted ch'in, plain flute—to their tangle of thin-water sound,
a dance in autumn dust, flowered skirts rustling silk and sigh.

Cinnamon leaves brushing wind, cinnamon scattering seed.
Black-azure puma-cat weeping blood, fox dying a cold death,

an opalescent dragon on ancient walls, tail inscribed in gold,
then the rain god riding it down into a lake's autumn waters,

and that ancient hundred-year-old owl—it's a forest demon
now: sound of laughter, emerald fire rising up out of its nest.

OLD MAN MINING JADE SONG

Mining jade, mining jade—all they want is water-emerald
for *lilt-in-her-stride* hairpins, beauty for beauty's sake,

though he's so hungry and cold even the dragons grieve,
and the pure clarity of Indigo Stream's breath is no more.

Foraging ridgetops on rainy nights, he dines on hazelnuts,
his old man's tears blood rife in a bitter cuckoo's mouth.

The water of Indigo Stream has had its fill of we the living,
and those drowned a thousand years still despise its water.

Mountains askew, cypress gales, howling rain. His ropes
hang down to headwaters—azure twisting, swaying. Cold

village, bleached house: he worries for his pampered girl.
Ancient terraces and stone cliffs—heart-gut dangle grass.

PAST AND FOREVER ON AND ON CHANT

Lucent-Lumen returns to western mountains,
Emerald-Blossom rises deep into far-off depths:

past and present—where will they ever end?
Years whirl away on wind by the thousands,

and ocean sands turn to stone. Fish froth up
sighs along ruins of a sea-bridge to the sun.

Bits of radiance roam empty distances, skies
propped on pillars worn away into the years.

WIVES OF THE RIVER HSIANG

Bamboo blood-flecked a thousand years, old but never dying:
it bounds the Hsiang, companion still to those spirit beauties.

Tribal girls sing and play, music filling cold southern skies.
Nine-Doubt Mountain tranquil green, tears stain blossoms red,

Nine-Doubt, where those phoenix lovers parted and set out
into distances, always intimate, making clouds-and-rain love.

Autumn *ch'i*, secret with grief, rises into green-azure maples,
and among waves in the icy night, ancient dragons cry out.

BORDERLAND SONG

Mongol horns stretch north wind longer.
Thistle Gate plain glistens clear as water.

Sky swallows the road to Azure-Deep Seas,
Great Wall a thousand miles of moonlight,

and dew drifting, misting over our flags,
cold metal calls the quarter hour all night.

Tribal armor intricate as serpent scales,
horses calling out, Ever-Grass Tomb bare,

we watch Banner-Tip stars. Autumn quiet.
Far reaches of sand this grief of distant

wandering. Sky ending north of our tents.
Gone beyond borderlands, river-murmurs.

LAMENTATION CHANT

South Mountain's peopled with such grief.
Ghost-rain keeps sprinkling empty grasses,

and autumn fills Ch'ang-an past midnight:
how many are turning old in all its wind?

Yellow-twilight paths blurred deep away,
streets of black-azure oak twist and sway,

trees standing in shadow beneath a moon.
Pellucid dawn will cover whole mountains.

Lacquer candles welcome new arrivals to
dark tombs. Confusions of fireflies flicker.

THE CHILL OF CANYON TWILIGHT

A pellucid fox facing the moon howls mountain wind:
autumn cold sweeps clouds away, empties emerald sky.

Jade mist trails white pennants into wet azure-greens.
At dawn, Star River's curling, flowing east of the sky,

a brook-egret asleep, dreaming swans into long flight,
the current swelling delicate and full, saying nothing.

Peak above snaking ridgeline peak—tangled dragons,
and for a traveler, bitter bamboo cries singing flutes.

DRAGON-CRY IMPERSONATION SONG

Stones grating across brass bowls,
a faint cry withered and worried.

Azure-deep eagles splattering blood,
lungs ripped from a white phoenix,

and cinnamon seed scattering away,
clouds carriage-canopies buffeting.

Foul canyon island all dead trees and crumbling sand
where the immortal Goddess Queen stopped growing old,

crystalline dragon spit rinsed away in dark caverns,
and golden claws buried along shoreline cove-shallows,

ash-azure cliff-steps mourning moss. Two river spirits
drying tear curtains, breaking blood-flecked bamboo.

Lotus-Dragon Emperor gone a thousand years, stench
lingering on after rain, and scent of dragon-bane iron.

TU MU

(803 to 853)

TU MU WAS born into a very wealthy and illustrious family presided over by his grandfather, who held no less a position than prime minister, and he spent his childhood in the most privileged of circumstances. The young Tu Mu spent much time at the lavish family estate in their ancestral village on the slopes of the Whole-South Mountains just south of the capital. There he moved in a world of natural beauty, political and literary celebrity, and seductive entertainments of beautiful courtesans, with their exquisite music and dance. But the family fortunes soon declined precipitously, and he spent much of his youth in relative poverty. In spite of this hardship, he somehow managed to gain the erudition required for government service. He had a relatively successful lifelong career, ever concerned with the people's welfare, which led to many poems of social conscience, though they functioned more as official protests than as art. He also became something of an expert in military strategy, authoring the standard commentary on Sun Tzu's *The Art of War.*

Tu is popularly remembered as an aesthete devoted to wine and music and courtesan romance, interests mingled with a strong nostalgia for the splendors he had known when young. But there are not, in fact, all that many poems of this type in the Tu Mu corpus, and Tu was not necessarily proud of those that do exist: he excluded most of them when he assembled a collection of his work. They were only added to the collection later, and many may not be authentic.

Tu Mu's work combines many influences, most notably Li Ho's sensuous textures and the extreme distillations of poets such as Wang Wei. Tu's most celebrated poems are short, rarely more than eight lines, and his quatrains are especially renowned for their clarity and concision, which grew out of the Ch'an (Zen) poetics that began with Meng Hao-jan and Wang Wei. His accomplishment was to add Li Ho's sense of interiority and emotional atmospherics to the distilled imagism of these landscape poets. Tu cultivates the enigmas of history and landscape in images of striking clarity, often combined to create surprising shifts and startling juxtapositions that open new interior depths, and these depths open in turn the fundamental human enigmas of consciousness and mirrorlike perception, revealing their organic relationship to the rivers-and-mountains realm.

EGRETS

Robes of snow, crests of snow, and beaks of azure-jade,
they fish in shadowy streams. Then startling up into

flight, they leave emerald mountains for lit distances.
Pear blossoms, a tree-full, tumble in the evening wind.

ANCHORED ON CH'IN-HUAI RIVER

Mist mantling cold waters, and moonlight shoreline sand,
we anchor overnight near a winehouse entertaining guests.

A nation lost in ruins: knowing nothing of that grief, girls
sing "Courtyard Blossoms." Their voices drift across the river.

AUTUMN EVENING

Autumn silver-moon candlelight chills painted screens,
gauze bed-curtains. Our fans buffet streaming fireflies.

On steps of sky the color of silken robes cold as water,
we sit watching Star River's Weaver-Girl and Ox-Herd.

SPRING SOUTH OF THE YANGTZE

A thousand miles of oriole song, reds setting greens ablaze,
river villages with mountains for walls, wineshop flags, wind.

Of those four hundred eighty Southern Dynasty monasteries,
how many towers and terraces remain in this mist and rain?

THOUGHTS AFTER SNOW IN HSIANG-YANG

My long-ago life rises into lone thoughts
and drifts windblown—too much for me.

Shoreline sounds echo night restlessly.
Cold lamplight thick with snow glistens.

Three years—a dream so bright and real,
thread stretching away into the furthest

distances. Dawn light on Ch'u Mountain:
no need to climb those wide-open heights.

INSCRIBED ON RECLUSE DARK-ORIGIN'S LOFTY PAVILION

Water joins West River to sounds beyond heaven.
Outside the study, pine shadow sweeps clouds flat.

Who taught me to sound this long flute, bamboo
borrowing spring wind to play radiant moonlight?

GOODBYE

It seems the fiercest love is no love at all, in the end.
Sipping wine together, we feel nothing now but absent

smiles. Candles, at least, still have hearts. They grieve
over goodbye, cry our tears for us until dawn-lit skies.

POND IN A BOWL

Breach cut in green-moss earth,
it steals a distant flake of sky.

White clouds emerge in mirror;
fallen moon shines below stairs.

CLIMBING JOY-ABROAD PLATEAU

A lone bird vanishes in the endless sky's empty tranquillity.
And all boundless antiquity too: it's disappearing right here.

You can see it in the Han, dynasty of unrivaled achievement,
now just five imperial tombs, treeless, autumn winds rising.

UNSENT

Distant clouds, trees deep into mist,
autumn bathed in a river's clarity.

Where is she tonight, so beautiful?
Moonlight floods the mountaintops.

INSCRIBED ON THE TOWER AT VENERATION MONASTERY

Late-light shadow across thousand-mountain
snows. In cold spring, a hundred-foot tower.

I climb up alone, and then back down alone.
Who can manage such distances of the heart?

AUTUMN DREAM

Frosty skies open empty depths of wind.
Moonlight floods fulling-stone clarities.

As the dream ends, I am dying at night:
I am beside a beautiful woman, thoughts

deepening—a leaf trees shed in the dark,
a lone goose leaving borderlands behind.

Then I'm in travel clothes, setting out,
heart and mind all distances beyond sky.

A MOUNTAIN WALK

Climbing far into cold mountains, the rocky path steepens
and houses grow rare. Up here where white clouds are born,

I stop to sit for a while, savoring maple forests in late light,
frost-glazed leaves lit reds deeper than any spring blossom.

CLOUD

I see a cloud at day's end and just can't look away.
It has no mind at all, no mind and surely no talent:

a sad flake of bright jade radiant with color, drifting
ten thousand miles of clear sky, nowhere it began.

PASSING CLEAR-GLORY PALACE

Great peace can fill ten thousand kingdoms with wine and song,
moonlight flooding through temples and towers touching sky.

An Lu-shan's dance beats a confusion of time among the clouds,
and winds crossing ridgeline peaks carry laughter drifting down.

AUTUMN LANDSCAPE AT CH'ANG-AN

On a tower beyond frost-filled forests,
I gaze into a flawless mirror of sky.

South Mountain and its autumn color:
ch'i-form breathed into such heights.

BACK HOME AGAIN

Kids keep tugging at my robes, asking:
Why did it take you so long to come back?

And who were you fighting those months
and years to win all that silk-white hair?

SENT FAR AWAY

These mountains emerald clouds at the far end of distance.
In tonight's clarity, one sound: a whisper of white snow.

I'm sending thoughts of you a thousand miles of moonlight:
scraps of light along canyon streams, haze of steady rain.

THE HAN RIVER

Steady and full, all surging swells and white gulls in flight,
it flows springtime deep, a green so pure it should dye robes.

Going south and coming back north, I've grown older, older.
Late light lingers, farewell to a fishing boat bound for home.

A CLEAR STREAM IN CH'IH-CHOU

I've played all day in the stream. Now twilight's yellow
lights autumn's destined coming, root of this white hair.

What is it I've trusted you to rinse a thousand times away,
until now, the dust fouling my brush-tip leaves no trace?

LI SHANG-YIN

(c. 813 to 858)

LI SHANG-YIN IS traditionally described as the last great poet of the T'ang Dynasty, and his work represents a departure in Chinese poetry for two primary reasons. First is his interest in romance, a subject that had rarely appeared in Chinese poetry, except in the *yüeh-fu* tradition of stock female figures. Romance had begun to appear in the work of Tu Mu and Li Ho, but with Li Shang-yin it becomes a central preoccupation, though in the more experimental poems translated here, it appears primarily as a sensuous atmosphere. And after Li, romance and eroticism continued as the principal concern of *tz'u*, a new form of poetry written by courtesans and their male admirers (see pp. 335–37).

Li Shang-yin's second innovation is the way his poems create more a mood or atmosphere than a clear statement. Li thought a poem should embody the mysterious origins (literally "dark-enigma," for which see Key Terms: *hsüan*) and inner patterns (see Key Terms: *li*) of the cosmos. Although he wrote many conventional and straightforward poems, his most innovative poems succeed in this aspiration: they are so mysterious, in fact, that it is often impossible to say just what they are about. In Li's most important and experimental poems—many of which offer no title to help orient the reader—this elusiveness is created by the surprising juxtaposition of discontinuous ideas and images, a poetics of collage or fragmentation that feels especially modern.

Many critics over the centuries have argued that Li's poems are commentaries on either contemporary politics, his romantic intrigues, or his relationships to powerful patrons. They have assumed that the poems are saying something clear but in a veiled way, because he is either criticizing the political establishment or writing about clandestine love affairs. There is no doubt some truth to this, but as a poet calculating each gesture and its effect, Li clearly intended a poetry of elusive ambiguity, and that elusiveness is indeed the work's great strength.

The most discussed and debated aspect of Li's enigmatic work is how thick with allusion it is. All Chinese poets used allusions to literary or historical precedents to enrich their writing, but in his more experimental poems, Li Shang-yin pushed this practice to its limit. Nearly every line contains some kind of literary or historical reference. However, in the more radical poems, those references do not form a unified system that resolves a poem's ambiguities into a clear statement. They are as fragmented as the poem's immediate ideas and images, so they simply add another layer of elusiveness, one that is not available to us without losing the poems in a flood of scholarly explanation. Reading these poems in translation, one can imagine behind every strange image a strange story, and that is enough to experience the overall effect of the poems, for they are not poems that depend on allusion for their meaning but symbolist poems that create their own mysterious worlds. In doing this, they fulfill Li's primary intent: to both suggest and frustrate coherence. This poetics offers the reader depths beyond the conventional self, which is shaped by linguistic coherence. It represents Li's Taoist/Ch'an (Zen) practice in the poetic realm, opening that space between linguistic coherence and silence, where the human blends into the mysterious origins and inner patterns of the cosmos.

THE BROCADE *CH'IN*

The brocade *ch'in* has fifty strings: there's no reason for it,
each string and bridge conjuring up another bloom of youth:

in a morning dream, Chuang Tzu's confused with a butterfly,
and Emperor Wang's death left his spring passion to a nightjar

scattering blood: moonlight on vast seas—it's a pearl's tear:
far off, Indigo Mountain jade smokes in warm sun: up close,

smoke vanishes: can this feeling linger even in a memory:
never anything but this moment already bewildered and lost.

OFFHAND POEM

Idle sleep in a small pavilion clears away the ease of wine:
mountain pomegranate and sea cypress, branches tangled

together on a rippling-water bed-mat, pillows of amber:
and nearby, a fallen hairpin, a pair of kingfisher feathers.

LADY NEVER-GRIEVE GRIEVES, SINGING OF THE NORTHERN CH'I DYNASTY

Azure Dragon bright in the east, White Tiger in the west,
and in the center, an auspicious star guiding our affairs:

jar and river jade-pure—they laugh at a crystalline pool:
cutting a hole in heaven won't lead to the Ox-Herd's land:

when heaven's warhorses go thundering across clouds,
Ox Mountain tumbles into pieces, loud as shattered coral,

and the eyes of autumn beauties glisten, but cry no tears:
of twelve old jade-pure towers—not a single nail remains:

mist pushed apart spits out a moon cast thousands of miles,
crimson *wu-tung* trees dying ten times over in single file:

white poplars, farewell rooms, ghosts mingled with people:
no point lingering out dark memories like silkworm paper:

the sun sets into a wind herding cut threads of silk away,
blood clots together, blood scatters away, and no one's left.

UNTITLED

Coming is an empty promise, and departure leaves no trace:
moonlight slants across rooftops: a bell sounds the fifth watch,

and dreams make distant farewells no cry can summon back:
hurry to finish a letter, ink not ground thick enough to use:

candlelight enfolds half the bed-curtain's golden kingfishers:
scented musk drifts through embroidered lotus—faint, faint:

after her love, he resented the distance to Paradise Mountain,
and out beyond it, ten thousand more Paradise Mountains rise.

ON HISTORY

Lakes north and south brimmed over, vast waters in flood,
and a flag of surrender, lone scrap on a hundred-foot pole:

three hundred years of endeavor a single morning dream:
who'd believe there's a dragon coiled into Bell Mountain?

FISH-HUNT SONG

Someone's readied crossbow arrows, sharpened azure-stone tips,
and someone's a tribal chief, face tattooed, strong as three tigers:

searching the tide, backs to the sun, they watch fins and scales:
all loss and absence in the night, vermilion colors of whale stir,

light and delicate powder of arrow-shaft bamboo fragrant as cake:
green ducks may wander back to a pond that's harboring dragons,

but drifting at the far end of heaven, Star River voice full of ice,
why would it come wandering back here to die on a golden platter?

UNTITLED

The pellucid road winds back around into twilight clouds:
a seven-scented carriage, cry of a dappled horse cut short:

spring wind offers itself everywhere, opens into enticing
smiles that leave a country's ten thousand homes in ruins.

1 *Spring*

Wind-rinsed radiance opens landscapes, paths east and west:
how many days seeking a spirit, so lovely and never glimpsed:

the honeycomb's winged guest is all heart of spring passion:
it knows seductive leaves and enticing branches everywhere,

the sun's lavish warmth lingering west of those peach trees,
alluring hair gathered and tucked up into a peach-tree bun:

dragon lords and phoenix ladies frolic deep in dark distances:
tangled floss and buffeted gossamer—they confuse heaven too:

woman rising, a little drunk in faint light, and it's like sunrise,
sunlit blinds, dream cut short, and the drift of remnant voices:

when grief comes, you cast iron nets, hoping to catch coral,
seas vast, heaven wide open—that's where you lose your way:

robe and sash are heartless: some wide open, some pulled tight:
spring mists glistening emerald-green, autumn frost so white:

grind pure cinnabar or crush stone: heaven won't care which:
longing to roam Heaven-Jail stars, a cheated spirit locked inside:

she puts her thick gauze robe away, and puts on thin raw silk,
her cool slip gracing fragrant skin, her waist-jewels clittering

in this sunlight, too much for spring's east wind: it's become
a dark mystery-rinsed radiance sinking away into western seas.

2 Summer

Window-screens of rain in front: too much grief to roll them up:
and behind the house, trees in bloom cast pools of dark shadow:

when her home landscape is like the underworld's Yellow Springs,
what good is a stonethorn crossbow for a traveler past midnight:

a gauze fan calls down winds from the gate of heaven, whirlpools
churn on gossamer bed-curtains and kingfisher-green screens:

in isolate depths of quiet, a nightjar scatters dead passion's blood:
how many nights have malarial blossoms opened on cotton trees:

shadows drift the moon's Cinnamon Palace, radiance beyond reach:
enticing mists, broken orchids, and sweet words in faint whispers:

you long for the Star River to come pouring down into your heart,
yet live without Weaver-Girl to watch over meetings and partings:

rivers that flow murky and clear ought to share a single source,
but still, Great-Benefit River flows clear and the Yellow murky:

how can gossamer mist billow into dusk-gold skirts of a goddess,
how touch her curtained cloud-carriage calling, *O lovely wonder*?

3 Autumn

The moon's waves spread, drenching heaven's wide-open eaves,
then it sets with its icy moon-toad, and sparse stars drift inside,

cloud-screens motionless around eyebrows worried and alone:
all night long, kites on winds above west tower swoop and dive:

wanting to weave blossoms of longing and send them far away,
a longing for someone that lasts all day, choked with resentment:

hearing the Northern Dipper, the sound of it pivoting slowly,
without seeing the Star River, its crystalline shallows coursing

between lovers: a gold fish locks cinnamon broken from spring,
and dust of all antiquity sifts across ducks on cushions of love:

who could bear it, that little park of ours now just a long road,
and jade-pure trees feel nothing when you lose your homeland:

its Ch'u song hidden away, the jeweled *ch'in* grows still, still:
and daubed with gold, gauze robes from Yüeh are thin and cold

as night passes: startled by frost, a parrot on the curtain hook
calls southern clouds swelling up around Cloud-Dream lovers:

a pair of earrings is clittering, dangling from a foot-long silk
letter that speaks of a place where two met on the Hsiang River:

singing lips that will be seen for a lifetime in clouds and rain,
and sorrows over a fragrant scent held for a moment long ago.

4 Winter

The sun rises east of heaven: the sun sets west of heaven:
a phoenix-woman flying alone, a dragon-woman destitute:

among the cold creek's white stones, no one else is seen:
her room is further away than Emperor Shun's wilderness

tomb: on the frozen wall, secret blossoms of frost spreading:
the flowering root splits open, and the fragrant heart dies:

in a painted boat clinging to waves, thinking of the moon,
wondering: what if the moon-goddess isn't beautiful at all:

Ch'u flutes and tribal strings are grieving over the world:
in the empty city, her dance ends, but a willow-thin waist

remains: back in those long-ago days, they melted with joy
in your hands, those two sisters Peach-Leaf and Peach-Root:

hair tossed and tumbled to one side, she braves dawn cold:
hairpins elegant white-jade swallows, cicadas delicate gold:

wind-carriages and rain-horses never carry anyone away:
candles crying red tears resent dawn light filling the sky.

DAY AFTER DAY

Day after day, spring's radiance challenges the sun's radiance,
and apricots blossom, scenting steep roads in a mountain town.

How long before thoughts lose all purpose and drift, thread-ends
buffeted and trailed out hundreds of feet among gossamer floss?

UNTITLED

It's so hard to be together, and so hard to part: a tender
east wind is powerless: the hundred blossoms crumble:

the heart-thread doesn't end until the silkworm's dead,
and tears don't dry until the candle's burnt into ash:

she grieves, seeing white hair in her morning mirror,
and chanting at night, she feels the chill of moonlight:

exquisite Paradise Mountain—it isn't so very far away,
and that azure bird can show us the way back anytime.

INCENSE-BURNING SONG

Clouds inlaid with gold twist and curl around like fish teeth:
peacock wings and tails, flood-dragon beards and whiskers:

a Chang palace left incense-burner mountains, vast ideal:
a Ch'u beauty offered her smile, an opening lotus blossom:

silk floss from eight cocoons—it scatters into little flames,
and animals smolder faint crimson fragrance, cloud-mother

far away: white heaven's moon-lake cold but not yet frozen,
a golden tiger swallows autumn, vomits it up into the west:

jade-pure waist-jewels breathe radiance, sunset's bronze-lit
light filling window-screen waves, slanting through gates:

to come from the west wanting to climb forested ridgelines:
a spirit lost to cypress roofbeams out planting peach trees:

dew-drenched courtyard, moonlit well, crimson *ch'i*-mist:
light gowns and thin sleeves can take over your thoughts:

beautiful people in that Shu pavilion, their night together
grew deep: golden bells asking nothing of moving lamps:

so when will delicate wind sing all your joys and sorrows,
your heart of ash become earth, passions filling with dew?

East winds hush and sigh, and delicate spring rains arrive:
out beyond the lotus pond, there's the whisper of thunder:

the golden moon-toad gnaws a lock open: incense drifts in:
jade tiger circles back, pulling silk rope to draw well-water:

the secret love of Lady Chia and young Han led to marriage,
and the Lo River goddess shared her bed with a Wei prince:

don't hope for spring passion that rivals all those blossoms
burgeoning forth: an inch of longing's just an inch of ash.

YÜ HSÜAN-CHI

(c. 840 to 868)

WOMEN'S POETRY, TOO, made a resurgence in the T'ang Dynasty. With better education in general, more liberal attitudes toward women, and a great expansion in the numbers of well-educated courtesans and women nurtured in monasteries, more women than ever among the literate class were writing poetry. (For a larger discussion of women poets in China, see "Women's Poetry in Ancient China" on p. 451.) Still, only three female voices survive in collections containing more than a handful of poems. Of these, perhaps the most impressive is Yü Hsüan-chi.

Very little is known about Yü's brief life. According to legend, she was executed at the age of twenty-eight because she beat a servant girl to death in a jealous rage, suspecting the girl of an affair with one of her lovers. This story may or may not be true, and she may have been as young as twenty-four when she died. In any case, it is clear that she lived an exceptionally cultivated, independent, and self-determined life, availing herself of all three social options that made such a life possible for a woman. She was the "lesser wife" (concubine) of a wealthy official (Adept-Serene, see p. 324), who eventually abandoned her; a Taoist adept in a monastery; and a courtesan.

Yü Hsüan-chi's social and artistic skills, as well as her great beauty, made her quite successful as a courtesan, involving her in liaisons with a range of prominent political and literary figures. At the same time, her poetry is exemplary in the female tradition because hers is not generally the limited female voice constructed by the male poetry establishment: it is forceful, self-assured, and original, even directly challenging male privilege and domination at times. It is certainly no accident that the meaning of Yü's name, *Hsüan* + *chi*, is nothing less than cosmic in its designs: *Dark-Enigma* (see Key Terms: *hsüan*) + *Loom of Origins*.

ORCHID FRAGRANCE, SENT FAR AWAY

Drunk day and night, my body sings
all longing for you again this spring.

Messengers carrying letters in rain,
someone heartbroken at the window,

pearl blinds up, gazing at mountains:
grief's fresh as scented grasses again.

Since we parted, how much rafter dust
has fallen through our *ch'an* stillness?

FAREWELL

All those tender nights upstairs in the capital, hearts content
together—I never guessed my pure-spirit love would leave.

Now, dozing and waking, I don't mention drifting clouds gone
who knows where. The lamp burns low. A wild moth flutters.

IN REPLY TO LI YING'S "AFTER FISHING ON A SUMMER DAY"

We've lived a year in the same lane
without meeting once, and now you

send crystalline lines for old love,
all fragrance of broken cinnamon.

Way's nature is like snow and ice.
Ch'an mind laughs at gauze robes.

Star River heights? There's no path
through mist-strewn waves of love.

GAZING OUT IN GRIEF, SENT TO ADEPT-SERENE

Maple leaves color a thousand, fill ten thousand branches.
Evening sails creep through a bridge's drowned reflection.

Longing for you, my heart is like this west-river current
flowing east day and night—never ceasing, never ceasing.

RADIANCE, REGAL AND COMPOSURE WERE THREE
SISTERS ORPHANED YOUNG WHO BECAME GREAT
BEAUTIES. THEY WROTE A POEM OF THE MOST
PURE CLARITY, LIKE OLD HSIEH WRITING ABOUT
SNOW, AND QUITE BEYOND COMPARE. HOW COULD
ANYONE IMPROVE UPON IT? A TRAVELER FROM
THE CAPITAL SHOWED IT TO ME, AND I'VE
FOLLOWED ITS RHYMES

You hear about rare and glorious beauties from the south,
and now it's these eastern neighbors, these three sisters

admiring each other in rooms and writing parrot poems,
or embroidering phoenix gowns beside emerald windows,

their courtyard a crimson confusion of broken flowers,
green wine brimming cups raised sip by sip to their lips.

First gazing into the Goddess Queen's jasper-pure pool,
then banished to this world of dust, we'll never be men,

and if the poet's a woman, all they care about is how she
compares to Hsi Shih, so lovely and silent. It shames me

utterly. I sing all those enticing songs, my sweet voice
twittering, my *ch'in*'s babbling strings fingered lightly,

compete on terraces to offer the silkiest black-azure hair,
flaunting white-jade hairpins that challenge the moon.

From a childhood of dew dripping off pines in ravines,
I've grown to span the sky, to harbor willow-wisp mists,

easy in clouds-and-rain love. And mind simply abides.
Why not stumble through some ragged tune on a flute?

Momma hated me whispering among flowers. A perfect
poet-love, so handsome—I've only met him in dreams,

and working lines into sheer clarity cuts the spirit short.
It's like a lovely young girl aching for death so sweet—

too sad to watch. And where's all this beauty leading us?
Clouds drifting away home—they float north, float south.

VISITING ANCESTRAL-TRUTH MONASTERY'S SOUTH TOWER, WHERE THE NEW GRADUATES HAVE INSCRIBED THEIR NAMES ON THE WALL

Cloudswept peaks fill my eyes, opening clear springtime skies,
and fingertips give birth to words, stroke by brawny stroke.

I hate it that these silky gauze robes keep my poems shut away,
leave me gazing at men's names, all my yearning for nothing.

THOUGHTS AT HEART, SENT TO HIM

I long to send on red-stringed *ch'in* song
this tired tangle of thought and feeling.

We made clouds-and-rain love early on,
but never shared an orchid-scent heart:

the radiant peach and plum in my bloom
couldn't slow your quest for high renown,

and azure-deep pine-and-cinnamon green
couldn't still your longing for admiration.

Moon colors moss all clarity on the steps.
Song drifts depths of courtyard bamboo.

Red leaves lie thick at the gate. I'd sweep
for a man who fathoms my *ch'in* utterly.

LATE SPRING

My simple gate's worn-out. In this deep lane, no one stops by.
That handsome long-ago poet-love lingers only in my dreams:

gauze robes swirl, scented dance at the bed-mat in whose home,
and song drifts off towers, bidding wind farewell where, where?

Here, war-drums in the streets fill sleep with their dawn racket,
and in courtyard idleness, magpie chatter tangles spring grief.

How can I fathom a world of human care, when I'm on my own
ten thousand long miles away, an unmoored boat drifting free?

AFTER HIS POEM, FOLLOWING ITS RHYMES

Men robed purple and red make this world a din of confusion.
Here, alone amid colors of moonlight, I offer crystalline chants,

done wanting some jade-pure man, done chasing elegant ideas.
I just scribble out poems, go around visiting brushwood gates,

and even simple blossoms bring on hymns of praise and thanks.
I'm another Yen Hui mastering delusion deep in a meager lane,

and not aching to see you, not a creeper in need of a tall pine:
to live the loftiest of lives, all I need is the mountain out front.

Nothing needs doing. I'm idle and free now,
wandering landscapes all wind-rinsed light,

river moon floating among broken clouds,
boat unmoored and drifting some vast lake.

I play my *ch'in* in a Buddhist temple's quiet,
chant poems off an ancient general's tower,

or take thickets of flute-bamboo for friends
and flakes of chime-stone as kindred spirits.

Done chasing after silver-and-gold fortunes,
I make swallows and sparrows all my wealth,

fill cups with the greens of springtime wine
and face moon in a window's dark mystery,

or circle a pool, depths clearing. A reflection
in water flowing thin, I take out my hairpins,

then lie in bed with books scattered around,
maybe rise half-drunk to comb out my hair.

INSCRIBED ON A WALL AT HIDDEN-MIST PAVILION

Spring blossoms and autumn moons slip so easily into poems.
Bright days and crystalline nights—they're sage immortals

scattered here. Aimless, I raised pearl blinds for emptiness
and moved my bed-mat to stay. I sleep facing mountains now.

SORROW AND WORRY

A confusion of falling leaves scatters in warm evening rain.
I play vermilion strings alone, and singing crystalline songs

let go of heartsick longing for kindred spirits. I cultivated
true nature: why cast it away on swelling seas of bitterness?

Their carriages clattering outside the gate, sage elders visit.
And my bed is littered all over with Taoist books and scrolls.

Simple people wander blue cirrus-traced sky in the end. Azure
mountains and green rivers: barely here before they're gone.

Sung Dynasty:
The Mainstream Renewed

(c. 1000 to 1225)

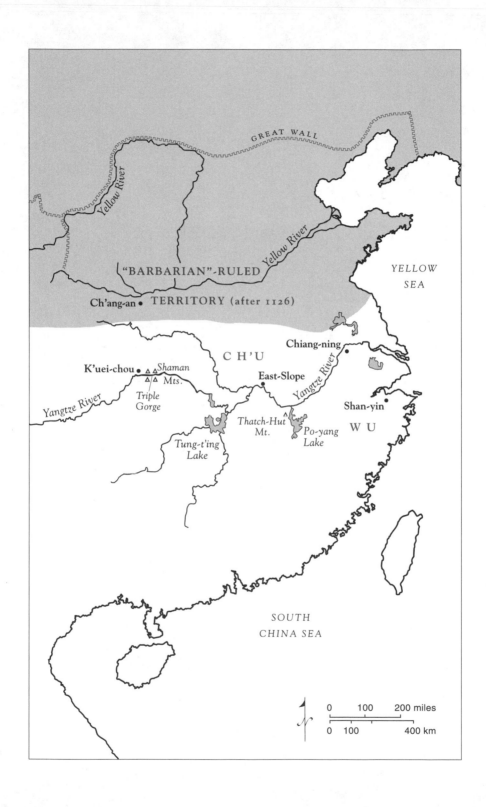

GREAT WALL

Yellow River

Yellow River

"BARBARIAN"-RULED

Ch'ang-an • TERRITORY (after 1126)

YELLOW
SEA

CH'U

Chiang-ning

K'uei-chou • △ △ Shaman

△ △ Mts.

East-Slope

Yangtze River

Yangtze River

Triple
Gorge

Shan-yin •

Thatch-Hut
Mt.

Po-yang
Lake

WU

Yangtze River

Tung-t'ing
Lake

SOUTH
CHINA SEA

0   100   200 miles

0   100   400 km

THE LAST HALF CENTURY of the T'ang Dynasty produced a generally mediocre and derivative poetry of three distinctive types: highly refined landscape poetry, in the style of Wang Wei; a dense hermetic poetry, written in the style of Li Shang-yin and representing the last flickerings of the experimental tradition; and finally, poetry from the romantic world of courtesans (see the discussion of *tz'u* below). These preoccupations reflected the political enervation of the T'ang, and they continued through the half century of instability that followed the T'ang's collapse and into the early decades of the Sung.

As the Sung returned the country to stability, peace, and prosperity, Sung poets reacted against the precious and self-involved poetries of the late T'ang years, returning the art to its mainstream commitment to clarity and empirical immediacy. Critics have wanted to define a distinctive Sung style that can be contrasted decisively to the T'ang, but it is better to see the Sung as an extension of trends already existing in T'ang poetry. And the great Sung poets are of course quite singular, so broad generalities about them are hardly more accurate than they are for T'ang poets. Any attempt to define a period style denies them their individuality and tends to blur them all into one poet, but it is perhaps possible to suggest some orientations that most of the poets share.

Sung poets had little patience for mere poetic effect, be it the pure insights of spiritualized landscape poems or the self-involved ambiguities of Li Shang-yin's evocative atmospherics. Rather than looking to a carefully constructed realm of artifice for insight, they looked to the workaday world in which we live our actual lives. Their commitment was to reality in all its stuttering imperfections, so their poems often focused on precise physical description and attention to the most ordinary, even unsavory aspects of everyday life. They felt little need to poeticize what we call reality and the Chinese called *tzu-jan* (see Key Terms), an attitude profoundly informed by Ch'an (Zen) Buddhism. Now fully assimilated, less a posture to be perfected and declared in a poem than the simple fabric of experience for the intelligentsia, Ch'an taught that enlightenment is nothing other than a clear mind's attention to everyday actuality, an insight that inspired a broad empirical trend not only in Sung arts but also in philosophy and science.

This Ch'an attention to *tzu-jan* is reflected in the imagistic texture of these realistic poems, but it was also deepened, for Sung poets typically spoke with a kind of calm artlessness, which they considered the essence and most fundamental value of poetry. This artlessness, central to the revitalization that made the Sung poetic era rival even the T'ang, offers an alternative, and perhaps finally more profound engagement with *tzu-jan* than that found in T'ang poetics. Sage belonging to Lao Tzu's wilderness cosmology had typically been embodied in the subject matter of the poem, in the poem's explicit statement. But the major Sung poets *enact* that belonging in the form of the poem rather than simply *portray* it in the poem's subject matter. There is an easygoing, even bland feel to the artless language and relaxed movement of such poems. As with Po Chü-i, this strategy integrates the movements of thought into the movements of *tzu-jan*. Profoundly influenced by their Ch'an practice, Sung poets had seen through the need to assert a powerful individuality by shaping a singular vision of the world, for such an assertion isolates the individual outside natural process. So Sung poetry traded the singular poetries typical of the T'ang Dynasty for a plainspoken, uncrafted simplicity.

This approach is of course radically antipoetic, for what appears to be an unassuming mediocre poem becomes a great poem, and what seems to be a very original and striking poem becomes a mediocre and uninsightful poem. (This makes it difficult to decide which Sung poems are truly important: the most interesting poems may not represent Sung poetics accurately, and poems that best represent the poetics may not be terribly interesting.) In fact, it may very well be that the greatest poets of the Sung are actually among the least remembered poets of the Sung. In later centuries, this conundrum often led critics to question which is the greater poetry, the intense and virtuosic poetry of the T'ang's major poets or the plain and mundane poetry of the Sung, for the Sung's simplicity of voice is actually quite complex: it is the voice of a poet participating in the indifferent process of *tzu-jan* burgeoning forth from the undifferentiated unity of absence (*wu*: see Key Terms). This represents a culmination of the poetics developed by T'ao Ch'ien and Po Chü-i, the poetics of an egoless ego, accepting the self with all its delusions and clumsiness as a part of *tzu-jan*'s unfolding.

The Sung revitalization represents both a mature stage of Ch'an practice and a return to beginnings, to Lao Tzu and the lazybones understanding of T'ao Ch'ien. Su Tung-p'o described Sung poems as revealing a serene inner richness concealed within a withered exterior. And Huang T'ing-chien, expressing his own poetic values as much as anything, said of T'ao Ch'ien: "When you've just come of age, reading these poems seems like gnawing on withered wood. But reading them after long experience in the world, it seems the decisions of your life were all made in ignorance."

Tz'u

The primary form for serious poetry throughout the written tradition had been the *shih*, which grew out of the folk tradition in the "Nineteen Ancient-Style Poems" (p. 85) and the Lady Midnight collection (p. 89), but during the Sung a new form came into widespread use: the *tz'u*, or song-lyric. The *tz'u* has a looser, more spontaneous feel, as it has lines of varying length, rather than the rigid uniformity of the *shih*, in which all lines are the same length (either five or seven characters). Another difference is in the titles: while *shih* employ titles that somehow reflect the subject matter of the poems, *tz'u* are simply titled after the tunes they were written to accompany. (Rather than use misleading and arbitrary titles, *tz'u* are left untitled in this translation.)

The *tz'u* form emerged during the T'ang Dynasty, when a new type of music migrated into China with female entertainers from central Asia. In the folk tradition, *tz'u* filled the same function as Music-Bureau *yüeh-fu* poetry (see pp. 72–73), but with a new feel to the music, and it addressed a similar range of peasant themes in a similarly straightforward way. No Chinese music from this period survives, but this exotic foreign music apparently had more emotive force than the indigenous music of China and so was quickly adopted by courtesans for their seductive songs. These courtesans soon began inventing lyrics to fit their purposes—sensuous lyrics they could sing to entertain and entice their male clients.

The new culture of romance that arose with the increasing popularity of courtesans proved very appealing for poets during the late T'ang years, notably Li Ho, Tu Mu, and Li Shang-yin. In a culture governed by propriety and arranged marriages, this courtesan romance offered a new emotional stimulus and a sense of romantic freedom that we now take for granted. With a few early exceptions (pp. 185, 282, e.g.), the *tz'u* form entered the establishment male tradition in the mid-eighth century, when male poets began writing *tz'u* lyrics to be sung by courtesans. Naturally, they were just what the men wanted to hear: suggestive songs about beautiful women languorously longing for men, such as this *tz'u* by Wen T'ing-yün (812–870), who became the first notable *tz'u* poet in the male tradition by infusing the form with the sensibility of experimentalists such as Li Ho and Li Shang-yin:

UNTITLED

Willow floss on and on,
delicate spring rain,
and out beyond blossoms, the sound of a waterclock's drip.
Borderland geese startled,
crows lift off city walls.
Golden partridge gracing painted screens.
Thin mist fragrant
entering bed-curtains,
these ponds and pavilions of passion are all forlorn sorrow.
Embroidered curtains
behind a red candle.
I dream on and on, my love: you won't know how far.

Tz'u poetry became a significant part of the "decadence" that typified poetry in the later T'ang, and being limited to scenes of courtesan romance, it was not generally considered part of the "high art" tradition. It remained the realm of emotional self-indulgence that many associated with the end of the T'ang in the form of Li Yü (937–978), who was the last significant T'ang poet and the one who opened the *tz'u* form to topics beyond romance. Li Yü was also the T'ang emperor (actually of the Southern T'ang, last vestige of the destroyed T'ang Dynasty) who lost his nation to the Sung because, rather than attending to the business of his country, he devoted his energies to the beauties of art and romance. As they illustrate this moral interpretation of late T'ang cultural history, Li's most widely known poems are those he wrote at the end of his life, while imprisoned by the Sung conquerors, and they are filled with intense nostalgia and regret:

UNTITLED

Spring blossoms and autumn moons—when will they end?
Things happened: who knows few or many?
Last night in this little tower, still more spring wind,
I couldn't bear to turn and look at my old country flooded with moonlight.

Carved railings, jade staircases—they must still be there:
the rouged faces will be new, that's all.
How much grief can there be in a single person?
It's like a great river swollen with springtime water surging east.

The range of subject matter in *tz'u* writing continued to expand, and in the Sung Dynasty the *tz'u* came to be seen as a serious poetic form like the *shih*, a transformation often attributed to Su Tung-p'o (p. 364). Virtually all great Sung poets wrote at least some *tz'u*, thus bringing to fruition in the male "high art" tradition yet another infusion of poetic energy from the folk tradition and, indeed, as in the Lady Midnight poems, from the female folk tradition.

MEI YAO-CH'EN

(1002 to 1060)

MEI YAO-CH'EN WAS tall and good-natured, with bushy eyebrows, large ears, and red cheeks. This odd character, poor and faltering in his career, came to be called the great "mountain-opening patriarch" of Sung Dynasty poetry. Mei summarized his poetics in the term *p'ing-tan*, which became a touchstone for Sung poetry. *P'ing-tan* translates literally as "even and bland," and as a spiritual disposition, *p'ing-tan* extends to other possible translations of the two terms: "ordinary/tranquil" and "blank/thinned-out-and-flavorless" (for the philosophical sense of *tan*, see poems on pp. 370 and 419, where it is translated as "blank"). It is an extension of T'ao Ch'ien's "idleness" (see Key Terms: *hsien*) via Po Chü-i's "idle and bland" (*hsien-tan*), for a *p'ing-tan* poem *enacts* the spiritual posture of idleness in the movement of the poem rather than merely taking it as the subject of the poem. This is something Mei and other Sung poets recognized in the poems of T'ao Ch'ien, Wei Ying-wu, Po Chü-i, and others, but they made it the primary criterion for poetic insight. A *p'ing-tan* poem takes experience as it is, without straining to extract from it profound emotional or philosophical insights, and so tends to be realistic, plainspoken, free of exaggerated poetic sentiment, calm and subdued whatever the topic, descriptive, socially engaged.

Central to Mei's *p'ing-tan* poetics is his realism. Poetry in China, as in any other culture, traditionally functioned as a privileged realm containing only the most essential of human utterances: the most complex or intense thoughts or emotions, reflections on spirituality or urgent social issues, and so on. One compelling poetic strategy is to bring seemingly unworthy material into this privileged realm, for this gives a certain eminence to the seemingly unworthy and, at the same time, challenges the idea that some things are loftier than others. In Taoist terms, this means that one is beyond choosing what to value and not value, an act that separates a person from the indifferent unfolding of *tzu-jan* (see Key Terms). Earlier poets (especially Tu Fu) had played on this tension to a certain extent, but Mei Yao-ch'en took it as the very heart of his poetics, including the most mundane aspects of experience in his poems. This opened his poetic vision to everything equally, the lofty realm of mountain peaks and Ch'an (Zen) insight together with the unsavory everyday realm of lice and latrines.

By replacing the striving for profound and exquisite effects typical of serious poetry with an artless simplicity, Mei elevated that simplicity into complex wisdom. *P'ing-tan* as the embodiment of profound spiritual insight echoes back through the tradition to Chapter 35 of the *Tao Te Ching* (p. 49), where *tan* ("bland") appears:

> Music and savory food
> entice travelers to stop,
> but the Way uttered forth
> isn't even the thinnest of bland flavors.

So *p'ing-tan* means moving in profound harmony with the unfolding of Way (natural process) in a poem: already being Way, rather than writing poems that try to make one a part of it. And as in the work of T'ao Ch'ien, whom Mei and later Sung poets recognized as the first master of *p'ing-tan*, however unassuming this poetic Way may appear, it reflects a deep wisdom that comes only after long cultivation.

8TH MONTH, 9TH SUN: GETTING UP IN THE MORNING, I GO OUT TO THE LATRINE AND FIND CROWS FEEDING ON MAGGOTS THERE

Crows flapping around before sunup,
no telling which are male or female:

rat-carcass meals must be rare indeed
for them to come peck at shit-worms.

Soon stuffed, they rise into treetops,
cock their heads, cry into west wind.

I'm done listening to your evil omens.
Your feathers must reek with stench,

and divinities keep clean if they can
see into the origin and end of things.

STAYING OVERNIGHT IN HSÜ'S LIBRARY, HSIEH SHIH-HOU AND I ARE DRIVEN CRAZY BY RATS

Lamp-flame low and blue, everyone asleep,
hungry rats come sneaking out of holes

and send plates and bowls crashing over,
startling us from our dream-filled sleep.

Bang—an ink-stone tumbles off the table,
and we panic. Next they're on the shelves

gnawing at books. Suddenly my silly boy
starts meowing like a cat! Goofy plan, eh?

THE BOAT-PULLERS

Leg broken on the sandy shore, a goose
hobbles along like a man, wings splayed:

what will it do when evening rains come
and the cold wind starts ripping through?

Sodden feathers mud-stained, arched neck
shrinking back—it doesn't utter a sound.

That's their life exactly. Guess it's better
than lugging weapons around some war.

A LONE FALCON ABOVE THE BUDDHA HALL AT UNIVERSAL-PURITY MONASTERY

I just rented a place that looks out over the monastery's Buddha Hall,
and all that gold and emerald bathes my tumbledown house in light.

Gazing up over the rooftops, I watch a flock of pigeons nesting, busy
fussing and feeding their young, no idea how far gone the year is.

Their shit's everywhere, all over the carved eaves and painted walls,
even splattered across clay heads and shoulders of sacred Buddhas,

but monks don't dare take crossbows out and start picking them off.
Suddenly, an ash-dark falcon drifts over, flaunting ruthless claws,

crows crying out, magpies shrieking, mynahs cackling. Pure passion,
the falcon wheels around, then catching a glimpse of fragrant meat,

plunges headlong and cold-blooded, outnumbered but wildly fearless,
and in a flash it's shattered a braincase, terrifying the whole flock.

The dead bird tumbles through air, but it never reaches the ground:
in a flurry of wings and feathers, the falcon whirls down to snag it,

then settles on rooftop Buddha heights, rips and tears at it with gusto,
gulps down hunks of meat, slashes the liver, scatters intestines away.

Tired old vultures, skulking and cruel and without the hunter's skill,
circle overhead waiting for their chance, hungry eyes glaring down.

When the glutted falcon finally lifts away into flight, they cower back,
then scuttle down into a frenzy, no telling vultures and ravens apart.

A crowd of kids gathers to gawk and point. People in the street laugh.
And I keep chanting whatever comes to mind beside an autumn river.

1ST MOON, 15TH SUN: I TRY GOING OUT TO THE LANTERN FESTIVAL, AND QUICKLY RETURN

If I stay home, the gloom only gets worse,
so I go out and wander the festival for fun,

but rich and poor alike stroll beside wives,
driving any joy further and further away.

Once you're old, anything's overwhelming.
I want to keep on, but it's wearing me out,

so I go back home to the kids, and no one
says a word. You can smell the acrid grief.

Last year they went out with their mother,
smeared on paint and rouge just like her:

now she roams the Yellow Springs below,
and they're dressed in tatters, faces dirty.

Remembering how young they both are,
I hide my tears, not wanting them to see,

push the lamp away and lie facing the wall,
a hundred sorrows clotting heart and lung.

FARMERS

Towering trees shade a brushwood gate,
emerald moss dappled with falling light.

They hoe lotus, a mountain moon rising,
and then, searching thin mist for a trail,

the old man leads a child, eyes following
their starveling ox taking its calf home.

And for dinner, back home in lamplight,
they savor white garlic pan-fried in dew.

HSIEH SHIH-HOU SAYS THE ANCIENT MASTERS NEVER WROTE A POEM ABOUT LICE, AND WHY DON'T I WRITE ONE

It's so easy to get ratty clothes dirty,
so easy, and so hard to get lice out.

Thronging inside folds at the belt,
wandering up along the fur collar—

who can find them, so nicely hidden,
dining on blood all cozy and snug?

If my life's a mere blink of the eye,
what's there to contemplate in yours?

344

ON A FAREWELL JOURNEY FOR HSIEH SHIH-HOU,
WHO'S RETURNING HOME TO NAN-YANG, WE
ENCOUNTER A VAST WINDSTORM, SO WE SPEND
THE NIGHT AT SOLAR-HEIGHTS MOUNTAIN
MONASTERY, THEN CONTINUE ON THE NEXT
MORNING TO CHIANG INN

Long ago I traveled out to send you off in spring wind,
spring wind a lavish delight, apricots in radiant bloom,

and now we share a farewell journey in autumn wind,
autumn wind clattering leaves down, rivers full of sand.

Frost knots our horses' fur, their manes buffeted out.
The servants shuffle along, scowls set against the cold,

and our rag coats blow open, cold cutting bone-deep
among dead trees scraping together, threatening fire.

Suddenly, from a cliff's belly, an old monastery appears,
and we dismount at last, happy to stay the night among

temples and halls terraced up and down the mountain,
majestic pine and cedar towering into ridgeline clouds,

where fallen leaves sweep swirling down long hallways
and curtains shaken clean beat in the abbot's window.

A terra-cotta mother-goddess nurses nine sweet babies,
hugging and caressing them, charming them with play:

it carries this distant traveler's thoughts back to family,
makes me burn with longing to see my little ones again.

We huddle around a brazier as twilight sky turns black,
then borrow monk beds and sleep lit by shrine lamps,

but even under quilts aplenty, we're soon cold as iron.
It's nothing like home, though I can't afford blankets,

and soon awake, we wait out dawn, pillowed on arms
as our legs turn numb with cold, muscles cramped tight.

Finally clappers ring out: wooden fish marking dawn.
And rising, we watch the Pleiades and Hyades arc west

as the wind's howl dies away and the east brightens.
Our doubtful servants pack, and we're about to set out,

when an old monk comes carrying ink-stone and brush,
sweeps a wall clean, and asks me to write out the year.

After leaving the gates, we travel to a mountain inn,
its thatch roof blown off. It's just beams and rafters,

but we stay. Opening camp-chairs, we laugh and talk,
and though you've given up wine, we spread our mats.

Hardly five hundred miles left on your journey home,
and surely you have a purse of coins in your satchel,

but you shake out robes, eager to go while there's sun,
and no wonder: a devoted mother is waiting anxiously.

I, on the other hand, leave for vistas of rivers and seas,
thoughts haunted even there by these places we shared.

SHEPHERD'S-PURSE

People call shepherd's-purse food of poverty,
think it's shameful. But I call it a rare treat.

I've watched families gather shepherd's-purse.
They start at National Gate and head south:

carrying lean iron knives, blades rust-eaten,
frost-battered baskets of azure-green bamboo,

they go plodding out, deep into frozen land,
and scrape around there for roots and leaves.

Hands so raw they can't feed themselves, they
live in hunger, and you're ashamed to eat it?

Dining on juicy lamb and red-tailed fish, fine
fragrant meats—that, that's what poverty is.

A maid comes running into the house
talking about things beyond belief,

about the sky all turned to blue glass,
the moon to a crystal of black quartz.

It rose a full ten parts round tonight,
but now it's just a bare sliver of light.

My wife hurries off to fry roundcakes,
and my son starts banging on mirrors:

it's awfully shallow thinking, I know,
but that urge to restore is beautiful.

The night deepens. The moon emerges,
then goes on shepherding stars west.

EAST RIVER

Reaching East River, I gaze across the water,
then sit facing a lone island. Boats creep forth.

Wild ducks, thoughts idle, sleep along the bank,
and in ancient trees, every limb is blossoming.

Pebble shorelines perfectly smooth, sieve-pure,
reed thickets bloom short and scissor-smooth.

So much to feel, but I can't stay. Night's come,
and my tired horse keeps looking toward home.

A LITTLE VILLAGE

On the broad Huai, among many islands, a village appears:
thorn-date fences, their tattered openings the only gates.

Squawking back and forth, cold chickens scuffle for food,
and old-timers without clothes cradle their grandchildren.

Sparrows nest in ragged rigging on battered little boats,
and the river's gnawed at mulberries until the bank's all

roots dangling in air. O, this is how they live. It's fantasy
listing them in tax books alongside some emperor's people.

EYES DARK

A darkness disease has seized my eyes.
On bright clear days, I walk through fog,

and whatever I see is double. It's scary.
My writing brush scrawls around, lost.

People coming toward me look like haze,
and birds soaring past are a quick blur.

No telling what's what in this confusion,
I'm suddenly free of likes and dislikes.

AUTUMN MEDITATION

Wu-t'ung trees spread above the well,
yellow, and crickets hide under beds.

Absence keeps deepening in presence.
No more false promise in the season.

Hushed wind starts leaves fluttering,
then blown rain clatters on roof-tiles:

the ear hears, but mind is itself silent.
Who's left now all thought's forgotten?

WANG AN-SHIH

(1021 to 1086)

WANG AN-SHIH WAS a remarkable figure—not only one of the great Sung Dynasty poets but also the most influential and controversial statesman of his time. The deep commitment felt by intellectuals in ancient China to both the Confucian realm of social responsibility and the Taoist realm of spiritual self-cultivation gave rise to a recluse ideal that answered both of these imperatives. In one mythic version of this ideal, a sage recluse living contentedly in the mountains recognizes that the nation is in crisis and needs his wisdom. He reluctantly joins the government after being summoned by the emperor, resolves the crisis, and then, having no interest in the wealth and renown associated with that life, returns to cultivate his simple life of spiritual depth in the mountains. This ideal was enacted by countless intellectuals in ancient China, though in a more realistic form. They devoted themselves to public service, always watching for a chance to spend time in mountain seclusion, often at Ch'an (Zen) Buddhist monasteries, and then at some point retired permanently from government service to live as recluses. Wang An-shih was one of the great exemplars of this recluse ideal. A devoted civil servant, frugal almost to a fault and completely immune, even hostile, to the grandeur of high office and political power, Wang rose to no less a rank than prime minister. As prime minister, he instituted a controversial system of radically egalitarian social reforms in an effort to improve the lives of China's dispossessed peasants. And once these reforms were securely in place, he left the government in the hands of trusted compatriots and retired to a reclusive life in the countryside near Chiang-ning (River-Serene), on the south shore of the Yangtze River.

It was after his retirement that Wang wrote the poems on which his reputation is based. He spent those later years practicing Ch'an Buddhism and wandering the mountains around his home, a Taoist/Ch'an cultivation of the rivers-and-mountains realm that shapes his poems. But however profound the Ch'an wisdom in Wang's late poetry, it was haunted by the failure of his political dream. Wang's compatriots eventually lost power in government, and he had to watch helplessly as conservative elements dismantled the social reforms he had worked so hard to put in place.

In dramatic contrast to his stature as the most powerful statesman in China, Wang's position as one of the Sung Dynasty's greatest poets is largely based on the short landscape poems that he wrote during these years, most notably quatrains (*chüeh-chu*), and it is those poems that are represented in this selection. The quatrain form was ideal for the Sung's poetics of artlessness. The larger the poem, the larger the interpretive structure it imposes on the landscape of reality. Such is the case in the West, where a human-centered culture has meant that great poems tend to be large, even epic, in their proportions. In contrast, China's great poetry tends to be quite short. As the briefest of China's poetic forms, the Ch'an-inspired quatrain does not impose a structure on the world so much as open an emptiness, a place in consciousness to let that world enter. And the fact that a man of such majestic public stature would focus on quatrains is an indication of the grandeur inherent in that humble gesture.

MIDDLE YEARS

Middle years devoted to the nation, I lived a fleeting dream,
and home again in old age, I wander borderland wilderness.

Looking south to green mountains, it's clear I'm not so alone
here: on spring lakes, they crowd my little-boat life all adrift.

EVENTS AT BELL MOUNTAIN

Water soundless, a wandering stream skirts bamboo forest.
And west of bamboo, wildflowers delight in gentle spring.

Facing all this under thatch eaves, I sit through the day.
Not a single bird. No song. Mountain quiet goes deeper still.

FOLLOWING THOUGHTS

Following thoughts all brush-bramble my hands open through,
I trace ridgelines, cross creeks, climb out onto terraces beyond:

the simplest wind-and-dew bridge, a little-boat moon all adrift,
lost birds, widowed birds—their comings and goings at an end.

SELF–PORTRAIT IN PRAISE

Things aren't other than they are.
I am today whoever I was long ago,

and if I can be described, it's as this
perfect likeness of all these things.

WRITTEN ON A WALL AT HALFWAY-MOUNTAIN MONASTERY

1

When I wander, heaven starts raining,
and when I'm done, rain's gone again.

How could rain be my own wandering?
Pure chance brought us together here.

2

If it's cold, I just sit somewhere warm,
and if it's hot, I wander somewhere cool:

all beings no different from Buddha,
Buddha precisely all beings themselves.

WANDERING BELL MOUNTAIN

Gazing all day into mountains, I can't get enough of mountains.
Retire into mountains, and mountains become your old masters:

when mountain blossoms scatter away, mountains always remain,
and in empty mountain streamwater, mountains deepen idleness.

RIVER RAIN

All dark and distant mystery, river rain soaks yellow twilight.
Heavens enter recluse islands, brimful, misting them together,

and North Creek pours through South Creek waters. Suddenly,
South Mountain's meandering around North Mountain clouds.

ABOVE THE YANGTZE

North of the Yangtze, autumn shadow spreads halfway open.
Evening clouds heavy with rain hang low across the land.

Rambling tangled in green mountains, all roads surely lost,
I suddenly see a thousand sails shimmering in and out of view.

GAZING NORTH

Hair whiter still, I ache to see those long-ago northlands,
but keep to this refuge: goosefoot cane, windblown trees.

Pity the new moon—all that bright beauty, and for whom?
It's dusk. Countless mountains face each other in sorrow.

INSCRIBED ON MASTER LAKE-SHADOW'S WALL

Thatch-eave paths are always well-swept, pure, free of moss,
and with your hands, flowering orchards planted themselves.

A creek meanders by, snug curve cradling jade-green fields.
Two mountains push a door open, sending azure-green inside.

HYMN

Dawn lights up the room. I close my book and sleep,
dreaming of Bell Mountain and full of tenderness.

How do you grow old living with failure and disgrace?
Just go back to the cascading creek: cold, shimmering.

EAST RIVER

East River's swollen current surges around fallen trees;
and yellow reeds cut, island shallows open away, empty.

In late light at South Creek, smoke rises. Vast and silent,
western mountains hover between presence and absence.

READING HISTORY

Renowned achievement's been bitter business from the beginning.
Who can you trust to tell the story of all you've done and not done?

Whatever happens is already murky enough, and full of distortion,
then small minds muddle the truth further and it's utter confusion:

they only hand down dregs. Their azure-green and cinnabar inks
can't capture the fresh kernel of things, the quintessential spirit,

and how could they fathom a lofty sage's thoughts, those mindless
sentinels guarding thousand-autumn dust on their pages of paper?

LEAVING THE CITY

I've lived in the country long enough to know its many joys.
I'm starting to feel like a child back in my old village again.

Leaving the city today, I simply leave all that dust behind,
and facing mountains and valleys, I feel them enter my eyes.

AFTER VISITING A MASTER OF THE WAY ON
BELL MOUNTAIN, I RETURN AT DUSK

Through a thousand, ten thousand peaks,
this road between presence and absence

wanders—bees sampling open blossoms,
gibbons climbing trees to dine on fruit.

I search for the Way across a cold creek.
I'd hoped dusk might light the way home,

but the sky's gone dark, no moon rising.
My houseboy will be out closing the gate.

SUN WEST AND LOW

Sun west and low: stair-shadow, churning *wu-t'ung* trees.
Blinds raised: green mountains, and half-empty bamboo.

Ducks blurred in fire drift, gold on the chill of deep water.
Dreams a ruins of distance and worry among this birdsong.

AT LUMEN RIVER HEADWATERS

West of Lumen City, a hundred mountains rise ridge beyond ridge.
All trace of my life buried in these dark depths of haze and cloud,

it's perfectly empty: that worry over white hair, over all I've done
and not done. In spring wind, the river lights up a ravaged face.

EAST RIDGE

Together we climb to this East Ridge lookout on New Year's Eve
and gaze at the Star River, its length lighting distant forests.

Earth's ten thousand holes cry and moan. That wind's our ruin,
and in a thousand seething waves, there's no trace of a heart.

ABOVE THE YANGTZE

A letter from long-ago shores arrives, saying
our village is tangled in sickness and hunger.

Why are they telling me, a ten-thousand-mile
wanderer, swelling my hundred-year sorrow?

No one cares about patching up ruined lives
now, and my lifework's only turned to shame.

My sick eyes gaze off toward them. Night falls.
I trust myself to this little-boat life all adrift.

IN BAMBOO FOREST

In bamboo forest, my thatch hut's among stone cliff-roots.
Out front, through thin bamboo, you can glimpse a village.

I doze all day, all idleness. And no one stops by here to visit.
Just this spring wind come sweeping my gate-path clean.

CUT FLOWERS

Getting this old isn't much fun,
and it's worse stuck in bed, sick.

I draw water and arrange flowers,
comforted by their scents adrift,

scents adrift, gone in a moment.
And how much longer for me?

Cut flowers and this long-ago I:
it's so easy forgetting each other.

SU TUNG-P'O

(1037 to 1101)

Su Tung-p'o (Su Shih) was born into a common family from the lower
reaches of the educated class but rose to become one of China's greatest
intellectuals, traditionally considered the Sung Dynasty's greatest poet, and
no less renowned for his calligraphy (which followed the same philosoph-
ical principles as his poetry). He was at times quite influential in govern-
ment, but because he opposed Wang An-shih's radical policies and never
stopped voicing his criticisms, he spent most of his life in the provinces, in-
cluding many years in especially arduous exile. He was also tried for trea-
son (on the journey north to his trial, Su's wife burned many of his poems
on the deck of a boat, fearing they would be used to implicate him), jailed
and beaten, and very nearly executed. It was said that great poetry grows
out of hardship and exile, and indeed Su consolidated his mature poetics
during his first exile. In fact, he took his literary name, Tung-p'o (East
Slope), from the site where he lived during that exile as a subsistence
farmer: East-Slope Su.

Su Tung-p'o's work represents a striking extension of Mei Yao-ch'en's
p'ing-tan poetics (see pp. 338–39), for he added a subjective dimension to
Mei's realism. Su's poems enact consciousness wandering like water—Lao
Tzu's operant metaphor for *Tao*—taking shape according to what it en-
counters. His mastery of this poetics derives in part from a lifelong devo-

tion to Ch'an (Zen) Buddhism, for Ch'an no-mind allows a spontaneous and crystalline responsiveness to whatever experience one encounters. But as with water, there is an inner nature to the poet that endures through all the transformations. This enduring inner nature returns us to the concept of *li*, or inner pattern (see Key Terms), that was so important to Hsieh Ling-yün (see p. 127). And the different roles *li* plays in the thought of these two poets summarize the transformation that had taken place in Chinese poetics.

For Hsieh Ling-yün, *li* is primarily manifested in the empirical world, and the goal of poetry is to render empty mind mirroring the vast dimensions of *li* in the rivers-and-mountains realm, thereby bringing its dynamic energy inside consciousness. But Su Tung-p'o's poems weave together the empirical world and wandering thought, and for him both aspects are manifestations of *li*, the "inner pattern" of *tzu-jan*'s (see Key Terms) unfolding. In other words, wilderness is not simply out there in the mountains, it is always already here within us as well. Consciousness is itself already wild—so every gesture in a poem is wilderness, whether it is a philosophical insight, a whimsical metaphor, or an egret taking flight.

This poetics gives the poems a light and effortless feel. Rather than struggling with poetic material to extract an earnest poetic statement, concise and compelling, Su's poems tend to move with a kind of easy spontaneity as their statement slowly emerges—a movement that renders consciousness in its true nature as a form of *tzu-jan*'s perennial movement and transformation. This happens not only in individual poems but also through the entire body of his work. He wrote easily and on most any topic (hence the large number of poems in his corpus: 2,400 surviving), each poem open to a new perspective, never sounding like the last word, and therefore feeling like part of that ongoing organic process from which emerges not just poetry but the entire cosmos. Su's poetics in turn reflects a philosophical disposition that allowed him a profound emotional balance in the face of considerable hardship and disappointment. And that balance is something for which he is especially remembered in the Chinese cultural legend: a detached tranquillity, even lightheartedness, that grows out of an acceptance of both sorrow and joy as equally inevitable aspects of *tzu-jan*'s unfolding.

12TH MOON, 14TH SUN: A LIGHT SNOW FELL
OVERNIGHT, SO I SET OUT EARLY FOR SOUTH CREEK,
STOPPED FOR A QUICK MEAL AND ARRIVED LATE

Snowfall at South Creek: it's the most priceless of things,
so I set out to see it before it melts. Hurrying my horse,

pushing through thickets alone, I watch for footprints,
and at dawn, I'm first across fresh snow on a red bridge!

Houses in shambles beyond belief, nowhere even to sleep:
it's a village of starvation, voices mere murmurs. I gaze.

Only the evening crows know my thoughts, startled into
flight, a thousand flakes tumbling through cold branches.

UNTITLED

Forests end in mountain light, and bamboo hides walls.
A confusion of cicada cries, dry grasses, a small pond.

An occasional bird wings white through empty sky,
and delicate in scent, waterlilies shine across water.

Out beyond the village, along
ancient city walls, I'll stroll
till dusk, staff in hand, then turn back in slant light.

Thanks to rain that came last night in the third watch,
I get another cool day in this drifting dream of a life.

INSCRIBED ON A WALL AT THE PREFECTURAL COURT

On New Year's Eve I should be home early,
but this office full of business keeps me.

Writing-brush in hand, hiding my tears,
I face all these bound prisoners, helpless

little people scrambling for food, snared
in the law's net, and no reason for shame.

I'm no different: adoring a meager salary,
I follow orders, losing my chance to live

quiet and far away. No telling who's noble,
who vile: we're all just angling for a meal.

Could I free them for the holiday at least?
I brood in shame before ancients who did.

A light boat one lone leaf,
a startled swan two oars—

water and sky are pure clarity
reflecting deep. Waves smooth,

fish roil this duckweed mirror
and egrets dot misty shorelines.

We breeze past sandy streams,
frostfall streams cold,
moonlit streams aglow,

ridge above ridge like a painting,
bend beyond bend like a screen.

Here I think back to
Yen Tzu-ling's empty old age,

lord and recluse one dream.
Renown's empty then as now,

just mountains stretching away:
cloud mountains erratic,
dawn mountains green.

SIPPING WINE AT THE LAKE: SKIES START CLEARING, THEN RAIN

It's gorgeous under clearing skies, a lake all billows and light,
and lovely too in rain, mountain colors among empty mists.

I can't help comparing West Lake to Lady West, her makeup
just barely there or laid on thick: she's exquisite either way.

INSCRIBED ON A WALL AT A SMALL MONASTERY ON CRAGGED HEIGHTS OF BLUE-OX RIDGE, A PLACE HUMAN TRACKS RARELY REACH

Hurrying our horses home last night, passing river dikes of sand,
we found kitchen smoke trailing fragrance out across ten miles,

and this morning we wander Blue-Ox Ridge, walking-sticks in hand,
cliff-wall cascades drumming the silence of a thousand mountains.

Don't laugh at the old monk.
It's true he's deaf as dragons,
but at the end of this hundred-year life, who isn't a pitiful sight?

And tomorrow morning, long after we've set out again for the city,
he'll still be here among the white clouds of this poem on the wall.

Bamboo scratches at the window-screen,
and rain clattering in bamboo clatters.

Shutters wide-open tranquillity, no dust,
mist rises from a table's cold ink-stone.

You relish this solitude in quiet mystery,
and returned to origins, wanting nothing,

sit *ch'an* stillness on sackcloth and mat,
stand listening to wind's voice in a bowl.

Presence and absence blank here, in cold
cap and sandal, you sprinkle and sweep,

offer thick tea rinsing depths of night,
light incense drifting all worry away,

and on my way home, fireflies meander
north-hall darkness one by one by one.

This life tangled in sorrow and trouble
somehow offers such repose in idleness.

Roaming vultures regret former laughs,
earthworms lament their late awakening,

and I'm no T'ao Ch'ien for quiet integrity.
But where's karma in all this idleness?

AFTER LI SZU-HSÜN'S PAINTING *CRAGGED ISLANDS ON THE YANGTZE*

Mountains all azure-green,
the river all boundless away,
Lone-Spires loom up out of the water, Greater beside Lesser,

and the road ends among fallen cliff-walls, gibbons and birds
scattered away, then nothing but trees towering up into sky.

Where's that river-trader sailing from?
Its oar-songs rise and fall midstream in the river's current

as a gentle breeze plays across shoreline sand, too faint to see.
And Lone-Spires always plunge and swell with passing boats:

majestic summits two slave girls in mist,
they adorn themselves in dawn's mirror.

That merchant there on the boat—he's hardly mean and cruel.
Year before last, his housegirl married an awfully handsome man.

6TH MOON, 27TH SUN: SIPPING WINE AT LAKE-VIEW TOWER

1

Black clouds, soaring ink, nearly blot out these mountains.
White raindrops, skipping pearls, skitter wildly into the boat,

then wind comes across furling earth, scatters them away,
and below Lake-View Tower, lakewater suddenly turns to sky.

2

Setting animals loose—fish and turtles—I'm an exile out here,
but no one owns waterlilies everywhere blooming, blooming.

This lake pillows mountains, starts them glancing up and down,
and my breezy boat wanders free, drifts with an aimless moon.

MIDSUMMER FESTIVAL, WANDERING UP
AS FAR AS THE MONASTERY

I was going wherever I happened to go,
giving myself over to whatever I met,

when incense drew my recluse steps to
mats spread open and pure, tea poured.

Light rain delayed my return, quiet
mystery outside windows lovelier still:

bowl-dome summits blocking out sun,
grasses and trees turned shadowy green.

Climbing quickly to the highest shrine,
I gazed out across whole Buddha-realms,

city walls radiant beneath Helmet Peak
and cloudy skies adrift in Tremor Lake.

Such joy in all this depth and clarity,
such freedom in wide-open mountains,

my recluse search kept on after dusk
cook-smoke rose above distant villages.

Back home now, this day held in mind
shines bright and clear. I can't sleep,

and those monks are sitting awake too,
sharing a lamp's light in *ch'an* stillness.

I live here between heaven and earth,
a lone ant wandering a vast millstone:

I struggle feebly on toward the right,
but the wind-wheel just hauls me left.

I hurry along, all Humanity and Duty,
and still wind up ice-cold and hungry.

Cooking rice on a sword-blade is risky,
and you can't sit on a rug full of pins,

but rivers and mountains are exquisite,
fleeting as an afternoon thunderstorm,

and when young, who's daring enough
to leave the world for a fieldland home?

What luck to be sent here, abandoned,
a horse liberated from saddle and bags.

The family together, we've taken over
a river post-station in this far-off place

heaven opened to us. Hunger and want
come and go. Why celebrate or mourn?

Pure repose, free of all sorrow and joy,
I won't make a lament of my sad words.

EAST SLOPE

1

Who would choose such deserted ruins,
broken walls choked in brambleweed,

who wear themselves out on this land,
work all year to harvest some pittance:

no one but a lone wanderer heaven's
condemned. No escape, I found myself

here cleaning away broken roof-tiles,
soil parched with drought, precarious

paths all tangled thorn-bramble grass.
And now I hope to scrape out a living.

I pause at the plow to catch my breath
and imagine the granary stacked full.

2

These abandoned weed-infested fields
high and low, they all have their use:

valley wetlands perfect for fine rice,
eastern uplands for date and chestnut.

An old friend living south of the river
promised to send some mulberry seeds,

and lovely bamboo isn't hard to start.
The only worry is how fast it spreads.

I still need to find the best house-site,
and as I survey *ch'i*'s movements here,

the houseboy burning off dry grasses
comes running: he's uncovered a well!

I can't promise a feast anytime soon,
but the drinking-gourd's a breeze now.

4

We got the rice in before Bright-Clarity,
and now I'm counting the joys to come.

Rain-feathered sky will darken spring
ponds, shouts welcoming green needles,

and we'll transplant them by summer,
rejoice as windblown leaves tower up,

shimmering with dew in the moonlight,
each one dangling silk-threaded pearls.

Seed-clusters heavy with autumn frost,
they'll topple over against each other,

then we'll listen to it: locust song adrift
all across the fields, like wind and rain.

And soon the rice-pot's full, fresh-hulled
jade-white kernels lighting the basket.

I've always been paid government fare,
rust-rot rice no better than gritty mud,

but now, at last, I'll savor such flavors:
it's a promise made to belly and tongue.

The great river flows east,
its current rinsing
all those gallant figures of a thousand ages away.

West of the ancient battlements,
people say, are
the Red Cliffs of young Chou from the Three Kingdoms:

a confusion of rock piercing sky
and wild waves pounding cliff-walls,
roiling up into a thousand swells of snow.

It's like a painting, river and mountains
where how many august heroes once came together,
and I can almost see it back then, when Lord Chou was
here with lovely Ch'iao, his young new bride:

his bright and fearless presence
with feather fan and silk turban,
talking and laughing
as masts and hulls became flying ash and vanished smoke.

Surely spirits of that ancient time
roam here, smiling at all these feelings
and my hair already turning white.
Our life's like dream,
so pour out the whole cup, offering to a river and its moon.

PRESENTED TO ABBOT PERPETUA ALL-GATHERING AT EAST-FOREST MONASTERY

A murmuring stream is the tongue broad and unending,
and what is mountain color if not the body pure and clear?

Eighty-four thousand *gathas* fill a passing night. But still,
once day has come, how could I explain them to anyone?

INSCRIBED ON A WALL AT THATCH-HUT MOUNTAIN'S WEST-FOREST MONASTERY

Seen from one side, it's a ridgeline. From another, it's a peak.
Distant or near, high or low—it never looks the same twice.

But if I just can't recognize Thatch-Hut Mountain's true face,
here's why: I am myself at the very center of this mountain!

INSCRIBED ON A PAINTING IN WANG
TING-KUO'S COLLECTION ENTITLED *MISTY
RIVER AND CROWDED PEAKS*

Heartbreak above the river, a thousand peaks and summits
drift kingfisher-green in empty skies, like mist and cloud.

At these distances, you don't know if it's mountain or cloud
until mist thins away and clouds scatter. Then mountains

remain, filling sight with canyoned cliff-walls, azure-
                                        green, valleys in cragged shadow,
and cascades tumbling a hundred Ways in headlong flight,

stitching forests and threading rock, seen and then unseen
as they plunge toward valley headwaters, and wild streams

growing calm where mountains open out and forests end.
A small bridge and country inn nestled against mountains,

travelers gradually work their way beyond towering trees,
and a fishing boat drifts, lone leaf on a river swallowing sky.

I can't help asking where you found a painting like this,
bottomless beauty and clarity so lavish in exquisite detail:

I never dreamed there was a place in this human
                                        realm so perfect, so very lovely.
All I want is to go there, buy myself a few acres and settle in.

You can almost see them, can't you? Those pure and remote
                                        places in Wu-ch'ang and Fan-
k'ou where I lingered out five recluse years as Master East-Slope:

a river trembling in spring wind, isolate skies boundless,
and evening clouds furling rain back across lovely peaks,

crows gliding out of red maples to share a boatman's night
and snow tumbling off tall pines startling his midday sleep.

Peach blossoms drift streamwater away right here in this
human realm, and Warrior-Knoll wasn't for spirit immortals.

Rivers and mountains all empty clarity: there's a road in,
but caught in the dust of this world, I'll never find it again.

Returning your painting, I'm taken by sighs of sad wonder.
I have old friends in those mountains,

and their poems keep calling me home.

BATHING MY SON

People all hope their kids will grow up to be so clever and wise,
but I've been consumed by clever-and-wise. It's ruined my life.

Plain and simpleminded—that's what I want most for my son.
Then he'll live free and easy, reign as some high state minister.

AT BRAHMA-HEAVEN MONASTERY, RHYMED WITH A SHORT POEM OF CRYSTALLINE BEAUTY BY THE MONK ACUMEN-HOARD

You can only hear a bell out beyond mist:
the monastery deep in mist is lost to sight.

Straw sandals wet with the dew of grasses,
a recluse wanders. Never coming to rest,

he's simply an echo of mountaintop moon—
light coming and going night after night.

AFTER MY BROTHER'S "THOUGHTS OF LONG AGO AT FROG-RIVER POND"

A person's life lived out somewhere: do you know what it's like?
It's like a wild goose flying free that lands in mud-crust snow,

its web-toed feet leaving a chance print there in the mudpack,
and then sets out again, soaring east or west, who knows where.

Our old monk friend is dead now, the grave's shrine-tower built,
and the monastery wall's in ruins, those poems we wrote there

gone. Remember how we came here back then, mountain roads
precarious and long, people desperate, that lame mule yowling?

WRITING-BRUSH AT LEISURE

My hair white, a wispy tangle full of frost-fallen wind,
I trust my sick body to a thatch hut, a bed woven of vines.

Someone told him this old-timer's spring sleep is lovely,
that wisdom monk: he strikes the dawn bell lightly now.

AFTER T'AO CH'IEN'S "DRINKING WINE"

5

This little boat of mine, truly a lone leaf,
and beneath it, the sound of dark swells:

I keep paddling in depths of night, drunk,
pleasures of home, bed and desk forgotten.

At dawn, when I ask about the road ahead,
I'm already past a thousand ridges rising

beyond ridges. O where am I going here,
this Way forever leaving ever returning?

Never arriving, what can we understand,
and always leaving, what's left to explain?

LI CH'ING-CHAO

(c. 1084 to 1150)

LI CH'ING-CHAO IS traditionally described as the greatest female poet in the Chinese tradition. Unlike Yü Hsüan-chi and so many other women who scraped together minimally educated and self-determined lives as concubines, courtesans, and monastics, Li Ch'ing-chao was born to an aristocratic family that gave its daughters the same opportunities as its sons. Her family married her to a no less enlightened man, with whom she lived a very happy and active life as a full intellectual equal. Together they amassed and studied a vast collection of books, paintings, calligraphy, and antiquities. But this blissful life crumbled when invaders conquered northern China. Li and her husband were forced to flee the fighting several times, losing more and more of their collections with each move. Then, in the midst of this desperate situation, her husband died of a sudden illness. Thus, in her mid-forties, Li was stripped of the resources that had protected her from a virulently sexist society: her art collections (with their huge monetary value) were gone, and her husband was dead, as were her father and brothers. Although she apparently had some money left, at least initially, she was a woman alone, without any male protectors. Little is known of the last two decades of her life, but it is generally thought that she spent much of that time homeless and impoverished.

At her death, Li left nearly a thousand poems. But as with so many female poets in ancient China, this collection was completely lost. The collection we now have, cobbled together from diverse secondary sources, contains fewer than a hundred poems, and half are of dubious authorship. So as far as the poetry is concerned, Li Ch'ing-chao is almost as much a construct of literary legend as Lady Midnight. The poetry of women, even a woman as privileged as Li, continued to operate almost as a folk tradition that survived only insofar as the male establishment chose to preserve it. (For a larger discussion of women poets in China, see "Women's Poetry in Ancient China" on p. 451.)

Nearly all of Li Ch'ing-chao's surviving poems are *tz'u* (see pp. 335-37), the form for which she is renowned. While men such as Su Tung-p'o had expanded the *tz'u* to include virtually all of the topics that had traditionally appeared in *shih*, Li remained quite conservative, arguing that the *tz'u* was a genre women could claim as the vehicle for their own distinctive concerns, and that it should not be absorbed into the male tradition. So readers have admired not so much her innovation as the sheer depth of feeling in her poems, and her ability to render emotion in surprisingly concrete and immediate images. Li Ch'ing-chao came to be seen as the quintessential female *tz'u* poet, the exemplar of *tz'u* written by women in its mature phase, after it had freed itself from the clichés of the lovelorn courtesan, and her poems reveal a woman who is fully self-possessed and intellectually powerful.

UNTITLED

As the day comes to an end, a passing breath of wind and rain
rinses away the sun's blazing heat.
The music of earth's inner pattern falls silent.
Facing a chestnut-blossom mirror, I brush on a wisp of powder,

and through gossamer robes of crimson silk, my jade skin glistens
sleek and fragrant as tender snow.
I smile and say to my sandalwood love:
tonight, inside gauze bed-curtains, pillow and mat will be cool.

UNTITLED

I can't forget that river pavilion as the sun sank away,
so profoundly drunk we didn't know the way back home.
Out on a boat returning late, making such love
we happened into depths of blooming lotus,

and flailing through,
flailing through,
startled up a sudden shoreline full of wild-winged gulls and egrets.

The last blossoms tumble down,
scattering the same reds that shade a woman's rouge:
another year's springtime affair.
Airy willow catkins drift skies,
and shoots promise lavish bamboo.

In quiet rooms of isolate depths,
I sit facing the delicate greens of our little garden:
there's no point climbing summits
when my sad love comes home only long enough to leave.

It's like a crystalline dream, that year
we wandered a thousand miles and more
along the stream north of the city,
meandering beside those icy ripples
where you'll find my eyes still lingering for you.

UNTITLED

Thin mist and thick cloud, a sorrow lingering on all day,
incense buffeted from a golden animal . . .
It was the 9/9 celebration again today.
Inside gauze bed-curtains: jade pillows
and a chill starting to drift in after midnight.

Skies yellow at sunset, I sipped wine at my eastern fence,
and a dark fragrance filled my sleeves.
Don't say it wouldn't buffet a spirit away:
opening blinds to the west wind,
I was the frailest of yellow blossoms.

UNTITLED

Tired of my thousand-autumn swing,
I wander off, lazily stretching my slender hands,
dew still thick on frail blossoms,
faint beads of sweat staining gossamer robes.

When I see him coming,
I flee, embarrassed,
stockings slipping, gold hairpin loose,

then pause at the door, turning back
to savor the scent of azure-green plums.

UNTITLED

Wind freshens on the lake, sending broad swells across these vast expanses.
It's already late autumn,
blossoms rare, their scents sparse.

Mountains mirrored here in radiant waters—they're in love with us,
can't stop talking about us,
can't stop admiring us.

Lotus seeds are already ripe, lotus leaves old and worn and withered.
Crystalline dew rinses duckweed blossoms pure, and shoreline grasses.
Gulls and egrets sleeping on beaches of sand don't even turn their heads:
you'd think they were angry at us for going home so soon.

UNTITLED

Who's with me sitting alone at a moonlit window?
There's just the two of us, my shadow and I,
and when the bedside lamp goes out,
shadow's gone, leaving me abandoned here.

Nothing more?
Nothing more?
Just this amazing thing, all grief and worry, that I am.
My very own grief and worry: amazing!

UNTITLED

A lovely wind, dust already fragrant with fallen blossoms:
      it's sunset, and I can't even comb my hair.
Things go on and on. People don't: all our great plans vanish.
      Now, if I try to speak, nothing comes but tears.

I hear spring along Twosome Creek is still exquisite, my love,
      and I ache to go drifting there in a light boat,
but I'm afraid those frail little Twosome-Creek boats
      couldn't bear up all this grief and sorrow.

UNTITLED

Night comes, and I'm so drunk it takes forever to undo my hair,
      plum-blossom petals stuck to dying branches.
A haze of wine thinning away shatters spring sleep,
      and once the dream's broken, there's no going back:

      it's all silence, silence,
      moon drifting closer, closer,
      kingfisher blinds rolled down.
Again a last few ravaged petals dying,
      again fondling a remnant fragrance,
      again inhabiting this very moment.

UNTITLED

I planted a banana tree outside the window, and already
its shade fills the courtyard,
its shade fills the courtyard.
Leaf after leaf, heart after heart
so full of feeling, some furled and some open

in third-watch rain, it's wounding a heart among pillows
drop by drop of icy clarity,
drop by drop of icy clarity,
with grief, and ruin, a far-off stranger
who can't get used to the sound.

UNTITLED

Year after year, a little drunk
out in snow, we tucked white blossoms into our hair,
plum blossoms. And later we ravaged them, thoughts far from pure,
so many petals drenching our robes in crystalline tears.

This year, beside a distant sea at the edge of heaven
in wind-scoured silence, the white streaks my old hair.
It's late, I know, and the wind is fierce:
there won't be a plum blossom in sight.

UNTITLED

These courtyard depths feel deep, deep, so utterly deep here beyond
cloud windows and rooms of mist, doors left always closed,
willow tips and plum blossoms opening little by little their radiance.
Spring is returning to city trees in Mo-ling,
and I'm a stranger to these serene, far-off walls.

Moonlight once filled my thoughts, wind my song—so much wonder,
and now it's all old, gone away, nothing finished.
Who cares anymore about this withered scatter of haggard grief?
I'm way past flirting at the Lantern Festival:
I'm not even tempted by a walk in the snow.

LU YU

(1125 to 1210)

THE SEMINAL MOMENT of Lu Yu's life and poetic career came only a few months after his birth, when invaders captured China's northern heartland and forced the Sung government into the south, thereby ending what came to be known as the Northern Sung Dynasty and beginning the Southern Sung. For his first eight years, Lu's family lived as impoverished refugees fleeing the fighting (much as Li Ch'ing-chao had done). The family finally settled at their ancestral village in the south, and as an adult, Lu became an outspoken advocate of military confrontation, arguing passionately that the Sung government needed to reclaim the north in order to reunify the country and rescue the people suffering under "barbarian" rule.

This put Lu at odds with the faction that controlled the government and followed a policy of appeasement. Hence, Lu's life was driven by intense frustration in his career, which was undermined at every turn by the faction in power, and in his unfulfilled aspiration for a unified China. He lived a self-consciously wild and reckless life, almost as an act of protest (he took the literary name Wild Old Man); traveled a great deal, moving from one minor post to another; and was several times stripped of office because of his critical stance toward government policy and his irresponsible behavior. Lu's poems during those years were wide-ranging and often wildly imaginative, including many passionate calls to arms and poems of social criticism, and they were widely read.

Through it all, Lu was also drawn to the personal cultivation of Taoist and Ch'an (Zen) Buddhist practice. When he was removed permanently from government office at the age of sixty-four, he returned to spend his last two decades as an increasingly impoverished recluse on the family farm at Shan-yin (Mountain-*Yin*), his ancestral village. There, his long practice of Ch'an no-mind coming to fruition, he cultivated a profound transparency to experience. During these two decades he wrote no fewer than 6,500 poems (about one per day), which were arranged chronologically in his collection. As a whole, these poems have the feel of a notebook or journal describing the concrete details of village life and tracing the wanderings of a person's attention through the days and seasons of a life.

In this late poetry, the Sung interiorization of *tzu-jan* (see Key Terms) came to another of its logical conclusions, for the mastery of the poems lies more in their form than in any particular statement they make. They don't just *portray* wisdom, they *enact* it by following the provisional insights of every-day life, and so demonstrating his understanding that ordinary experience is always already enlightened, that enlightenment resides in the everyday move-ment of perception and reflection, rather than in the distillation or intensifi-cation of experience into privileged moments of insight. It is this day-to-day transparency that represents Lu Yu's distinctive way of weaving consciousness into the fabric of natural process, of making every gesture in a poem wild.

To suggest this transparency, the poems on pages 401 through 405 are a consecutive sequence from an arbitrarily chosen moment in Lu Yu's life: a few days in the autumn of 1205, his eightieth year.

ON THE WALL-TOWER ABOVE K'UEI-CHOU AT NIGHT, THINKING OF TU FU

Done advising emperors, hair white—no one cared about
old Tu Fu, his life scattered away across rivers of the west,

chanting poems. He stood on this tower once, and now he's
gone. Waves churn the same isolate moon. Inexhaustible

through all antiquity, this world's great dramas just rise
and sink away. Simpleton and sage alike return in due time.

All these ice-cold thoughts, who'll I share them with now?
In depths of night, gulls and egrets lift off sand into flight.

LOOKING AT A MAP OF CH'ANG-AN

My hair's turning gray, but this devotion to our country remains.
South of the peaks, I've been gazing north into southern mountains

all year. To mount a horse, spear athwart: that's where my heart is,
laughing at those chicken-shits digging moats around our capital . . .

Sun sinks away. Smoke comes windblown over ridges. It's autumn,
and the sound of watchmen banging cookpots fills tumbling clouds.

Ravaged fathers in Ch'ang-an country go on grieving, and looking
looking for the emperor's armies coming back through the passes.

FLOWING-GRASS CALLIGRAPHY SONG

I've terrorized my family making three thousand jars of wine,
but ten thousand bucketfuls couldn't ease such restless grief,

so this morning, drunken eyes ablaze with cliff-top lightning,
I grab a brush and gaze out, all heaven and earth grown small,

then suddenly send strokes flying, forgetting who I ever was,
windy clouds filling my thoughts, heaven lending me strength,

and divine dragons battle in landscapes of dark rancid mists,
unearthly spirits topple mountains over, the moon goes black.

Before long I've driven off the grief that infected my chest,
I bang on the bed and hoot, wildly fling my cap to the ground

realizing even exquisite Wu paper and Shu silk aren't enough:
I'll send ink sprawling across the great hall's thirty-foot walls!

AT CLOUD-GATE MONASTERY, SITTING ALONE

Northern mountains, and southern too—I've wandered them all,
and if I look back, I see sixty-seven years of springtime festivals.

Today, given this far away into old age, all battered and broken,
I sit alone, lit incense fragrant, and listen to the sound of water.

THE SOUND OF RAIN

The sound of rain keeps drumming on from morning till night,
voice of a poet chanting lines far from the dust of this world,

"Cloud-Gate" and "Unity-Pond," ancient songs a thousand forevers
gone, tunes broken, notes forgotten: they survive right here.

The sound of rain keeps drumming on all through the night,
lament of Ch'ü Yüan, so full of grief leaving his own country

for Nine-Doubt Mountain's tangled ridges and the cold autumn
waters of that Hsiang River, loyalty sincere, tears welling up.

Grown old, frail and sick and not a scrap of thought anywhere,
I lie facing an azure-green lamp-flame's last sputtering blaze,

lean up in bed, focus on breathing in and out like a cold turtle,
chant long incantations on cushions, laugh at my lone sword.

The sound of rain keeps on and on, sleep ever more delicious,
and when windows brighten and crows cry, I rise and dress,

calling my son to roast some rabbit and pour out leftover wine,
then settle into a camp-chair and sit amid the sounds of rain.

MONKS NEED HOMES

Monks need homes, timber beams and plasters of emerald and gold,
so the petition flies in every direction, like a feathered call to arms,

and it's nothing to rich merchants and grand officials with their
hordes of money. They can fling gold away like broken roof-tiles.

But poor families scraping by on beans and rice: if their crops fail
they're suddenly corpses withering away in some ditch, and if not

they're whipped at tax time, blood spattering magistrate courtyards,
and still, they'll happily give those monks everything they have.

The ancients nurtured our people the way they nurtured children,
encouraged them in farmwork, worried that they might go hungry:

Emperor Wen wouldn't give a hundred in gold for dewfall terraces,
and he felt humbled by the Duke of Chou writing "Seventh Moon."

But these shit-for-brains can't fathom such things. They believe
it's perfectly normal: people all around them wounded and broken,

majestic Buddha halls and statues on and on. Our people long since
worn to the very bone—how will they ever elude hunger and death?

INVOKING THE GODS

Drums throb and throb,
pipes wail and wail,

and an old shaman appears, green cloak and scholar-tree staff,
then a young girl dancing, crimson tunic and embroidered skirt.

Tallow-tree candles burning so bright even wax can't compare,
carp stews fragrant and delicious enough for any god's kitchen,

the old shaman comes chanting prayers,
the young dancer offering jars of wine:

We invite you here, O gods, to enjoy abiding peace and pleasure,
and ask for glistening grain harvested in cartfuls without end,

for oxen and sheep crowding through our village gates at dusk,
chickens and ducks tending a hundred newborn chicks apiece.

Grant us harvest after harvest
free of taxes year after year,

spare us their bulrush whips
and let prisons stand empty.

Tie thatch into officials, mere figures, just the way we like them,
carve wood into clerks without their damned ledgers and books,

return us to the pure ways our first emperor gave us long ago
before anyone knotted ropes or cooked up useless complications.

Arm in arm, happily drunk after the gods leave, people scatter
into depths of night, singing and dancing along country lanes.

RESOLUTION

Years ago, leaving capital gates, vowing
it was forever, I came to this resolution,

and it's fiercer still, now I'm so suddenly
old and frail as a wisp of reed or willow,

my wife and kids sick of cold and hunger,
neighbors laughing at my oddball ways.

Singer of sad songs out harvesting grain,
angry recluse at ease gnawing on snow,

I'll lie a thousand years under pine roots,
shadowy wind scouring the empty tomb

until fierce heart and liver alone remain,
fused and transformed into golden iron

and cast into a cosmic sword. It offers up
blood of those clever-tongued ministers,

then lifted from its case in the armories
it's carried forth by glorious front ranks,

three feet of blazing starlight ridding our
ten-thousand-mile peace of vile demons.

Once you see this divine marvel, you see
all that Mongol filth isn't even fit to kill.

THE RIVER VILLAGE

What a joke that scholar's office cap was. Not another word:
my hair's white now, and I'm happy dozing in a river village,

though birds roosting in deep forests call one after another,
and boats moving through locks kick up that racket all night.

I'm sick, but get up and rummage all day in tattered old books,
and when sorrow comes, I just pour a little crystalline wine,

but how secluded is this life anyway? Just listen to this place!
It's late, and still some monk's out knocking at a moonlit gate!

A MOUNTAIN WALK

Heading south from my brushwood gate, I start climbing
this mountain, grass sandals tattered among white clouds,

forgetting I'm so poor I may never repay my wine debts.
Ignoring a monk's stone inscription, I abide in idleness,

my ancient three-foot *ch'in* a last trace of cook-smoke,
my *ch'an* staff a lone tree-limb of Hsiang River ripples.

I gaze north from my little hut here, into mist and cloud,
friends all scattered away, birds returning for the night.

TAKING A TRAIL UP FROM DEVA–KING MONASTERY TO THE GUESTHOUSE WHERE MY FRIEND WANG CHUNG–HSIN AND I WROTE OUR NAMES ON A WALL FIFTY YEARS AGO, I FIND THE NAMES STILL THERE

Meandering these greens, azure all around, you plumb antiquity.
East of the wall, above the river, stands this ancient monastery,

its thatched halls we visited so long ago. You a mountain sage,
I here from Wei River northlands: we sipped wine, wrote poems.

Painted paddle still, I drift awhile free. Then soon, I'm nearing
home, azure walking-stick in hand, my recluse search ending.

Old friends dead and gone, their houses in ruins, I walk through
thick bamboo, deep cloud, each step a further step into confusion.

OFFHAND POEM AT MY EAST WINDOW

I pass the whole day in utter tranquillity at my east window,
all that mirage and illusion of a lifetime gone, mind empty.

Autumn *ch'i* isn't baring trees yet. But I'm old, and already
thinking of that first time I felt the hundred insects calling.

The ridges of a folding screen recall Thatch-Hut mountains,
and my wife's high-peaked hat sacred Little-Forest summits,

but how could that flush of young health and strength last?
A simple vine finds recluse quiet wherever the place allows.

7TH MOON, 29TH SUN, *YI* YEAR OF THE OX: I HAD A
DREAM LAST NIGHT IN WHICH I MET A STATELY
MAN, AND AT FIRST SIGHT WE WERE LIKE OLD
FRIENDS. HE HAD WRITTEN MANY PAGES OF
LOVELY POEMS LONG AGO, ALL PERFECTLY PURE
AND SIMPLE. I STARTED READING THROUGH
THEM, BUT WOKE BEFORE I COULD FINISH. TO
RECORD WHAT HAPPENED, I'VE WRITTEN THIS IN
LONG LINES.

The traveler is an instant friend, utterly clear and true:
even before we dip out wine, we share kindred thoughts.

The pillow is cold, but I don't understand it's all a dream
in the clear night. I just savor that vision of an old sage.

Star River tipped, Dipper sunk, ancient histories empty,
mist scatters and clouds leave. Our two bodies are mirage,

and mind is perfect clarity. It sees through this illusion.
But even that wide awake, who can avoid our acrid fate?

TO MY SON, YÜ

An old-timer's just a worn-out child. I can't manage alone.
Though this mind is companion to sage ancient masters,

everything's gone: firewood and water, servants, strength.
And I've even pawned my *ch'in* and books. It's that bad.

Mortar and pestle are silent: I'm too sick to grind medicine.
The granary's swept out: there's nervous talk of hunger.

I still have a few years left. You'll need to look after me.
Those misty ten-thousand-mile views will just have to wait.

LIGHT RAIN

Blazing summer days: no force could bring them back.
Clouds suddenly rising off the river, lovely, so lovely,

ducks leave a bridge's shadow, paddling into fine rain,
and butterflies flutter out, frolicking in field breezes.

The willow won't survive nights and days much longer,
and waterlilies will only open two or three more times.

If the changing sights of a single year haunt your eye,
why wonder that Ch'ang-an is now ash among kalpas?

ON A BOAT

1

A three-plank boat, its sail made of ragged bamboo mats,
a fishing lantern anchored overnight at heaven's gate:

forty-eight thousand acres of misty lakewater, where
the Maker-of-Things hurries jonquil flocks into bloom.

2

Scents of mountain vegetables and tender herbs everywhere,
the view's regal down to sheep coddled for the emperor's table.

I trust my thoughts to that voice of the ancient Liu Wen-shu:
it's soy gruel that's always been the most enduring of flavors.

AT DRAGON-INCEPTION MONASTERY, VISITING
TU FU'S OLD HOUSE

We've tossed aside the tranquil peace of those northern grasslands:
Mongol dust overran both capitals, left defenses burning, burning.

Adviser no more, grown old, your ten-thousand-mile life wandering . . .
Come here under cold skies, I listen to the sound of a river flowing.

DEATH-CHANT

Brushwood gate closed, I've sung death-chants half a year
now, life somehow destined to linger on, *ch'i*-strength faint.

All that evil karma—how could I avoid meals of horse-feed,
or living in such poverty, ragged clothes cut from ox-cloth?

Amid muddy and clear, who knows sagehood from pretense,
and who's seen through it, gotten past *yes this* and *no that*?

Still, there's this radiant enlightenment you mustn't forget,
this one essential understanding: *no-thought is true return.*

NEAR DEATH, GIVEN TO MY SON

Once you're dead and gone, the world's ten thousand affairs are empty.
I know that. But never seeing our nation whole again still grieves me.

When the emperor's armies reclaim our northern plains, don't forget:
that very day at the family altar, you must send word to your old father.

YANG WAN-LI

(1127 to 1206)

LIKE HIS FRIEND Lu Yu, Yang Wan-li was an adamant opponent of the government's policy of appeasing the foreigners controlling north China. But in spite of the problems this position caused, Yang had a relatively successful official career—a trusted adviser to prime ministers and emperors at times, and at others banished to the provinces. He once even led government forces in a brief war against a small army of bandits and rebels. But unlike Lu Yu, Yang rarely wrote about politics. He was interested in poetry primarily as a form of Ch'an (Zen) Buddhist practice, and indeed he had a more thoroughly Ch'an conception of poetry than any other poet in the tradition.

Like an adept practicing directly under Ch'an masters, Yang studied the poetic masters of the past assiduously, trying to match his poetic insights to theirs. Then finally, when he was fifty, this "practice" led to a moment of sudden enlightenment. He began working spontaneously in his own style from immediate experience, and *tzu-jan*'s ten thousand things (see Key Terms) seemed to present themselves to him in poems written effortlessly. In the three decades after his enlightenment, Yang wrote with the same spontaneity as Lu Yu did during his two decades of retirement, producing no fewer than 3,500 poems, a rate that rivals Lu Yu's when one considers that Yang was not in retirement for the first half of this period and so had much less time available for writing.

Yang Wan-li's poetic enlightenment seems to have been part of a fundamental Ch'an awakening that is reflected in his poems. A typical Yang poem attends to the passing moments of immediate experience with a resounding clarity, and this attention usually leads to a moment of sudden enlightenment: a startling image or turn of thought, a surprising imaginative gesture, a twist of humor. And he could make poems out of nothing more than a crystalline attention to things themselves. Like Mei Yao-ch'en and Lu Yu, Yang often attends to the most mundane aspects of life, and he does this in the most profound way—empty mind completely occupied with nothing special: a fly, for instance, sunning on a windowsill.

ON THE SUMMIT ABOVE TRANQUIL-JOY TEMPLE .

Who says poets are so enthralled with mountains? Mountains,
mountains, mountains—I've raved on and on, and they're still

clamoring for attention. A thousand peaks, ten thousand ridges:
it's too much for me. If I climb an hour, I need to rest for three.

When your desk is piled full, you just can't add anything more,
and when your withered stomach is full, who can keep eating?

So what good's even a faint scrap of mist or kingfisher-green?
I'll wrap it all up, send the whole bundle off to my city friends.

INSCRIBED ON A WALL AT LIU TE-FU'S
ABSOLUTE-MEANING PAVILION

When T'ao Ch'ien saw what all this means, he forgot words.
His absolute was a place, and today it's taught by this place

here. If someone stops by to ask about absolute meaning,
it's easy: a face in depths of mirror, sky in depths of water.

WITH CHÜN YÜ AND CHI YUNG, I HIKE TO UNIVERSAL–COMPLETION MONASTERY, THEN RETURN LATE, SAILING ACROSS WEST LAKE

1

The screen's shade is faint, too faint to hide clear skies,
and a goosefoot staff is keeping me fresh. It's time to go,

but lakeside mountains have gracious plans to keep me,
leaving distant bells silent, sound itself as yet unknown.

2

As our boat lacing mists angles off the cove's willow shores,
cloud mountains appear and disappear among the willows.

And the beauty of climbing a mountain while adrift on a lake?
It's this lake's mind—that gaze holding the mountain utterly.

EARLY SUMMER, DWELLING IN IDLENESS, I WAKE FROM A NOON NAP

Sour plums at lunch left my teeth feeling all feathery.
Banana trees cast green across gauze window-screens.

A long day. I wake from a noon nap empty of thought,
all idleness, watch kids catch falling willow blossoms.

A COLD FLY

Chance sight on a windowsill, the fly sits warming its back,
rubbing its front legs together, savoring morning sunlight.

Sun nudges shadow closer. But the fly knows what's coming,
and suddenly it's gone—a *buzz* heading for the next window.

WATCHING A LITTLE BOY GLEEFULLY BEATING THE SPRING OX

He breaks the clay head first, like old-timers who set spring
free into the world then sow their fields with leftover shards.

The yellow ox has yellow hooves and a couple of white horns,
the ox-herd a green rain-cloak and hat of azure-blue bamboo,

and they forecast the earth's *ch'i*-veins will pulse with rain.
Last year wasn't so happy, not like this year of plenty will be,

so when the boy hears of a year without hunger, he's thrilled.
When his ox hears about plenty, it worries about staying fat.

Wheat fields will look like clouds, tassels swaying like brooms,
and rice will abound, filling baskets with perfect little pearls:

first they'll plow the broad fields, then start in the mountains.
O that poor yellow ox: when will it ever get a moment's peace?

COLD SPARROWS

A hundred thousand sparrows descend on my empty courtyard.
A few gather atop the plums, chatting with clear evening skies,

and the rest swarm around, trying to kill me with their racket.
Suddenly they all startle away, and there's silence: not a sound.

UNTITLED

I happen to hear wings beat in pine treetops
and realize it's a beach gull come for the night.
Keep that racket quiet, I whisper, afraid
kids will scare it off,

but after a while it suddenly breaks into flight,
breaks into flight heading who knows where.
I quit my job! Quit and came home,
I call to the gull!

LIGHT RAIN

Lonely and depressed, words absent, I lean against the door
alone: plum blossoms and light rain, dusk verging on yellow.

Rain drips off the eaves, sad excuse for a sage lofty and free.
Just one drop after another: won't it ever try anything new?

BREAKFAST AT NOONDAY–ASCENSION MOUNTAIN

These thousand peaks offer the beauties of spring again,
and what do I offer them? Nothing but mounting alarm.

Clouds plunder cragged cliffs where birds sing in trees,
rain swells mountain streams, cascades scattering petals,

and I can't see past thatch roofs, a wisp of kitchen smoke,
but I know exactly how starvation will look in this village.

I knew there'd be no meat for breakfast. But they barely
even manage bamboo shoots: just two or three wisps each.

ON A BOAT CROSSING HSIEH LAKE

I pour out a cup or two of emerald wine inside the cabin.
The door swings closed, then back open onto exquisite

ranged mountains: ten thousand wrinkles unseen by anyone,
and every ridge hand-picked by the late sun's slant light.

The gorge's river all empty clarity, rain sweeps in,
cold breezy whispers beginning deep in the night,

and ten thousand pearls start clattering on a plate,
each one's *tic* a perfect clarity piercing my bones.

I scratch my head in dream, then get up and listen
till dawn, hearing each sound appear and disappear.

I've listened to rain all my life. My hair's white now,
and I still don't know night rain on a spring river.

TEASING MY LITTLE ONE

We're stuck on a boat in rain, all cooped up inside.
My little one, the one who's never sad: he's morose,

just sits there, eyes falling closed, then sound asleep.
Finally I suggest bed, and he shakes his head *no, no.*

2

To see them, look at mountains revealed and unrevealed.
If you don't, even looking at mountains is pure delusion.

Ten thousand peaks of blue keep me enthralled all day,
and at dusk, I linger out twilight's last few purple spires,

but how many people venture forth on these riverboats
to gaze at mountains, and who can see them *absolutely*?

Let those boatmen keep their reckless talk to themselves:
if you scare the children, they'll refuse to go anywhere.

3

Always wanting to fill a poet's eyes to the brim, old heaven
worries that autumn mountains are too washed-out and dead,

so it measures out Shu brocade, unfurls flushed clouds of Wu,
and rubs them lush and low across these autumn mountains.

Before long, red brocade thins into kingfisher-green gauze
as heaven's loom weaves out evening crows returning home,

then evening crows and kingfisher-green gauze are gone:
nothing in sight but a clear river pure as sun-bleached silk.

THE TEMPLE-TOWERS AT ORCHID CREEK

The tall tower rises into a spire. The short one doesn't.
One sports a brocade robe, and the other a silver tunic.

I ask them why it is they never say a word, but they let
Buddha go on talking in the voice of a tumbling creek.

CROSSING OPEN-ANEW LAKE

A fisherman's taking his boat deep across the lake.
My old eyes trace his path all the way, his precise

wavering in and out of view. Then it gets strange:
suddenly he's a lone goose balanced on a bent reed.

THE SMALL POND

A spring's eye of shadow resists even the slightest flow.
Among tree shadow, its lit water adores warm clear skies.

Spiral of blades, a tiny waterlily's clenched against dew,
and there at the very tip, in early light, sits a dragonfly.

AT HSIEH COVE

The ox path I'm on ends in a rabbit trail, and suddenly
I'm facing open plains and empty sky on all four sides.

My thoughts follow white egrets—a pair taking flight,
leading sight across a million blue mountains rising

ridge beyond ridge, my gaze lingering near then far,
enthralled by peaks crowded together or there alone.

Even a hill or valley means thoughts beyond knowing—
and all this? A crusty old man's now a wide-eyed child!

ON A BOAT, CROSSING THROUGH PEACE-HUMANE DISTRICT

2

Distant mountains appear, like a painting, and I'm in love,
then suddenly they're furled away, blank as absence itself.

They can't fool this old-timer, sight still bright with clarity:
I can reach them in those depths of mist and cloud anytime.

3

Out on the merest wisp of a fishing boat, two small boys
give up the struggle. They ship their paddles and just sit.

It seems so strange. No rain in sight, they start opening
umbrellas. Not for shelter. They want to sail on the wind!

ON THE SECOND DAY AFTER 9/9, HSÜ K'O-CHANG AND I CLIMB UP INTO TEN-THOUSAND-BLOSSOM-RIVER CANYON, WHERE WE SHARE A CUP OF WINE

My old-timer's thirst is desperate, but moon's even worse.
When a little wine tumbles into my cup, moon's already

there, shepherding heaven's azure expanse deep inside,
both of them, heaven and moon, utterly stewed in wine,

so if the ancients deny *heaven treasures wine*, and say
moon has never understood wine—I know it's nonsense.

I lift a cup of wine and swill moon down in a single gulp,
then looking up to find moon still there in the heavens,

I laugh this grand old-timer's laugh and ask my friend:
Is the moon one orb or two, or is it both at the same time?

Once wine gets into a poem's gut, wind and fire swell up,
and once moon gets in, there's ice and snow everywhere,

then before a single cup's dry, the poem's already done,
me chanting it out, startling heaven itself. And how do I

know all boundless antiquity's a bare pile of dry bones?
I just ladle out a fresh cup and swill down another moon.

NO LONGER SICK, I FEEL SO OLD

When I was sick I forgot all about age,
but now I'm well again, I feel so old.

No one stays hale and hearty forever.
The ruins of age take over in no time:

mountain thoughts freeze cold suns,
autumn light infects withered poems,

and little pines grow heartless, aping
my palsied shake as I chant these lines.

12TH MOON, 27TH SUN, SEASON SPRING BEGINS: A NIGHT WITHOUT SLEEP

Resenting endless winter nights, I was longing for spring,
and now spring nights are worse, so what is there to say?

I scrunch my eyes closed, but it doesn't help. I can't sleep.
I rub the soles of my feet together, but they're no warmer.

And all night there's wind in the pines. I listen till dawn,
watching the lamp's clear light grow darker and darker:

finally I sit up, grab the quilts and pull them over my head,
only to realize it's me casting that shadow of a sick monkey.

Don't read books,
don't chant poems:

read books and your eyes wither until they see bones,
chant poems and every word's vomited from the heart.

People say it's delightful to read books,
they say it's wondrous to chant poems,

but it means lips hissing on and on like autumn insects,
and makes you thin and frail, ravages you with old-age.

Thin and frail, ravaged with age—that may not be much,
but it's pretty annoying for anyone close enough to hear.

It's nothing like closing your eyes and sitting in a study:
lower the blinds and sweep away dust, light some incense,

then listen to wind, listen to rain: they have such flavors.
When you're strong, walk. And when you're tired, sleep.

Notes

These translations follow the basic structure of the original poems. As evidenced in the translations, the couplet is the basic building block of most classical Chinese poetry. Line lengths are rendered, relative to one another, as in the original. Generally they are either five or seven characters long. Exceptions to this rule are clear from line-lengths in the translations. Otherwise, I have freely used the resources available in English, even when they do not correspond to anything in the original: enjambment, for instance, is rare in classical Chinese poetry.

INTRODUCTION

xxv Normally, the absent subject must be filled in with an "I" in English. Chinese poets will occasionally say "I," but usually an "I" in English is translating that open space in the grammar where the poet exists as a kind of absent presence—an unavoidable and egregious distortion of the original.

EARLY COLLECTIONS: THE ORAL TRADITION

Line lengths in *The Book of Songs* are generally four characters, with lines occasionally running longer.

THE BOOK OF SONGS

9 **Dark-Enigma:** See Key Terms: *hsüan.*

9 **Heaven:** See chapter introduction, p. 6.

9 **Shang:** China's earliest historical dynasty (traditional dates 1766–1122 B.C.E.) and its people. See chapter introduction, pp. 5–6.

9 **Celestial Lord:** Shang Ti, for whom see chapter introduction, p. 6.

9 **T'ang:** Renowned first emperor (regnant c. 1766–1753 B.C.E.) of the Shang Dynasty.

In Chou times this story of T'ang was embellished, in light of the Chou's emphasis on the idea of a Mandate of Heaven, and Emperor T'ang came to be known as the leader who overthrew the corrupt and unworthy Hsia, the quasi-historical dynasty that preceded the Shang.

9 **Mandate:** The Mandate of Heaven, the right to rule, bestowed by Heaven and dependent upon the ruler's wise and benevolent actions. See also chapter introduction, p. 6.

9 **Wu Ting:** Much celebrated later Shang ruler (regnant 1324–1265 B.C.E.). It is said that this poem was composed for a memorial ceremony several years after he died. It had clearly evolved considerably by the time it was collected in the Chou, as it speaks of Heaven and the Mandate, which were Chou concepts.

10 **wine:** There is no accurate translation for *chiu,* which is so prevalent in Chinese poetry. It was essentially the same as Japanese sake, whose recipe was imported from China. *Chiu* was made of fermented grains and had an alcohol content similar to that of wine. It was also similar to wine in the epicurean culture that surrounded it, for it was produced in a wide variety of styles and flavors, the finest of which were much valued by connoisseurs. Simple types of *chiu* could also be produced at home, and they often were by poor recluse poets.

11 **Millet God:** Millet was the staple grain in early Chinese culture, which was centered in the north. It was later replaced by rice, which was originally cultivated only in the south.

14 **T'ai:** Tan-fu (literally "True-Father") was a celebrated early ruler of the Chou. He was the grandfather of Emperor Wen, who appears at the end of this poem and in the following one.

14 **Tortoise shells:** The ventral shells of tortoises were used in ancient China to seek divine guidance. They were inscribed with what is the earliest surviving form of Chinese writing, then pierced with a hot instrument until they cracked. The orientations of the cracks in relation to the inscriptions were taken to indicate answers to the questions posed.

15 **Yü and Jui:** Neighboring states. They pledged peace after seeing how perfectly ordered the Chou state was, and according to legend, this led another forty states to declare allegiance to the Chou ruler.

15 **Emperor Wen:** Wen (literally "Cultured") is the Chou emperor who, through his exemplary rule, set the stage for the Chou conquest of the Shang. It was his eldest son, Emperor Wu (literally "Martial"), who actually overthrew the Shang. His other son, the Duke of Chou (see chapter introduction, p. 7) ruled after Wu's early death, and it was under his leadership that the Chou empire was consolidated and expanded.

18 **Seventh Moon:** The primary Chinese calendar is lunar. The beginning of the year comes with the second new moon after the winter solstice and corresponds to the beginning of spring, when the earth is reborn. It falls somewhere between January 20 and February 20, so the first month corresponds roughly to February and the twelfth to January. Hence, months one through three are spring, four through six are summer, seven through nine are fall, and ten through twelve are winter. In Chinese, the word for "month" is *moon,* and the word for "day" is *sun,* both of which are clear pictographic images: 月 (early form showing a crescent moon: 𝔇) and 日 (early forms showing a bright, hot sun: 🜚 ☉).

18 **Fire Star:** Also known as the Year Star, Fire Star begins to decline in the seventh month, an event that was used to mark the annual cycles. Hence, the poem's title and the repetition of "seventh moon" and "Fire Star" in the first three stanzas.

19 **Silkworm moon:** Silk was a basic industry in ancient China. The silkworm moon was the fourth lunar month, when the silkworms hatch out and feed on mulberry leaves. The reeds in line 2 were woven into baskets for gathering mulberry leaves and into frames where silkworms were kept as they were feeding.

29 **He built his hut:** This is the earliest surviving instance of the mountain-recluse poem that was to become so common in later Chinese poetry.

30 *ch'in*: A very ancient stringed instrument much revered by Chinese intellectuals as a means for attaining enlightenment, often appearing in poems and used as accompaniment when Chinese poets chanted their poems. In the hands of a master, a *ch'in* could voice with profound clarity the rivers-and-mountains realm, empty mind, even the very source of all things. For other descriptions of this spiritual aspect of *ch'in* music, see poems on pp. 150, 182, and 275. See also *The Resonance of the Qin in East Asian Art* by Stephen Addiss (New York: China Institute, 1999).

TAO TE CHING

40 **perennial absence . . . appearance:** An especially noteworthy instance of the rich linguistic ambiguity in ancient Chinese and how well Lao Tzu exploits it, for these lines are often read

> Free of perennial desire, you see mystery,
> and full of perennial desire, you see appearance.

40 **dark-enigma:** See Key Terms: *hsüan.*

40 **absence . . . presence:** See general introduction, pp. xxii–xxiii.

41 **nothing's own doing:** See Key Terms: *wu-wei.*

44 **spirit . . . drifting away:** It was generally believed that a person's spirit drifts away after death.

44 *ch'i*: See Key Terms.

44 **mirror:** Empty mind or pure awareness. See Key Terms: *hsin.*

44 **heaven's gate:** Gateway through which the ten thousand things come into being and return to nothing.

44 *Integrity*: The *Te* of *Tao Te Ching, Integrity* means integrity to Tao in the sense of "abiding by the Way," or "enacting the Way." Hence, it is Tao's manifestation in the world, especially in a sage-master of Tao.

46 *occurrence appearing of itself*: See Key Terms: *tzu-jan.*

54 **knot ropes:** A very early system of writing in China.

THE SONGS OF CH'U

59 **The Question of Heaven:** It seems likely that the title originally applied only to the section translated here: the first twenty-two questions, which concern cosmology. Of course, it is very possible that there were many more such questions, and that the others were simply lost. The rest of the poem's 172 questions concern earthly legends and legendary heroes, beginning in deep mythological times and slowly progressing up to early historical times (concerns that are of much less poetic interest and require extensive explanatory notes).

60 *yin* **and** *yang*: The two fundamental forces of the universe: male and female, hot and cold, light and dark. They arose from an undifferentiated primordial unity, and their

interaction gave birth to the empirical universe, its ten thousand things, and their constant transformation. Here, *yin* and *yang* are the "blazing radiance and utter darkness" of the preceding section.

60 **tethered . . . axle-pole:** Legends tell how the center of the sky was supported by a celestial axle-pole, around which it revolved, held by ropes leading from the axle-pole to the edges of the sky.

60 **eight pillars:** In those same legends, the outer edge of the sky was supported atop eight mountains, one in each of the eight directions.

60 **southeast tilting down:** An early myth explains why the pole around which the heavens turn is not exactly overhead and why rivers all flow toward China's southeast. The story tells how, in the midst of a battle between two gods, the northwest pillar was knocked down, causing the sky and earth (that is, China, which was believed to be the whole of the world) to tilt together in the northwest and apart in the southeast.

61 **meanders:** The constellations are not so neatly arranged that they fit inside nine perfectly symmetrical regions divided by straight boundaries. The boundary lines had to "meander back and forth" around the protruding constellations.

61 **Boiling Abyss:** In one myth, the sun bathes after its daytime journey in the waters of night, its heat causing them to boil.

62 **rabbit inside its belly:** Early myth saw in the darker regions of the moon a rabbit grinding herbs into an elixir of immortality.

62 *ch'i:* See Key Terms.

63 **Great-Unity:** A deification of the undifferentiated primordial unity out of which arose *yin* and *yang* and the ten thousand things. As a divinity, T'ai-yi was a sky-god identified with the brightest of the circumpolar stars.

63 **spirit-one:** A shamaness.

65 **Solar-Perch Tree:** According to myth, the sun is ten crows, one for each day of the week (the Chinese week was ten days long). They perch in the huge Solar-Perch (*Fu-sang*) Tree in the east waiting for their turn to rise.

66 **waters of night:** See note to page 61, "Boiling Abyss."

66 **Northern Dipper:** The Big Dipper.

69 *from* **Confronting Grief:** This translation is composed of extracts chosen to create a much shortened version of the original while still reading like a poem. The original is over four times as long: 376 lines, compared with the translation's 84.

69 **P'eng Hsien:** A noble minister from the Shang Dynasty who drowned himself when the emperor refused to heed his counsel. He returns at the end of the poem.

70 **Emperor Shun:** Mythic ruler (regnant 2255–2208 B.C.E.) of great sagacity during the legendary golden age of China.

70 **K'un-lun Mountain:** A towering range of mythic proportions in the far east, filled with supernatural sites and populated with legendary goddesses and immortals.

70 **Solar-Perch Tree:** See note to p. 65.

71 **Shao K'ang . . . daughters:** Characters from the quasi-historical Hsia Dynasty (c. 2205 to 1766 B.C.E.). Ch'ü Yüan is now traveling not only through space, but through time as well, for he has returned to the time before Shao K'ang had married the daughters.

71 **P'eng Hsien . . . dwelling-place:** The Ch'ü Yüan legend does indeed end with

him drowning himself, like P'eng Hsien. Ch'ü Yüan does this in the Flood-Gauze (Mi-lo) River, an act of loyal protest against corrupt government that is still commemorated in the Dragon-Boat Festival (fifth day of the fifth lunar month), during which dragon-boats are paddled out onto waterways in imitation of the boats that reputedly went out searching for Ch'ü Yüan when he threw himself into the river.

LATER FOLK-SONG COLLECTIONS

76 **Earth-Drumming Song:** Reputed to be a poem dating to legendary Emperor Yao's reign (2357 to 2255 B.C.E.).

79 **We Fought South of the Wall:** Many Music-Bureau folk-songs exist in later variations, in both the oral and the written traditions. For an especially well-known later variation of this poem, see Li Po's "War South of the Great Wall" on p. 186.

81 **Great Wall:** The Great Wall became emblematic of the hardship people endured because of war. Building it to defend China's northern frontier caused vast amounts of suffering and death among the workers, and the soldiers sent to defend it against northern invaders also suffered and died in large numbers.

81 **love-carp:** A wooden container for letters made in the shape of paired carp, a symbol of marital joy and fertility.

82 **six dragons:** The sun was believed to be pulled by a team of six dragons.

87 **Ox-Herd:** One of China's best-known star myths, recurring often in poetry, involves the Ox-Herd and Weaver-Girl stars, which correspond to our Vega and Altair. The myth tells how the Weaver-Girl was so devoted to loom-work that her parents, the Emperor and Empress of Heaven, began to worry about her happiness. They married her to the Ox-Herd, but then she forgot her loom-work entirely, preferring the joys of their new life together. This so displeased her parents that the empress, with a single stroke of her great silver hairpin, created the Star River (Milky Way) between the lovers, separating them forever. But the emperor, seeing how unhappy the lovers now were, declared that they would be allowed to meet for one night each year, on the seventh day of the seventh month, when all the magpies on earth fly up and hover over the Star River, creating a bridge for the Weaver-Girl to cross. And the lovers' tears upon parting are said to account for the autumn rains. There is still a festival held on this day in honor of the lovers. Celebrants hope there will be no rain, for the Star River is always brimful, and even a little rain will push it over its banks, creating a flood that will wash away the magpie bridge, thus preventing the lovers from meeting.

87 **Star River:** The Milky Way, also known by a number of other appellations, such as Silver River and River of Heaven.

88 **pine and cypress:** Noteworthy because they stay green through the winter. Hence, they were traditionally planted in graveyards.

90 **Lady Midnight Songs of the Four Seasons:** There are 117 Lady Midnight songs, which are arranged in two collections: *Lady Midnight Songs* (42 songs) and *Lady Midnight Songs of the Four Seasons* (75 songs). This selection has incorporated a number of the *Lady Midnight Songs* in the seasonal cycle of the *Lady Midnight Songs of the Four Seasons* collection.

95 **ready winter robes . . . sticks beating:** In a grief-filled autumn ritual that often appears in poetry, the women of China would thicken cloth for winter clothes by spreading it on special stones and pounding it with a paddle, a process called "fulling." In poetry, this was usually a ritual of longing for lovers who had been taken far away

to fight in wars. The ritual's sexual connotations are especially clear in the following oral-tradition poem from the same era as the Lady Midnight songs:

THE RIVER-CROSSING AT AZURE-BRIGHTS

For my fulling-stone of emerald jade,
this gold-lotus stick of seven jewels:

I lift it high, let it fall gently, gently
its light strokes plunge for you alone.

100 *yin . . . yang*: See note to p. 60. In a landscape, *yin* corresponds to places shaded from the sun's light (north sides of mountains and south sides of rivers), and *yang* corresponds to places exposed to the sun's light (south sides of mountains and north sides of rivers).

FIRST MASTERS: THE MAINSTREAM BEGINS

SU HUI

107 This facsimile was prepared by Michèle Métail, the French sinologist who reconstructed the complex rules that govern this text.

T'AO CH'IEN

113 **dust:** An oft-used metaphor for insubstantial worldly affairs.

113 **gate:** Literally, the entrance gate in the wall or fence that surrounds the courtyard of a house or monastery. But throughout the recluse tradition, *gate* often carries the metaphoric sense of "awareness," that through which the empirical world enters consciousness. Hence, the home within the gates is not only a recluse's house but his mind as well. This added dimension recalls a passage in Chapter 52 of the *Tao Tè Ching*, where a kind of meditative practice is described:

If you block the senses
and close the gate,
you never struggle.
If you open the senses
and expand your endeavors,
nothing can save you.

The idea of "closing the gate" became a familiar motif in recluse poetry and recurs in Wang Wei's work, the literal point being that the recluse's house was very secluded and he was content in that seclusion, rather than longing for company. Other equally resonant motifs include leaving the gate open and sweeping the gate-path as a gesture of welcome for unexpected guests. See *hsien* in Key Terms for the role *gate* plays in that central spiritual posture, idleness.

113 **empty:** See Key Terms: *k'ung*.

113 **idleness:** See Key Terms: *hsien*.

113 **occurrence appearing of itself:** See Key Terms: *tzu-jan*.

115 During T'ao Ch'ien's life, the country was ravaged by civil war and widespread peasant rebellions. The devastation described in this poem was no doubt caused by this fighting, which had recently swept through the region, and it gives another dimension to T'ao Ch'ien's recluse life.

116 **12th Month, *Kuei* Year of the Hare:** January 404.

116 **cups and bowls:** A reference to Confucius's favorite disciple, Yen Hui, who is described in *Analects* 6.10:

> The Master said: "How noble Yen Hui is! To live in a meager lane with nothing but some rice in a split-bamboo bowl and some water in a gourd cup—no one else could bear such misery. But it doesn't even bother Hui. His joy never wavers. O, how noble Hui is!"

117 **Drinking Wine:** In Chinese poetry, the practice of drinking wine generally means consuming just enough to achieve a serene clarity of attention, a state in which the isolation of a mind imposing distinctions on the world gives way to a sense of identity with the world. Po Chü-i half-seriously claimed that wine rivaled Ch'an (Zen) Buddhism as a spiritual practice, and Li Po too thought wine could bring a kind of enlightenment, as in the poem on page 179. In fact, wine and "drunkenness" generally function in Chinese poetry almost as a symbol that says the poet has attained a certain level of (temporary) enlightenment. For the nature of Chinese wine (*chiu*) itself, see note to p. 10.

117 **a hundred years:** Conventional reckoning of a life span.

117 **Section 5:** This famous poem resonated through the tradition, as can be seen in Su Tung-p'o's "After T'ao Ch'ien's 'Drinking Wine'" (p. 383) and Yang Wan-li's "Inscribed on a Wall at Liu Te-fu's Absolute-Meaning Pavilion" (p. 409).

117 **chrysanthemums:** The petals of chrysanthemums were mixed with wine to make chrysanthemum wine, popularly believed to promote longevity. Chrysanthemums have always been identified with T'ao Ch'ien because of the central place they held in his poetic world. See also pp. 118 and 120.

117 **South Mountain:** Calling up such passages as "like the timelessness of South Mountain" in *The Book of Songs* (*Shih Ching* 166.6), South Mountain came to have a kind of mythic stature as the embodiment of the elemental and timeless nature of the earth. Given this pedigree, poets often used this name to refer to whatever mountain happened to be south of them.

120 **9/9:** Dominated by thoughts of mortality, this autumn festival is celebrated on the ninth day of the ninth lunar month because the word for "nine" (*chiu*) is pronounced the same as the word meaning "long-lasting" or "long-living," hence "ever and ever." Hiking to mountaintops and drinking chrysanthemum wine were the customary activities on this holiday.

121 ***Cha* Festival:** Ancient name for the *La* Festival, which in T'ao's time fell on the last day of the lunar year. It was the first day of New Year's festivities celebrating the arrival of spring and the rebirth of earth.

122 **Peach-Blossom Spring:** This famous and often alluded to prose piece is actually an introductory note to a poem on the same topic. The story probably existed already in the folk tradition, where it was a fantasy about immortals, but in T'ao Ch'ien's retelling it is about an idealized community of very real humans.

122 **Great-Origin years:** Chinese history is divided into reign periods, which were declared by the emperors. Great-Origin lasted from 376 to 397 C.E.

123 **asked the way:** An allusion to Confucius's *Analects* 18.6, where the "river-crossing" represents the Way through this "surging and swelling" world, which a sage masters:

> As Confucius passed by, Settled-Constant and Brave-Seclusion were in the field plowing together. He sent Adept Lu to ask them about the river crossing. "Who's that you're driving for?" asked Settled-Constant.

"Confucius," replied Adept Lu.

"You mean Confucius of Lu?"

"Yes."

"Then he must know the river-crossing well."

Adept Lu then asked Brave-Seclusion, but Brave-Seclusion replied, "So who are you?"

"I am Chung Yu," replied Adept Lu.

"You mean Chung Yu who follows Confucius of Lu?"

"Yes."

"It's all surging and swelling," continued Brave-Seclusion. "All beneath Heaven's foundering deep, and who's going to change it? To follow a man who stays clear of one person or another—how could that ever compare with following one who stays clear of the world?"

And folding earth back over seed, he went on working without pause.

124 **old home's on South Mountain:** Tombs were placed on mountain slopes.

125 **village of weeds:** Reference to the early burial song "Village of Weeds" (p. 80).

HSIEH LING-YÜN

130 **dragons:** As benevolent as it is destructive, the Chinese dragon is both feared and revered as the awesome force of life itself. Animating all things and in constant transformation, it descends in autumn into deep waters, where it hibernates until spring, when it rises. Because the dragon embodies the spirit of change, its awakening is equivalent to the coming of spring and the return of life to earth.

130 **new *yang* swelling, transforming old *yin*:** The ongoing process of change is produced by the intermingling of *yin* and *yang*. Winter is pure *yin*, but as *yin* declines and *yang* increases, the season moves through spring into summer, which is pure *yang*. Thereafter, *yang* declines and *yin* increases, moving the year back through autumn to winter. See also notes to pp. 60 and 100.

131 ***yes this*** **and** ***no that*:** That one should not choose *yes this* or *no that* is a recurring idea in *Chuang Tzu* (two examples among many are 2.8 and 5.6). Only by accepting the unfolding of *tzu-jan* as it is can one dwell wholly as a part of that unfolding. As soon as you begin to judge, approving of some things and disapproving of others, wishing they were otherwise, you have separated yourself from the selfless unfolding of *tzu-jan*.

132 ***ch'i*-sited:** It was thought that the different features of a landscape determine the movement of *ch'i*, the universal breath (see Key Terms). The best site for a house would be chosen by a diviner who analyzed how the local movements of *ch'i* harmonized with the particular characteristics of those who would live in the house.

adoration: See chapter introduction, p. 128.

133 **inner pattern:** See chapter introduction, p. 128, and Key Terms: *li*.

grandfather: Hsieh's ancestral estate in Shih-ning (Origin-Serene) was established by his renowned great-great-uncle Hsieh An. Ling-yün's grandfather was Hsieh Hsüan, who returned to this family estate to live in seclusion after an illustrious career that included leading the Chinese armies to a decisive victory at Fei River (383), thereby saving Chinese civilization from being completely overrun by the foreign invaders who already controlled the north. Hsieh Hsüan developed the estate, but it had been neglected from that time until Ling-yün came, a period of thirty-four years. During this time there were several peasant rebellions against the aristocracy, and the Hsieh estate had probably suffered extensive damage as a result.

Ch'ü Yüan: First major poet in the written tradition. See pp. 55–58.

Yüeh Yi: Like Hsieh's grandfather and Ch'ü Yüan, Yüeh Yi was a national hero who fell out of favor with his sovereign. Once the sovereign had turned against him because of slanders, Yüeh Yi decided to leave the country rather than risk execution.

idleness: See Key Terms: *hsien*.

133 **Master Pan:** Pan Szu (c. 1st century B.C.E.—1st century C.E.), a Taoist recluse known for his profound sayings.

133 **Master Shang:** A resolute recluse who eventually allowed himself to be coaxed into taking office to alleviate his desperate poverty. He served reluctantly and finally left to end his life traveling among China's famous mountains.

141 **Thatch-Hut Mountain:** Perhaps the mountain most cultivated in the Chinese poetic tradition, Thatch-Hut Mountain is a presence in the work of most major poets, especially those in the rivers-and-mountains tradition. It was also a major monastic center. Of the many monasteries on Thatch-Hut Mountain, East-Forest was the most famous. It was founded there by Prajñā-Distance (Hui Yüan, 334–416), a major figure in Chinese Buddhism who emphasized *dhyāna* (sitting meditation) as he taught a form of Buddhism that contained early glimmers of Ch'an (*ch'an* is the Chinese translation of the Sanskrit *dhyāna*). It is said that Prajñā-Distance was an acquaintance of both T'ao Ch'ien and Hsieh Ling-yün, and that it was a visit to East-Forest that first aroused Hsieh's devotion to Buddhism.

141 Ellipses indicate lacunae in the text.

T'ANG DYNASTY I: THE GREAT RENAISSANCE

MENG HAO-JAN

149 **Autumn Begins:** This poem is discussed at length in the general introduction.

150 *Ch'in:* See note to p. 30.

150 **Juan Chi:** Poet from the third century C.E.

150 **mind:** See Key Terms: *hsin*.

151 **Warrior-Knoll:** Location of the Peach-Blossom Spring in T'ao Ch'ien's tale on p. 122.

152 **five recluse willows:** An oft-used reference to T'ao Ch'ien, who wrote a playful autobiographical sketch entitled *Biography of Master Five-Willows*, in which he described himself as having "five willows growing beside his house" (see my *Selected Poems of T'ao Ch'ien*, pp. 13–14).

152 **North-Slope's sage master:** A master of the Way who visited Wang Hsi-chih, the great calligrapher and elder contemporary of T'ao Ch'ien. The purpose of his visit was to trade a flock of rare geese for a copy of the *Tao Te Ching* in Wang's calligraphy.

153 **dharma:** The Chinese term (*fa*) literally means "law," and as dharma it is the fundamental law governing the unfolding of reality, or in fact the very manifestation of reality. It is also the teaching of that law or manifestation of reality.

154 **Warrior-Knoll:** Here, Meng changes the focus of T'ao Ch'ien's "Peach-Blossom Spring" paradise to Ch'an immediacy.

155 **Thatch-Hut Mountain . . . Prajñā-Distance . . . East-Forest:** See note to p. 141.

155 **Deer-Gate Mountain:** Meng Hao-jan's legendary recluse home.

155 **Master P'ang:** A fabled recluse from the second century C.E., Master P'ang lived on Deer-Gate Mountain and never entered cities or took office.

156 **peach-blossom pure:** Another reference to T'ao Ch'ien's "Peach-Blossom Spring" (see p. 122).

156 **dark-enigma:** See Key Terms: *hsüan*.

WANG WEI

159 **find empty rivers and mountains:** Not in the sense that he finds nothing, but in the sense that "empty rivers and mountains" are "old masters," and that Meng's sagacity was almost indistinguishable from theirs.

160 *sangha:* A Buddhist community, especially a group of people gathered around a particular teacher.

160 **white cloud:** This image of white cloud recurs often in the Chinese poetic tradition, simultaneously describing an empty and free state of mind, the sense of secluded distances, and the sense of drifting free like a cloud.

161 **P'ei Ti:** P'ei Ti was Wang Wei's closest friend and kindred spirit. This friendship is famous for the poetic exchanges that resulted when they were together in the mountains. One would write a poem, then the other would try to write a reply that echoed or responded in some way to the first. The "Wheel-Rim River" sequence that follows this poem is a particularly well-known example. But this set is also quite famous. In it, the Wang Wei poem is responding to the following poem, which P'ei Ti had just written:

CAUGHT IN RAIN AT WHEEL-RIM RIVER'S SOURCE,
THINKING OF WHOLE-SOUTH MOUNTAIN

Clouds darken the river's meandering
emptiness. Colors adrift end in sand.

Wheel-Rim River flows distant away,
and where is Whole-South Mountain?

162 **Wheel-Rim River:** Perhaps Wang Wei's most famous poetry, the "Wheel-Rim River" sequence was written at his hermitage in the Whole-South Mountains. There was also a corresponding scroll-painting, which survives only in copies and imitations. As mentioned above, there is a corresponding set of poems by P'ei Ti.

163 **Autumn-Pitch:** The second note (*shang*) in the ancient pentatonic scale, which is associated with autumn and things autumnal.

168 *ch'in:* See note to p. 30.

168 **settle into breath chants:** A method of harmonizing oneself with natural process.

169 **second watch:** Between 9:00 p.m. and 11:00 p.m. There were five watches in the night, two hours each, beginning at 7:00 p.m. and ending at 5:00 a.m.

169 **unborn life:** A central concept in Taoist and Ch'an thought. Self is but a fleeting form taken on by earth's process of change—born out of it and returned to it in death. Or more precisely, never *out of it* but totally unborn. Our truest self, being unborn, is all and none of earth's fleeting forms simultaneously. This poem applies that insight directly to the issue of old age and death: if we are "unborn" in this sense, we

cannot die. This leads to the very core of Taoist thought and Ch'an practice. As natural process emerges from absence (*wu*: nonbeing), to say we are unborn is to say that we are most essentially absence. This is the reality that is experienced directly in Ch'an meditation. And indeed, in addition to not (*wu*) birth (*sheng*), *wu-sheng* might also be read as absence's (*wu*) life (*sheng*), which makes sense here because the ten thousand things are in fact absence's life, which is a constant birth or burgeoning forth of change.

171 **inner pattern:** See Key Terms: *li*.

171 **fundamental name:** This couplet can also be read: "but my names together are fundamentally true: / this mind has returned to the unknown." Wang Wei's names (given name Wei, and literary name Mo-chieh) are the Chinese translation of Vimalakirti, the central figure in the *Vimalakirti Sutra*, which is especially important in the Ch'an tradition.

LI PO

174 **newborn clouds:** The Chinese believed, at least popularly, that clouds were born on high mountain slopes and rose from there into the sky.

175 **Ch'ang-an:** The capital, whose name means "Enduring Peace."

175 **spirit in sad flight:** It was thought that the spirit often left the body and traveled on its own. People believed it could travel some distance during sleep, journeys that we experience as dreams, or when a person suffers some emotional trauma. According to this belief, the spirit could travel long distances after death.

176 **East-Forest Monastery:** See note to p. 141.

176 **kalpa:** A cosmic cycle extending from the creation of a world-system to its destruction—traditionally given as 4,320,000 years.

177 **Fear-Wall Gorge:** One of the three gorges in the Yangtze's Triple Gorge (see note to p. 207) and far upstream from Steady-Shield Village, which was on the Yangtze near where it empties into the sea.

179 **Star River:** The Milky Way.

183 **six sun-dragons:** See note to p. 82.

183 **ch'i:** See Key Terms.

183 **Hsi Ho:** Hsi Ho drove the sun-chariot (in some myths, she is the mother of the sun).

183 **Lu Yang:** Lu Yang's army was in the midst of battle as evening approached. Fearing nightfall would rob him of victory, Lu shook his spear at the setting sun, and it thereupon reversed its course.

183 **Mighty Mudball:** Chuang Tzu's name for the world in its primordial state. See note to p. 362.

184 **clouds-and-rain love:** From the legend of a prince who, while staying at Shaman Mountain, was visited in his sleep by a beautiful woman who said that she was the goddess of Shaman Mountain. She spent the night with him and as she left said: "At dawn I marshal the morning clouds; at nightfall I summon the rain."

185 **Dragon . . . :** See note to p. 130.

185 **Untitled:** An early example of the *tz'u* form, for which see pp. 335–37.

186 **War South of the Great Wall:** Cf. folk-song on p. 79.

192 **Sacred Peak:** There is one sacred mountain for each direction in China, and one at the center. Exalt (T'ai) Mountain in the east is the most sacred of these five sacred mountains.

192 **Change-Maker:** Tao. See Key Terms.

194 **son's birth . . . daughter's birth . . . :** Reference to untitled poem on p. 76.

195 **First-Devotion:** After struggling for years to obtain a government position, an impoverished Tu Fu finally succeeded. He thereupon left the capital and journeyed north to the district of First-Devotion, where he had left his family in a village. The An Lu-shan Rebellion broke out within days of his arrival. For the larger biographical and historical context of this and the poems that follow, see the chapter introduction, p. 190.

In this poem, Tu Fu describes passing by Clear-Glory Palace, the emperor's summer palace in the mountains near the capital. For another poem describing this palace a month or two later, after An Lu-shan's armies had captured the capital, see Tu Mu's "Passing Clear-Glory Palace" on p. 305.

196 **pillars holding up heaven:** See note to p. 60.

198 **Moonlit Night:** This is reputed to be the first explicitly romantic poem written by a poet about his wife (though typically for Tu Fu, the romance is integrated with the political urgency of the time). Language like that of the third stanza was generally reserved for seductive courtesans.

198 **Ch'ang-an:** The capital, where Tu Fu was hiding after the rebel armies conquered and sacked the city. Ironically, its name means "Enduring Peace."

198 **Beacon-fires:** In times of war, neighboring garrisons would light beacon-fires each night at the same hour to signal one another that they were still secure.

199 **Dreaming of Li Po:** Li Po had become unwittingly involved with the leader of a minor rebellion in the southeast. Once the rebellion had been put down, Li was accused of being a traitor and banished to a waste region in the far southwest—an exile few survived. Li Po and Tu Fu were friends, and they wrote a number of poems for each other.

199 **it is no living spirit I dream:** In popular belief, at least, if someone came into your dreams it meant that person's spirit had left their body during sleep and entered your dream. Tu Fu's worry comes from the belief that it is only in death that a person's spirit can travel long distances. See also notes to pp. 44 and 175.

199 **dragons:** See note to p. 130.

202 **monkey sage:** From *Chuang Tzu*, 2.13:

> To wear yourself out illuminating the unity of all things without realizing that they're the same—this is called "three in the morning." Why "three in the morning"? There was once a monkey trainer who said at feeding time, "You get three in the morning and four in the evening." The monkeys got very angry, so he said, "Okay, I'll give you four in the morning and three in the evening." At this, the monkeys were happy again. Nothing was lost in either name or reality, but they were angry one way and pleased the other. This is why the sage brings *yes this* and *no that* together and rests in heaven the equalizer. This is called taking two paths at once.

206 **watch:** See note to p. 169.

207 **Star River:** The Milky Way.

207 **Triple Gorge:** A set of three spectacular gorges formed where the Yangtze River cut its way through the formidable Shaman (Wu) Mountains, forming a two-hundred-mile stretch of very narrow canyons. Famous for the river's violence and the towering cliffs haunted by shrieking gibbons, they appear often in Chinese poetry. They were located on the very outskirts of the civilized world, in a part of south China inhabited primarily by aboriginal peoples and frequently encountered by traveling (often exiled) artist-intellectuals. Tu Fu was living in K'uei-chou, which was perched above the river at the beginning of these magnificent gorges (which have recently been inundated by a huge hydroelectric project).

207 **Slumber-Dragon, Leap-Stallion:** Chu-ko Liang and Pai-ti, well-known figures from Chinese history. The first was a great cultural hero, and the second an infamous villain.

209 **knotting ropes:** See note to p. 54.

209 **departure and return:** Departure and return is the movement of Way (Tao).

210 **Jade-String:** Constellation in Ursa Major.

210 **Strung-Pearls:** The five planets known by the Chinese: Mercury, Venus, Mars, Jupiter, and Saturn.

210 **mirror:** The moon.

212 *ch'i:* See Key Terms.

212 **Wandering Star:** After flowing out to sea in the east, the Yangtze and Yellow rivers were said to ascend and rarify, becoming the Star River. The Star River crosses the sky, then descends in the west to form the headwaters of the Yangtze and Yellow. "Wandering Star" refers to a story in which a Yangtze fisherman boards an empty raft floating past his home. The raft carries him downstream and eventually up onto the Star River, where it becomes the Wandering Star.

212 **Southern Darkness:** The *Chuang Tzu* begins:

> In Northern Darkness there lives a fish called K'un. This K'un is so huge that it stretches who knows how many thousand miles. When it changes into a bird it's called P'eng. This P'eng has a back spreading who knows how many thousand miles, and when it thunders up into flight its wings are like clouds hung clear across the sky. It churns up the sea and sets out on its migration to Southern Darkness, which is the Lake of Heaven.

COLD MOUNTAIN (HAN SHAN)

215 **Way:** *Tao*, meaning both "path or road" and Lao Tzu's philosophical concept. See Key Terms: *Tao*.

215 **white clouds:** See note to p. 160.

218 **wandering boundless and free:** This phrase recurs in *Chuang Tzu*. It is the title of Chapter 1, and Chapter 6 (6.11) includes this description of two sages:

> On loan from everything else, they'll soon be entrusted back to the one body. Forgetting liver and gallbladder, abandoning ears and eyes—they'll continue on again, tumbling and twirling through a blur of endings and beginnings. They roam at ease beyond the tawdry dust of this world, nothing's own doing [*wu-wei*] wandering boundless and free through the selfless unfolding of things.

219 **no-mind:** Mind emptied of all content, of self and its constructions of the world. In this state, a goal of Ch'an practice, absence (*wu*) as empty-mind mirrors the ten thousand things. See also p. xxiv.

WEI YING-WU

224 **Dharma:** See note to p. 153.

226 The six poems on pp. 226–29 are from a set that follows the seasons through the year after Wei Ying-wu's wife died, beginning in winter and ending in autumn. As Wei explains in a note introducing the set, they mourn not only his wife but also the country's dire social situation, and they were written at his "old home at Integrity-Alike Monastery."

228 **Mirror:** Mirrors were made of polished bronze in a circular shape and small enough to hold in the hand. This one was cast in the form of a water-chestnut blossom: the back would have been shaped like the whorl of petals, and the surface of the mirror would have been at the opening of the blossom, with the tips of the petals projecting slightly around the edge of the surface.

228 **moon:** In Chinese poetry, the moon is often described as a mirror. See Tu Fu's "Riverside Moon and Stars" (p. 210), for example.

229 **fulling-stones:** See note to p. 95.

T'ANG DYNASTY II: EXPERIMENTAL ALTERNATIVES

MENG CHIAO

239 **scales:** Beginning of the dragon motif that runs through this sequence, as well as "Laments of the Gorges," which follows. Here we have the hibernating dragon coming back to life in spring. For the dragon, see note to p. 130.

240 **Way:** For both "Cold Creek" and "Laments of the Gorges," it should be remembered that water is Lao Tzu's central metaphor for Way. It recurs often in the *Tao Te Ching*, taking many forms, as in Chapter 32:

> Way flowing through all beneath heaven:
> it's like valley streams flowing into rivers and seas.

240 **evens all things out:** A central, recurring concept in this sequence, drawn from the second chapter of the *Chuang Tzu*: "A Little Talk About Evening Things Out." For Chuang Tzu, "evening things out" means seeing the essential oneness of all things. Once you master that, you "move in the boundless, and the boundless becomes your home." You do this by embracing things directly, rather than being trapped in intellectual distinctions and categories. After speaking of how limited such a life of distinctions is, he says: "But this is not the sage's way: the sage illuminates all in the light of heaven." This concept, though, soon proves to be of little real value in the poem, for natural process is driven by difference.

245 **Triple Gorge:** See note to p. 207.

246 **dragons:** See note to pp. 239 and 130.

248 **Death-owls call:** The Chinese thought an owl's voice resembled that of a ghost or spirit, so they thought a calling owl was beckoning the spirit of a dying person away.

249 *Wu-t'ung* **trees:** Especially admired tree, the wood of which was used to make *ch'in*s.

249 *ch'in:* See note to p. 30.

253 **Tao:** Altogether different from the philosophical Taoism of Lao Tzu and Chuang Tzu, this is religious Taoism, which focused on the esoteric pursuit of immortality and boasted goddesses and immortals riding cranes and dragons through the heavens. For Han Yü's hostility to Buddhism and religious Taoism, see chapter introduction, p. 251.

256 **singing geese, junk trees:** In the first tale of Chapter 20 in the *Chuang Tzu*, Chuang Tzu sees a gnarled tree that is not cut because it is so useless, then a goose that is killed because it cannot sing (i.e., because it is useless). To resolve the contradiction, he suggests that we should not struggle to preserve our lives by being either useless or useful but that we abide in Way (Tao), and so let ourselves drift through the ongoing transformation of things, without clinging to arbitrary values such as life or death, good or bad, teeth or no-teeth.

257 *from* **South Mountain:** This translation is composed of extracts chosen to create a much shortened version of the original while still reading like a poem. The original is about twice as long.

257 **South Mountain:** Here, Han Yü is describing the Whole-South Mountains, just south of the capital, Ch'ang-an. These mountains appear often in Chinese poetry, most notably as the site of Wang Wei's recluse home. Han shortens the name to South Mountain for the ancient resonance it carries (see note to p. 117).

257 **P'eng bird:** From the fable that opens the *Chuang Tzu*, for which see note to p. 212, "Southern Darkness."

257 *yang*: See note to p. 60.

258 *ch'i*: See Key Terms.

259 **moxa:** Pressed leaves that are burned on or near the skin as a medical treatment.

261 *I Ching: The Book of Change*, an ancient philosophical and divinatory text.

267 **Empty Gate:** Empty mind, the gate through which enlightenment is attained. Also a name for Buddhism.

268 **New *Yüeh-fu*:** See chapter introduction, pp. 265–66.

268 **Heaven-Jewel reign:** For this system of reign periods, see note to p. 122. The Heaven-Jewel reign lasted from 742 to 756 C.E. (the time leading up to and including the beginning of the An Lu-shan Rebellion).

269 **Open-Origin reign:** Period lasting from 713 to 742, the "golden years" of the T'ang Dynasty.

275 *Ch'in*: See note to p. 30.

275 *ch'i*: See Key Terms.

279 **Ch'ang-an:** The capital, whose name means "Enduring Peace."

280 **dark-enigma:** See Key Terms: *hsüan*.

282 **Waves Sifting Sand:** An early example of the *tz'u* form, for which see pp. 335–37. This poem is noteworthy for an understanding of geologic process that the West would not come to for over a millennium. See also Li Ho's "Sky Dream" (p. 290) and "Past and Forever On and On Chant" (p. 292).

285 **ch'an:** The *ch'an* of Ch'an Buddhism, which is a translation of the Sanskrit *dhyāna*, meaning "meditation."

285 **Home:** *At home*, in Buddhist phraseology, means to be a lay practitioner, and *giving up home* means to become a monk.

LI HO

288 **Endless-Peace:** Site of a vast battle in 260 B.C.E. It is said that over 400,000 soldiers died, and relics were apparently still turning up in Li Ho's time, a thousand years later.

289 **Weaver-Girl and Ox-Herd:** See note to p. 87.

289 **Star River:** The Milky Way.

290 **moon's old rabbit and cold toad:** Mythic inhabitants of the moon. See also p. 62 and note.

290 **dust soon seawater:** Li Ho often evokes his timeless mythic realms by reference to the vast time-spans of geologic process that the West discovered only in the late nineteenth century: land rising from the sea, mountains eroding away into plains, and finally ocean floors again. See also Li Ho's "Past and Forever On and On Chant" (p. 292) and Po Chü-i's "Waves Sifting Sand" (p. 282).

290 **ch'in:** See note to p. 30.

290 **dragon:** See note to p. 130.

291 **heart-gut dangle grass:** Also called "child-worry vine" and "farewell grass."

292 **Lucent-Lumen . . . Emerald-Blossom:** Sun and moon.

292 **pillars:** A variation on the myth in note to p. 60.

292 **Wives of the River Hsiang:** The mythic Emperor Shun (note to p. 70) had two wives, both daughters of Emperor Yao. When Shun died, they buried him on Nine-Doubt Mountain. Their sorrow was so great that they wept tears of blood, hence the red-flecked bamboo that grows throughout the region. Eventually, they leapt into the Hsiang River and thereupon became the spirit-wives of the river god.

292 **clouds-and-rain love:** See note to p. 184.

292 **ch'i:** See Key Terms.

293 **Ever-Grass Tomb:** The tomb of Wang Chao-chün, a great beauty who was sent to a Mongol chieftain as a tributary bride. When she died after an unhappy life among "barbarian" people, she was buried in Mongol lands, north of the Chinese border. It was said that the grass on her tomb was always lush and green, but here it's been turned to dust by the grazing of Mongol warhorses.

293 **Banner-Tip:** A constellation corresponding to our Pleiades. It was believed that if its stars began to flicker, war was imminent with the Mongol people to the north.

294 **South Mountain:** Here referring to the Whole-South Mountains just south of Ch'ang-an, which had many graveyards on their slopes.

294 **Ch'ang-an:** The capital, whose name means "Enduring Peace."

295 **Two river spirits . . . blood-flecked bamboo:** See note to p. 292.

TU MU

299 **Weaver-Girl and Ox-Herd:** See note to p. 87.

299 **Southern Dynasty:** A series of short-lived dynasties that rose and fell in quick suc-

cession during the fifth and sixth centuries C.E. (three to four hundred years before Tu Mu's time), when northern China was controlled by foreign invaders.

301 **white clouds:** See note to p. 160.

303 **fulling-stone:** See note to p. 95.

304 **where white clouds are born:** For white clouds, see note to p. 160. For clouds being born on mountain slopes, see note to p. 174.

305 **Clear-Glory Palace:** The emperor's summer palace in the mountains near the capital. This poem is remembering the days when An Lu-shan (see p. 146) was carousing there after capturing the capital and declaring himself emperor, not long after Tu Fu passed by this same palace during the journey he describes in his "First-Devotion Return Chant" (p. 195).

305 **Ch'ang-an:** The capital, whose name means "Enduring Peace."

305 *ch'i:* See Key Terms.

LI SHANG-YIN

310 *Ch'in:* See note to p. 30. The *ch'in* was supposedly invented with fifty strings by Fu Hsi (2953–2838 B.C.E.), the first emperor in China's legendary period, an act that was tantamount to the invention of music. (Fu Hsi also taught people to hunt, fish, and keep livestock.) Fu Hsi told the goddess Lady Origin-Weave to play his newly invented instrument, but when she did, it was so unbearably moving that he broke the instrument in half. The *ch'in* normally has seven strings. The twenty-five-string variant is technically called a *se*. The *ch'in* came to be associated with courtesans and romantic/erotic love.

312 **fifth watch:** Between 3:00 a.m. and 5:00 a.m. See note to p. 169.

312 **ink not ground thick enough:** Ink was made by rubbing a dry ink-stick on a wet ink-stone.

313 **Star River:** The Milky Way.

316 **moon-toad:** See note to p. 290.

316 **Northern Dipper:** The Big Dipper.

316 **clouds and rain:** See note to p. 184.

319 *ch'i:* See Key Terms.

YÜ HSÜAN-CHI

323 *ch'an:* See note to p. 285.

324 **Star River . . . love:** See note for the Ox-Herd and Weaver-Girl myth on p. 87.

325 *ch'in:* Musical instrument associated with courtesans and romantic/erotic love. See also note to p. 30.

326 **clouds and rain love:** See note to p. 184.

326 **Graduates:** These are the men who had passed the national exams and so were on their way to illustrious careers. The exam was not open to women.

327 **fathoms my *ch'in* utterly:** From *Lieh Tzu* 5.12:

> Po Ya was a great *ch'in* player, and Chung Tzu-ch'i a great listener. Once, Po Ya's thoughts wandered up among high peaks while he played.
> "Exquisite!" cried Chung Tzu-ch'i. "Lofty as Exalt Mountain."

When Po Ya's thoughts wandered to flowing rivers, Chung Tzu-ch'i cried: "Exquisite! Boundless as the Yellow and the Yangtze."

Whatever filled Po Ya's mind, Chung Tzu-ch'i always understood perfectly.

328 **Men robed purple and red:** The elite statesmen who controlled the government.

328 **Yen Hui:** See note to p. 116.

Sung Dynasty: The Mainstream Renewed

mei yao-ch'en

343 **Yellow Springs:** The underworld where, according to popular legend, people go when they die. Mei's wife has just died.

wang an-shih

362 **Star River:** The Milky Way.

362 **ten thousand holes cry and moan:** From *Chuang Tzu* 2.1:

"This Mighty Mudball of a world spews out breath, and that breath is called wind," began Adept Piebald. "Everything is fine so long as it's still. But when it blows, the ten thousand holes cry and moan. Haven't you heard them wailing on and on? In the awesome beauty of mountain forests, it's all huge trees a hundred feet around, and they're full of wailing hollows and holes like noses, like mouths, like ears, like posts and beams, like cups and bowls, like empty ditches and puddles: water-splashers, arrow-whistlers, howlers, gaspers, callers, screamers, laughers, warblers—leaders singing out *yuuu!* and followers answering *yeee!* When the wind's light, the harmony's gentle; but when the storm wails, it's a mighty chorus. And then, once the fierce wind has passed through, the holes are all empty again. Haven't you seen felicity and depravity thrashing and flailing together?"

"So the music of earth means all those holes singing together," said Adept Adrift, "and the music of humans means bamboo pipes singing. Could I ask you to explain the music of heaven for me?"

"Sounding the ten thousand things differently, so each becomes itself according to itself alone—who could make such music?"

363 **sweeping my gate-path:** A traditional gesture of welcome for anticipated visitors. See note to p. 113.

su tung-p'o

366 **Untitled:** It was Su Tung-p'o who definitively established the *tz'u* (see pp. 335–37) as a form of serious poetry, a status previously reserved for the *shih*. One indication of this is that, rather than just tune titles, he begins using descriptive titles, as in the other examples of his *tz'u* translated here: pp. 368 and 378.

368 **Yen Tzu-ling:** To avoid the necessity of serving in the government when his old friend became emperor in 25 C.E., Yen Tzu-ling disappeared into the mountains. He was found fishing at Seven-Mile Rapids but refused the high offices that were offered him, preferring instead to live as a recluse-farmer.

369 **Lady West:** Hsi Tzu or Hsi Shih: a great beauty from the fifth century B.C.E.

370 *ch'an*: See note to p. 285.

370 **blank:** This is the *tan* of Mei Yao-ch'en's *p'ing-tan*, for which see p. 338.

372 **Setting animals loose:** In their reverence for the sanctity of life, Buddhists would go to the markets, buy captured animals, and set them free.

374 **Exiled, We Move . . . :** This poem was written early in Su Tung-p'o's first exile, just after he'd been tried for treason and very nearly lost his life.

374 **Humanity and Duty:** Touchstones of Confucian virtue. Humanity (*jen*) means a selfless and reverent concern for the well-being of others, and Duty (*yi*) means to put that moral sense into practice. Su Tung-p'o is saying that he's been a selflessly devoted public servant.

376 *ch'i*'s **movements:** See note to p. 132.

377 **Bright-Clarity:** The mid-spring festival.

378 **Red Cliffs:** Site on the Yangtze where an epochal naval battle was fought in 208 C.E. This battle marked the end of the Han Dynasty when Lord Chou defeated the vastly superior fleet of the Han general Ts'ao Ts'ao by tangling it in a series of burning barges, thereby setting the Han fleet on fire. Twelve years later, the moribund Han fell, succeeded by the Three Kingdoms period (220–280).

379 **Presented to Abbot Perpetua All-Gathering . . . :** This poem is said to record Su Tung-p'o's enlightenment and has been an oft-cited part of the Ch'an literature ever since. The story is that Perpetua All-Gathering (Ch'ang-tsung) had given Su Tung-p'o a koan proposing that inanimate things continuously express dharma. Su stayed up all night working on the koan, then at dawn wrote this poem as his answer. After reading it, Perpetua All-Gathering acknowledged Su's awakening.

379 **tongue . . . body:** The Buddhist literature speaks of Buddha's "tongue broad and unending," dharma's "body pure and clear," and the "eighty-four thousand" teachings of Buddha.

379 *gathas*: Sacred Buddhist texts in poetic form.

381 *Peach blossoms . . .* **Warrior-Knoll:** *"Peach blossoms drift streamwater away"* echoes Li Po's "Mountain Dialogue" (p. 178). The peach blossoms and Warrior-Knoll refer to T'ao Ch'ien's "Peach-Blossom Spring" (see p. 122).

382 **mountaintop moon:** The pure clarity of moonlight is a common metaphor for the clarity of a Ch'an master's empty mind. Cf. Cold Mountain's poem "199" on p. 217.

383 **After T'ao Ch'ien's "Drinking Wine":** For T'ao Ch'ien's original poem, see p. 117 (section 5). Su Tung-p'o wrote a poem following the rhymes of each of T'ao Ch'ien's 120 poems—an enormous project and sign of the deep respect Su (and all Sung poets) had for T'ao.

LI CH'ING-CHAO

386 **chestnut-blossom mirror:** See note to p. 228.

388 **9/9 . . . eastern fence:** The 9/9 Festival and yellow chrysanthemums at the east fence are famously associated with T'ao Ch'ien and allude to his poems on pp. 117 (section 5) and 120.

391 **third-watch:** Between 11:00 p.m. and and 1:00 a.m. See note to p. 169.

395 **Wall-Tower Above K'uei-chou . . . Tu Fu:** Tu Fu, the great T'ang Dynasty poet (see pp. 190–221), lived in and around K'uei-chou during one of his most productive periods. He spent some of that time in this tower, where he wrote many of his late dark poems, for which see pp. 207–11.

395 **Ch'ang-an:** Traditional capital that was lost to the Mongol invaders when they took control of the north. Ironically, its name means "Enduring Peace."

396 **Wu . . . Shu:** Ancient names for southeastern and western China.

397 **Ch'ü Yüan:** First major poet in the written tradition. See pp. 55–58.

397 **Nine-Doubt Mountain . . . Hsiang River:** Where Ch'ü Yüan wandered and finally committed suicide by drowning. See also note to p. 292.

398 **Emperor Wen:** See note to p. 15.

398 **Duke of Chou writing "Seventh Moon":** For this poem, see p. 18. For the Duke of Chou, see p. 7.

399 **first emperor:** Fu Hsi, for whom see note to p. 310.

399 **knotted ropes:** See note to p. 54.

For poems on pp. 401–405, see p. 394.

401 *ch'in:* See note to p. 30.

401 *ch'an:* See note to p. 285.

402 *ch'i:* See Key Terms.

402 **Thatch-Hut mountains . . . Little-Forest:** Buddhist monastic centers. For Thatch-Hut Mountain, see note to p. 141. One of China's most famous monasteries, Little-Forest (Shao-lin) is said to be where Chinese martial arts originated and where Bodhidharma, legendary founder of Ch'an Buddhism, sat in meditation for nine years.

403 **Star River:** The Milky Way.

403 **Dipper:** The Big Dipper.

404 **kalpas:** See note to p. 176.

405 **Maker-of-Things:** See Key Terms: *Tao*.

405 **Tu Fu's old house:** This is a house in western China where Tu Fu lived briefly during his travels. Tu Fu's short career advising the emperor ended when his honesty enraged the emperor, and he spent the rest of his life wandering. The Sung emperor likewise had little patience for Lu Yu's advice.

406 **muddy and clear:** Allusion to *Mencius* (7.8) and "The Fisherman" in the *Ch'u Tz'u* (*The Songs of Ch'u*), where *muddy* is a lack of personal integrity in government, causing social disorder, and *clear* means personal integrity, resulting in social order and prosperity:

> When Chill-Flood Creek flows clear
> I rinse my hat-strings clean.
> When Chill-Flood Creek flows muddy
> I rinse my feet clean.

406 *yes this* and *no that*: See note to p. 131.

409 **Absolute-Meaning . . . T'ao Ch'ien:** This poem plays on T'ao Ch'ien's famous "Drinking Wine," section 5 (p. 117; cf. also Su Tung-p'o's poem on p. 383), where the idea of "meaning something absolute" occurs.

412 *ch'i veins*: See note to p. 132 and Key Terms.

413 **beach gull:** According to legend, gulls will associate only with a true recluse.

416 *absolutely*: Again, from T'ao Ch'ien's "Drinking Wine," section 5 (p. 117).

419 **blank:** This is *tan* from Mei Yao-ch'en's *p'ing-tan*, for which see p. 338.

420 **On the Second Day . . . :** This poem echoes Li Po's "Drinking Wine" poems (pp. 179–80), from which the italicized passages in lines 5–6 are taken.

9/9: Holiday, for which see note to p. 120.

Key Terms

An Outline of Classical Chinese Poetry's Conceptual World

TAO

道 *Way*

Tao originally meant "way," as in "pathway" or "roadway," a meaning it has kept. But Lao Tzu and Chuang Tzu redefined it as a spiritual concept by using it to describe the generative ontological process (hence, a "Way") through which all things arise and pass away. As such, *Tao* can be divided into two aspects: presence (*yu*), the ten thousand living and nonliving things of the empirical world, and absence (*wu*), the generative source of presence and its transformations. The Taoist way is to dwell as a part of this natural process. In that dwelling, self is but a fleeting form taken on by earth's process of change. Or more absolutely, it is all and none of earth's fleeting forms simultaneously. See also: pp. xxii and 36–39, and my translation of *Tao Te Ching* pp. x and xvi–xvii.

See: passim.

TZU-JAN

自然 *Occurrence appearing of itself*

Tzu-jan's literal meaning is "self-ablaze," from which comes "self-so" or "the of-itself," which as a philosophical concept becomes "being such of itself," hence "spontaneous" or "natural." But a more revealing translation of *tzu-jan* is "occurrence appearing of itself," for it is meant to describe the ten thousand things burgeoning forth spontaneously from the generative source (*wu*), each according to its own nature, independent and self-sufficient; each dying and returning to the process of change, only to reappear in another self-generating form. Hence, *tzu-jan* is described as the mechanism or process of *Tao* in the empirical world. See also: pp. xxii–xxiii, and my translation of *Tao Te Ching* pp. xx–xxi.

See: pp. 46, 48, 113, 133, 180.

WU   無 *Absence (Nonbeing)*
The generative void from which the ever-changing realm of presence (see the following entry) perpetually arises. Although it is often spoken of in a general sense as the source of all presence, it is in fact quite specific and straightforward: for each of the ten thousand things, absence is simply the emptiness that precedes and follows existence. *Wu* is known immediately in meditation, widely practiced by ancient Chinese poets and intellectuals, where it is experienced as empty consciousness itself, known in Ch'an (Zen) terminology as "empty mind" or "no-mind." See also: pp. xxii–xxv.
   See: pp. 40, 41, 49, 50, 115, 211, 350, 359, 360, 370, 419.

YU   有 *Presence (Being)*
The empirical universe, which has its origin in *wu*. The ancients described *yu* as the ten thousand living and nonliving things in constant transformation. See also: pp. xxii–xxv.
   See: pp. 40, 41, 49, 50, 350, 359, 360, 370.

WU-WEI   無為 *Nothing's own doing*
Impossible to translate the same way in every instance, *wu-wei* means acting as a spontaneous part of *tzu-jan* rather than with self-conscious intention. Different contexts emphasize different aspects of this rich philosophical concept as writers exploit the term's grammatical ambiguity. Literally meaning "not/nothing (*wu*) doing (*wei*)," *wu-wei's* most straightforward translation is simply "doing nothing" in the sense of not interfering with the flawless and self-sufficient unfolding of *tzu-jan*. But this must always be conceived together with its mirror translation: "nothing doing" or "nothing's own doing," in the sense of not being separate from *tzu-jan* when acting. As *wu-wei* is the movement of *tzu-jan*, when we act according to *wu-wei* we act as the generative source, which opens to the deepest level of this philosophical complex, for *wu-wei* can also be read quite literally as "absence (*wu*) doing." Here, *wu-wei* action is action directly from, or indeed *as* the ontological source: absence burgeoning forth into presence. This in turn invests the more straightforward translation ("doing nothing") with its fullest dimensions, for "doing nothing" always carries the sense of "enacting nothing/absence."
   With the exception of the *Tao Te Ching*, this central term does not itself occur in the poems of this anthology. But it is a constant presence as a spiritual posture that all poets aspired to and most enacted in their poetry, each in his or her own unique way.
   See: pp. 41, 42, 44, 51, 53, 172–73.

HSÜAN   玄 *Dark-Enigma*
Dark-enigma came to have a particular philosophic resonance, for in the third and fourth centuries C.E. it became the name of a neo-Taoist school of philosophy: Dark-Enigma Learning, a school that gave Chinese thought a decidedly ontological turn and became central to the synthesis of Taoism and Buddhism into Ch'an (Zen) Buddhism. Like Lao Tzu, the thinkers of the Dark-Enigma Learning school equated dark-enigma with absence, the generative ontological tissue from which the ten thousand things spring. Or more properly, it is Way before it is named or known, before absence and presence give birth to each other—that region where consciousness and ontology share their source.

It is interesting to note that *Hsüan* is the name of the bird that gave birth to the Shang people in the very early *Shih Ching* poem "Dark-Enigma Bird" (p. 9).

See: pp. 9, 40, 44, 52, 156, 280.

·CH'I   氣 *Ch'i*
The universal breath, vital energy, or cosmic life-force. In its originary form, it is primal-*ch'i* (*yüan-ch'i*), which is present in *wu* and is perhaps the aspect that makes the primordial emptiness of *wu* pregnant with possibility. Primal-*ch'i* is made up of *yin* and *yang* completely intermingled and indistinguishable. Once primal-*ch'i* separated out into *yin* and *yang*, *yang* rose up to become sky and *yin* sank down to form earth. As the universal breath, *ch'i* is in constant motion, flowing through landscapes, animating all things, and so is a kind of tissue that connects us always to the empty source.

See: passim.

LI   理 *Inner Pattern*
The philosophical meaning of *li*, which originally referred to the veins and markings in a precious piece of jade, is something akin to what we call natural law. It is the system of principles or patterns that governs the unfolding of *tzu-jan*, or the manifestations of primal-*ch'i* as it takes on the forms of the ten thousand things. *Li* therefore weaves absence and presence into a single boundless tissue. But concepts at these ontological depths blur, especially in the intermingling of Taoist and Buddhist thought, and in the hands of various writers, *li* appears virtually synonymous with a host of other key concepts: even *Tao* or *tzu-jan*, and Buddha or *prajñā* (the Buddhist term for enlightenment, in which emptiness is understood to be the true nature of all things). See also pp. 128 and 365.

See: pp. 119, 133, 138, 156, 171, 386.

HSIN   心 *Heart-Mind*
In ancient China, there was no fundamental distinction between heart and mind: the term *hsin* connotes all that we think of in the two concepts together. This range of meaning often blends into the technical use of *hsin* in Taoism and Ch'an (Zen) Buddhism, where it means consciousness emptied of all content, or perhaps consciousness as empty awareness. The recurring terms *empty mind* and *no-mind* emphasize this meaning. And at this fundamental level, mind is nothing other than absence (*wu*), the pregnant emptiness from which all things arise.

See: passim.

K'UNG   空 *Emptiness*
This concept resonates in a number of Taoist and Buddhist ways. In general it is essentially synonymous with absence (*wu*). As such it is often used to describe mind itself—consciousness emptied of all content. When used in reference to the empirical world, it suggests that the ten thousand things are most fundamentally absence, and so "empty." From this follows the ecological principle that all things arise in their particular forms from the web of being, then dissolve back into it as the material that will reappear in future forms. Hence, there is no permanent selfhood, or self is "empty."

See: passim.

HSIEN   閑 *Idleness*

Etymologically, the character for idleness that T'ao Ch'ien used (*hsien*) connotes "profound serenity and quietness," its pictographic elements rendering a moon (see note to p. 18) shining through an open gate (pictograph showing the two doors of the gate), or in its alternate form, a tree standing alone within the gates to a courtyard (see note to p. 113 for the resonance in the term "gate"). Later, another character was also used: *lan*. The pictographic elements of this character are equally revealing: it is made up of the character for "trust"(*lai*) beside the character for "heart-mind" (*hsin*). Hence, the heart-mind of trust, the heart-mind of trust in the world. But this is trust of truly profound dimensions, for "idleness" is essentially a lazybones word for the spiritual posture known as *wu-wei*. Hence, idleness is a kind of meditative reveling in *tzu-jan*, a state in which daily life becomes the essence of spiritual practice.

See: passim.

Women's Poetry in Ancient China

As it survives in the written tradition, Chinese poetry is almost exclusively male, so the poetry of women demands special mention. Much remains unknown about lyric poetry written by women in ancient China, but some tentative outlines can be sketched. The question of female poets in the anonymous folk tradition is inaccessible to us, though it seems clear, for example, that many of the *Shih Ching* folk-songs were originally composed by women. More is known about women poets in the educated and privileged class that produced China's written literary culture, women whose situation was both a debilitating trap and, when compared with that of the overwhelming majority of women who were desperately poor peasants, great good fortune.

These women were generally literate, receiving enough education to run a household and provide primary education to their children. But from the age of seven, girls generally lived in strict seclusion within the inner rooms of the house, unseen by anyone but close family. This seclusion reduced their realm of experience to the domestic, an obvious hindrance in the development of a poet. The greatest tragedy is not, of course, the absent poetry but that women were not allowed the personal freedom and spiritual depth that men took for granted. Happily, there were exceptions: families who valued girls, provided more extensive educations, and otherwise allowed girls to pursue their talents and interests; and men who valued more sophistication in a wife. Su Hui (p. 105) and Li Ch'ing-chao (p. 384) apparently enjoyed situations like this.

Several social realms outside the family did emerge in which women had a chance of some further self-cultivation and development as poets. The first was the realm of the inner palace, the emperor's harem. Women were often chosen as imperial concubines because of their intellectual and literary abilities, and the inner palace provided a limited kind of intellectual community because these women were expected to charm the emperor not only with their beauty but also with their skills as musicians, dancers, and poets.

Wealthy men began to keep cultivated women in their houses to provide entertainment, intellectual companionship, and sexual satisfaction. Eventually this class of women split into two types: concubines, who were attached to a particular household, and courtesans, who entertained male clients in their own quarters (it was considered entirely normal for married men to spend time with such courtesans). Courtesans were perhaps the most independent women in ancient China. They were relatively well-educated, skilled in the arts, and economically independent, and they could choose the men with whom they associated (though economic pressure was obviously ever-present). Indeed, this world of courtesans created something resembling what we now take for granted: romantic relationships (as opposed to the arranged marriages that were the norm) between men and women who are intellectually sophisticated and free in their actions. This atmosphere of romance was precisely the appeal courtesans held for their wealthy clientele, and in the T'ang Dynasty, when this culture of romance became widely established, it affected poetry deeply—both formally, with the rise of the *tz'u* form (pp. 335–37), and in terms of content. Nevertheless, the freedom enjoyed by courtesans was counterbalanced by economic insecurity, especially as they grew older and their beauty faded, and by their status as compromised women not worthy of "acceptable society."

Supplementing the social institutions that supported concubines and courtesans, Taoist monasteries arose that provided more independent-minded women with an intellectual atmosphere and freedom from many of the restrictions society placed on them. Over the centuries, this monastic realm developed toward the world of courtesans, often hosting intellectual gatherings that entertained wealthy scholar-officials. And in addition to similar artistic and intellectual cultivation, the women in these monasteries were able to travel widely and choose lovers as they liked.

Even though these institutions no doubt fostered a substantial amount of poetry, only a very few poets are known to us. Some female poets were apparently quite well-known in their own time, and there was probably some sense of a women's tradition based on word-of-mouth reputations and contemporary collections. But for all that, female poets from the lettered class have vanished almost as completely as have those in the folk tradition. It was extremely rare for a female poet to survive in more than a handful of poems. Su Hui and the nebulous Lady Midnight are the only two notable exceptions before the T'ang Dynasty. From the T'ang, only three poets survive, with collections containing 50 to 100 poems; and from the Sung, only two survive, with collections containing 100 and 330 poems. These numbers pale when compared with those of prominent male poets of those dynasties: in the T'ang, Li Po is survived by 1,100 poems, Tu Fu by 1,400, and Po Chü-i by 2,800; and in the Sung, Su Tung-p'o is survived by 2,750, Lu Yu by 10,000, and Yang Wan-li by 4,200.

It may well be that more poetry surviving in the feminine voice was written by men than women. In fact, it was men who determined the themes that were allowed in women's poetry. They decided what types of poetry to preserve; what types of poetry they would write in the voices of women, thereby setting the parameters within which women could write; and what types of poetry were expected of concubines and courtesans (who were obliged to write such poetry out of economic necessity). Such poetry tends to emphasize certain male fantasies about women, centered on the woman as longing for an absent lover. It seems clear that independent-minded women must have written outside the limitations imposed by male expectations, but precious little of that work has survived.

The history of what does survive from the female tradition can be traced through this anthology in the following sections:

1. *Shih Ching* folk-songs (pp. 22, 23, and others?)
2. *Tao Te Ching* (pp. 36–54, Introduction and passim)
3. Music Bureau Folk-Songs (pp. 81, 84, and others?)
4. Nineteen Ancient-Style Poems (pp. 86 and 88)

Finding List for Poets

Tu Mu	Du Mu	296
Wang An-shih	Wang An-shi	351
Wang Wei	Wang Wei	157
Wei Ying-wu	Wei Ying-wu	222
Yang Wan-li	Yang Wan-li	407
Yü Hsüan-chi	Yu Xuan-ji	321

PINYIN WITH WADE-GILES EQUIVALENT

Pinyin	**Wade-Giles**	**Page**
Bai Ju-yi	Pai Chü-i (Po Chü-i)	265
Bo Ju-yi	Po Chü-i	265
Chu-ci	Ch'u Tz'u	55
Dao De Jing	*Tao Te Ching*	36
Du Fu	Tu Fu	190
Du Mu	Tu Mu	296
Han Yu	Han Yü	251
Han Shan	Han Shan	213
Lao-zi	Lao Tzu	36
Li Bai	Li Pai (Li Po)	172
Li Bo	Li Po	172
Li He	Li Ho	286
Li Qing-zhao	Li Ch'ing-chao	384
Li Shang-yin	Li Shang-yin	308
Lu You	Lu Yu	393
Mei Yao-chen	Mei Yao-ch'en	338
Meng Hao-ran	Meng Hao-jan	147
Meng Jiao	Meng Chiao	237
Qu Yuan	Ch'ü Yüan	55
Shi Jing	*Shih Ching*	5
Su Dung-po	Su Tung-p'o	364
Su Hui	Su Hui	105
Su Shi	Su Shih (Su Tung-p'o)	364
Tao Qian	T'ao Ch'ien	110
Tao Yuan-ming	T'ao Yüan-ming (T'ao Ch'ien)	110
Wang An-shi	Wang An-shih	351
Wang Wei	Wang Wei	157
Wei Ying-wu	Wei Ying-wu	222
Xie Ling-yun	Hsieh Ling-yün	127
Yang Wan-li	Yang Wan-li	407
Yu Xuan-ji	Yü Hsüan-chi	321

Finding List for Poets

Finding List for Chinese Texts

MUSIC-BUREAU FOLK-SONGS

1. *Yüeh-fu Shih Chi*. Kuo Mao-ch'ien, ed. c. 1125 (SPPY edition: *chüan*, page number, and leaf).
2. *Yüeh-fu Shih Chi*. Kuo Mao-ch'ien, ed. c. 1125 (1979 Beijing edition: page number).

3. *Ku-shih Yüan*. Shen Te-ch'ien, ed. 1719 (SPPY edition: *chüan*, page number, and leaf).
4. *Ku-shih Yüan Chien Chu*. Shen Te-ch'ien, ed. 1719 (Wang Ch'un-fu edition, 1959: *chüan*, page number, and leaf).

Page	1. *Yüeh-fu Shih Chi*	2. *Yüeh-fu Shih Chi*	3. *Ku-shih Yüan*	4. *Ku-shih Yüan Chien Chu*
76	83.2a	1165		
76	38.1a	555		
77	25.3a	365		
78	16.7a	231		
79	16.4b	228		
80	27.3b	396		
80	27.5a	398		
81	38.1a	555		
82	1.4a	5		
83	37.5b	550		
84			4.8a	2.4a

NINETEEN ANCIENT-STYLE POEMS

1. *Ku-shih Yüan*. Shen Te-ch'ien, ed. 1719 (SPPY edition: *chüan*, page number, and leaf).
2. *Ku-shih Yüan Chien Chu*. Shen Te-ch'ien, ed. 1719 (Wang Ch'un-fu edition, 1959: *chüan*, page number, and leaf).

Page	1. *Ku-shih Yüan*	2. *Ku-shih Yüan Chien Chu*
86	4.4b	2.4a

LADY MIDNIGHT SONGS OF THE FOUR SEASONS

The Lady Midnight collections begin on the following pages in the two editions of *Yüeh-fu Shih Chi* cited earlier: 44.3a and 641. They are also available in Ting Fu-pao's *Ch'üan Han San-kuo Chin Nan-pei-ch'ao Shih* (1927), in the *Ch'üan Chin Shih* section, 8.1a.

The numbers in the list here are the poem numbers from the original two collections: LM = *Lady Midnight Songs*; Sp, Su, Au, Wi = the seasons in the *Lady Midnight Songs of the Four Seasons* collection.

Page	*Yüeh-fu Shih Chi*
90	LM 24
	Sp 3
91	Sp 10
	Sp 19
92	LM 3
	LM 30
93	Su 1
	Su 3
94	Su 9
	LM 33
95	Au 1
	Au 2

96	Au 3
	Au 5
97	Au 8
	Au 17
98	Au 18
	Wi 9
99	Wi 11
	Wi 13
100	Wi 14
	Wi 16

T'AO CH'IEN

1. *Ching-chieh Hsien Sheng Chi.* T'ao Shu, ed. 1839. SPPY (*Chüan*, page number, and leaf).
2. *T'ao Yüan-ming Shih Chien Chu.* Ting Fu-pao, ed. 1927 (*Chüan*, page number, and leaf).

Page	1. *Ching-chieh Hsien Sheng Chi*	2. *T'ao Yüan-ming Shih Chien Chu*
113	2.4a	2.4a
116	3.11b	3.6a
117	3.15a	3.11b
119	4.4b	4.4b
120	2.3b	2.3b
121	3.29a	3.24b
122	6.1a	4.21a
124	4.4b	4.4a
125	4.17b	4.19b

HSIEH LING-YÜN

1. *Hsieh Ling-yün Chi Chiao Chu.* Ku Shao-po, ed. and comm. 1986 (Page number).
2. *Hsieh K'ang-lo Shih Chu.* Huang Chieh, ed. and comm. 1924 (*Chüan*, page number, and leaf).
3. *Ch'üan Sung Wen* (*Chüan*, page number, leaf).

Page	1. *Hsieh Ling-yün Chi Chiao Chu*	2. *Hsieh K'ang-lo Shih Chu*	3. *Ch'üan Sung Wen*
130	63	2.12a	
131	56	2.22b	
132	114	3.3b	
133	318	Sung Shu 67.7a	31.1a
138	178	3.14a	
139	183	3.14b	
140	121	3.17a	
141	194	4.4b	

MENG HAO-JAN

1. *Meng Hao-jan Chi.* SPPY (*Chüan*, page number, leaf).
2. *Meng Hao-jan Shih Chi Chien Chu.* T'ung P'ei-chi, ed., 2000 (Page number).

WANG WEI

1. *Wang Yu-ch'eng Chi Chu*. Chao Tien-ch'eng, ed. 1736. SPPY (*Chüan*, page number, and leaf).

LI PO

1. *Li T'ai-po Shih Chi*. Wang Chi, ed. 1759. SPPY (*Chüan*, page number, and leaf).
2. *Li Po Chi Chiao Chu*. Ch'ü Shui-yüan, ed. 1980 (Page number).

178	19.2b	1095
179	23.2b	1331
181	6.11a	448
182	24.19b	1416
183	3.28b	267
184	25.11a	1465
185	20.22b	1207
185	30.5b	1727 (3)
186	30.8b	1711
187	23.10a	1354
187	5.12a	374
188	8.1a	533
189	22.14b	1299 (2)
189	6.9b	443

Tu Fu

1. *Chiu Chia Chi Chu Tu Shih*. Kuo Chih-ta, ed. In William Hung's *A Concordance to the Poetry of Tu Fu* (*Chüan* and poem number).
2. *Tu Shih Ching Ch'uan*. Yang Lun, ed. (*Chüan*, page number, and leaf).

Page	1. *Chiu Chia Chi Chu Tu Shih*	2. *Tu Shih Ching Ch'uan*
192	1.5	1.1a
192	17.14 (1)	1.2a
193	1.12	1.21a
195	2.16	3.8a
198	19.6	3.18b
198	19.9	3.20
199	5.10 (1)	5.22a
200	3.11	5.16b
201	20.11	6.11a
202	6.16	7.6b
205	21.15	7.21a
206	21.25	7.29b
206	27.25	12.25b
207	31.43	15.10a
207	30.6	14.4b
208	30.29	17.15b
208	32.29	17.16a
209	13.19 (2)	18.4a
210	34.5a	19.4a
211	32.12	17.34a
212	35.1	19.19b
212	35.9	19.24a

Cold Mountain (Han Shan)

Poem numbers follow numbering in *Han Shan Tzu Shih Chi* and *Ch'üan T'ang Shih*. Depending on the edition of *Ch'üan T'ang Shih* consulted, the Cold Mountain collection is found in either *chüan* 806 or *han* 12, *ts'e* 1, *chüan* 1.

Wei Ying-wu

1. *Wei Su-chou Chi*. SPPY (*Chüan*, page number, and leaf).
2. *Wei Ying-wu Chi Chia Chu*. T'ao Min and Wang Yu-sheng, eds. 1998 (Page number).

Page	1. *Wei Su-chou Chi*	2. *Wei Ying-wu Chi Chia Chu*
224	8.11a	530
224	7.11b	468
225	3.10b	194
225	3.8a	173
226	6.8b	397
227	6.9a	400
227	6.9a	401
228	6.10a	405
228	6.12a	421
229	6.10a	407
230	7.5b	433
230	7.12a	470
231	7.7a	442
231	7.4b	427

Meng Chiao

1. *Meng Tung-yeh Shih Chi*. Hua Ch'en-chih, ed. (Page number).
2. *Meng Tung-yeh Chi*. SPPY (*Chüan*, page number, and leaf).
3. *Meng Tung-yeh Shih Chu*. Ch'en Yen-chieh, ed. (*Chüan*, page number, and leaf).

Page	1. *Meng Tung-yeh Shih Chi*	2. *Meng Tung-yeh Chi*	3. *Meng Tung-yeh Shih Chu*
239	88	5.6b	5.8b
245	185	10.4b	10.6a
249	58	4.1a	4.1a

Han Yü

1. *Han Ch'ang-li Shih Hsi-nien Chi Shih*. Ch'ien Chung-lien, ed. (Page number).
2. *Han Ch'ang-li Chüan Chi*. Liao Ying-chung, ed. SPPY (*Chüan*, page number, and leaf).

Page	1. *Han Ch'ang-li Shih Hsi-nien Chi Shih*	2. *Han Ch'ang-li Chüan Chi*
253	482	6.3b
255	81	4.11b
257	194	1.17b
262	415	9.11b
264	237 (8)	1.22b

Po Chü-i

1. *Po Chü-i Chi Chien Chiao*. Chu Chin-ch'eng, ed. and comm. 1988 (Page number).
2. *Po Chü-i Chi*. Ku Hsüeh-chieh, ed. 1979 (Page number).
3. *Po Hsiang-shan Shih Chi*. Wang Li-ming, ed. 1703. SPPY (*Chüan*, page number, and leaf).

Page	1. *Po Chü-i Chi Chien Chiao*	2. *Po Chü-i Chi*	3. *Po Hsiang-shan Shih Chi*
267	776	265	13.12b
267	725	251	13.5a
268	165	61	3.4a
271	221	78	4.3b
272	227	79	4.4b
273	92	33	2.4a
274	96	34	2.4b
275	302	103	5.7b
276	336	120	6.7a
277	647	232	12.5a
278	401	143	7.10a
278	1163	382	18.3a
279	1031	343	16.12b
280	448	161	21.5a
281	624 (2)	225	11.10b
281	1976	646	30.11a
282	2169	715	32.13a
284	2485	822	24.15b
285	1710	558	28.2b
285	2426	802	36.8b

LI HO

1. *Li Ch'ang-chi Shih Chi*. Wang Ch'i, ed. and comm. 1760. SPPY (*Chüan*, page number, and leaf).
2. Poem number in standard collection and Frodsham's complete translation.

Page	1. *Li Ch'ang-chi Shih Chi*	2. *Poem number*
288	4.18a	150
289	3.21a	110
290	1.9b	20
290	4.12b	137
291	2.8b	51
292	2.2a	47
292	1.19b	44
293	4.19b	152
294	2.22b	69.3
294	4.17b	148
295	wai chi 2a	170

TU MU

1. *Fan-ch'uan Shih Chi Chu*. Feng Chi-wu, ed. and comm. 1798. SPPY (*Chüan*, page number, and leaf; *pc* indicates the *pieh chi* section, and *wc* the *wai chi* section).

Page	1. *Fan-ch'uan Shih Chi Chu*
298	3.26a
298	4.10b

299	wc 11b
299	3.7b
300	4.7b
300	4.17b
301	4.28a (2)
301	4.31a
302	2.16a
302	4.31b
303	3.28a
303	pc 3a
304	wc 8b
304	3.27a
305	2.15a (3)
305	2.30b
306	wc 6a
306	4.28a
307	4.7b
307	3.14a

LI SHANG-YIN

1. *Yü-hsi Sheng Shih Chien Chu.* Feng Hao, ed. and comm. 1780. SPPY (*Chüan*, page number, and leaf).

Page	1. *Yü-hsi Sheng Shih Chien Chu*
310	4.28a
310	5.15b (1)
311	2.38a
312	3.42b (1)
312	6.8a
313	3.42a
313	5.46a
314	5.34a
318	6.14b
318	3.47b
319	5.25b
320	3.42b (2)

YÜ HSÜAN-CHI

1. *Yü Hsüan-chi Shih.* SPPY (Page number and leaf).
2. Poem number in *Ch'üan T'ang Shih.*

Page	1. *Yü Hsüan-chi Shih*	2. Poem number
323	1b	3
323	11a	42
324	4b	15
324	10b	40
325	12b	47
326	5b	19
327	7b	28

Finding List for Chinese Texts

328	9b	35
328	12a	46
329	8a	31
330	7a	25
330	6a	20

MEI YAO-CH'EN

1. *Wan-ling Chi.* SPPY (*Chüan*, page number, and leaf).

Page	1. *Wan-ling Chi*
340	36.4b
341	11.5a
341	43.7a
342	11.6a
343	11.7a
344	7.3a
344	24.5a
345	7.6a
347	31.3a
348	19.1a
349	34.5b
349	34.1b
350	30.2a
350	22.1b

WANG AN-SHIH

1. *Lin-chuan Chi.* SPPY (*Chüan*, page number, and leaf).

Page	1. *Lin-chuan Chi*
353	28.8b
353	30.5a
354	27.6a
354	26.4b (1)
355	3.2a
356	30.10a
356	32.6a
357	30.8b
357	33.9b
358	29.5a
358	32.4a (3)
359	33.9a
359	25.7a
360	31.7b
360	14.7a
361	30.5b
361	33.4a
362	27.4a
362	16.5a (2)
363	27.6a
363	2.2b

Su Tung-p'o

1. *Su Shih Shih Chi*. Feng Ying-liu and Wang Wen-kao, eds. (Page number and *chüan*).
2. *Tung-p'o Ch'i Chi*. Ch'eng Tsung, ed. SPPY (Collection, *chüan*, page number, and leaf).
   Chi = Tung-p'o Chi
   Hsü = Tung-p'o Hsü Chi
3. *Ch'üan Sung Tz'u*. T'ang Kuei-chang, ed. (Page number).
4. *Su Tung-p'o Tz'u*. Ts'ao Shu-ming, ed. 1968 (Poem number).

Page	1. *Su Shih Shih Chi*	2. *Tung-p'o Ch'i Chi*	3. *Ch'üan Sung Tz'u*	4. *Su Tung-p'o Tz'u*
366	183 (4)	*Chi* 2.4a		
366			288	150
367	1723 (32)	*Chi* 18.11a		
368			303	3
369	430 (9)	*Chi* 4.7a		
369	580 (12)	*Chi* 6.5b		
370	831 (16)	*Chi* 9.6a		
371	872 (17)	*Chi* 10.1b		
372	339 (7)	*Chi* 3.6b		
373	951 (18)	*Chi* 11.5a		
374	1053 (20)	*Chi* 12.2a		
375	1079 (20)	*Chi* 12.4a		
378			282	130
379	1218 (23)	*Chi* 13.10b		
379	1219 (23)	*Chi* 13.10b		
380	1607 (30)	*Chi* 17.9b		
381	2535 (47)	*Hsü* 2.23b		
382	380 (8)	*Chi* 4.1a		
382	96 (3)	*Chi* 1.1a		
383	2203 (40)			
383	1881 (20)	*Hsü* 3.7b		

Li Ch'ing-chao

1. *Li Ch'ing-chao Chi* (Page number).
2. *Li Ch'ing-chao Chi Chien Chu*. Hsü P'ei-chün, ed. and comm. (Page number).
3. *Ch'üan Sung Tz'u*. T'ang Kuei-chang, ed. (Page number).

Page	1. *Li Ch'ing-chao Chi*	2. *Li Ch'ing-chao Chi Chien Chu*	3. *Ch'üan Sung Tz'u*
386	43		
386	1	927	
387	51		189
388	11	929	
388	42		1
389	13	929	
389	47		
390	9	931	
390	6	930	111
391	9	930	97

391	7	926
392	18	929

LU YU

1. *Lu Fang-weng Ch'üan Chi.* SPPY (*Chüan*, page number, and leaf).

Page	1. *Lu Fang-weng Ch'üan Chi*
395	2.15b
395	5.13a
396	14.11b
396	22.6b
397	24.2a
398	27.1a
399	29.1b
400	35.10b
401	63.1a
401	63.1b
402	63.1b
402	63.1b
403	63.2a
404	63.2a
404	63.2a
405	63.2a
405	10.3b
406	85.3a
406	85.6b

YANG WAN-LI

1. *Ch'eng-chai Shih Chi.* SPPY (*Chüan*, page number, and leaf).
2. *Ch'üan Sung Tz'u.* T'ang Kuei-chang, ed. (Page number).

Page	1. *Ch'eng-chai Shih Chi*	2. *Ch'üan Sung Tz'u*
409	35.11b	
409	4.9a (2)	
410	2.6a	
411	3.10b	
411	12.3a	
412	13.5a	
412	12.7a	
413		1666
413	13.4b	
414	14.4a	
414	16.4b	
415	20.6b	
415	27.2b	
416	28.12b	
417	28.11a	
417	31.8a	
418		

Finding List for Chinese Texts

Further Reading

For poets I have translated, I list only my books because they are the next place to go after the selections in this volume. For readers wanting to investigate the poets in more depth, those books contain extensive bibliographies (any books that have appeared since those bibliographies are included here).

GENERAL

Birch, Cyril. *Anthology of Chinese Literature: From Early Times to the Fourteenth Century.* New York: Grove Press, 1965.

Bynner, Witter. *The Jade Mountain: A Chinese Anthology Being Three Hundred Poems of the T'ang Dynasty 618–906.* New York: Alfred A. Knopf, 1929.

Cheng, François. *Chinese Poetic Writing: With an Anthology of T'ang Poetry.* Donald Riggs and J. P. Seaton, trans. Bloomington: Indiana University Press, 1982.

Hinton, David, ed. and trans. *Mountain Home: The Wilderness Poetry of Ancient China.* New York: Counterpoint Press, 2002. Reprint, New York: New Directions, 2005.

Lin, Shuen-fu, and Stephen Owen, eds. *The Vitality of the Lyric Voice: Shih Poetry from the Late Han to the T'ang.* Princeton: Princeton University Press, 1986.

Liu, James J. Y. *The Art of Chinese Poetry.* Chicago: University of Chicago Press, 1962.

Liu, Wu-chi, and Irving Yucheng Lo. *Sunflower Splendor: Three Thousand Years of Chinese Poetry.* Bloomington: Indiana University Press, 1975.

Mair, Victor, ed. *The Columbia History of Chinese Literature.* New York: Columbia University Press, 2001.

Neinhauser, William. *The Indiana Companion to Traditional Chinese Literature.* Bloomington: Indiana University Press, 1986.

Owen, Stephen. *An Anthology of Chinese Literature: Beginnings to 1911*. New York: W. W. Norton, 1996.

———. *Traditional Chinese Poetry and Poetics*. Madison: University of Wisconsin Press, 1985.

Red Pine. *Poems of the Masters: China's Classic Anthology of T'ang and Sung Dynasty Verse*. Port Townsend, Wash.: Copper Canyon Press, 2003.

Rexroth, Kenneth, ed. and trans. *Love and the Turning Year: One Hundred More Poems from the Chinese*. New York: New Directions, 1970.

———. *One Hundred Poems from the Chinese*. New York: New Directions, 1956.

Sze, Arthur, ed. and trans. *The Silk Dragon: Translations from the Chinese*. Port Townsend, Wash.: Copper Canyon Press, 2001.

Waley, Arthur. *Chinese Poems*. London: George Allen & Unwin, 1946.

Watson, Burton. *Chinese Lyricism: Shih Poetry from the Second to the Twelfth Century*. New York: Columbia University Press, 1971.

———. *The Columbia Book of Chinese Poetry: From Early Times to the Thirteenth Century*. New York: Columbia University Press, 1984.

———. *Early Chinese Literature*. New York: Columbia University Press, 1962.

Weinberger, Eliot, ed. *The New Directions Anthology of Classical Chinese Poetry*. New York: New Directions, 2003.

INTRODUCTION

Chuang Tzu. *Chuang Tzu: The Inner Chapters*. David Hinton, trans. Berkeley: Counterpoint Press, 1997.

Pound, Ezra, and Ernest Fenollosa. *The Chinese Written Character as a Medium for Poetry*. San Francisco: City Lights Books, 1964. (First printing 1920, expanded edition 1936.)

EARLY COLLECTIONS: THE ORAL TRADITION

THE BOOK OF SONGS

Confucius. *The Analects*. David Hinton, trans. Berkeley: Counterpoint Press, 1998.

Granet, Marcel. *Festivals and Songs of Ancient China*. E. D. Edwards, trans. London: Routledge & Sons, 1932.

Karlgren, Bernard. *The Book of Odes: Chinese Text, Transcription, and Translation*. Stockholm: Museum of Far Eastern Antiquities, 1950.

Legge, James. *The She King or the Book of Poetry. The Chinese Classics*, vol. 4. Oxford: Oxford University Press, 1871. Reprint, Hong Kong: Hong Kong University Press, 1960.

McNaughton, William. *The Book of Songs*. New York: Twayne Publishers, 1971.

Mencius. *Mencius*. David Hinton, trans. Berkeley: Counterpoint Press, 1998.

Pound, Ezra, trans. *The Confucian Odes: The Classic Anthology Defined by Confucius*. New York: New Directions, 1954.

Waley, Arthur. *The Book of Songs*. London: George Allen & Unwin, 1937. Revised edition (Joseph Allen, ed.), New York: Grove Press, 1996.

Wang, C. H. *The Bell and the Drum: Shih Ching as Formulaic Poetry in an Oral Tradition*. Berkeley: University of California Press, 1974.

TAO TE CHING

Lao Tzu. *Tao Te Ching.* David Hinton, trans. Berkeley: Counterpoint Press, 2000.

THE SONGS OF CH'U

Field, Stephen. *Tian Wen: A Chinese Book of Origins.* New York: New Directions, 1986.

Hawkes, David. *Ch'u Tz'u: Songs of the South.* Oxford: Oxford University Press, 1959. Reprinted as *The Songs of the South.* Harmondsworth: Penguin Books, 1985.

Waley, Arthur. *The Nine Songs.* London: George Allen & Unwin, 1955. Reprint, San Francisco: City Lights Books, 1973.

LATER FOLK-SONG COLLECTIONS

Allen, Joseph. *In the Voice of Others: Chinese Music Bureau Poetry.* Ann Arbor, Mich.: Center for Chinese Studies, 1992.

Birrell, Ann. *New Songs from a Jade Terrace: An Anthology of Early Chinese Love Poetry.* London: George Allen & Unwin, 1982. Reprinted as *Chinese Love Poetry: New Songs from a Jade Terrace.* Harmondsworth: Penguin Books, 1986.

Lady Midnight. *A Gold Orchid: The Love Poems of Tzu Yeh.* Rutland, Vt.: Charles E. Tuttle, 1972.

FIRST MASTERS: THE MAINSTREAM BEGINS

Owen, Stephen. *The Making of Early Chinese Classical Poetry.* Cambridge, Mass.: Harvard University Press, 2006.

SU HUI

Métail, Michèle. *La Carte de la Sphère Armillaire de Su Hui: Un Poème Chinois à "Lecture Retournée" du Quatrième Siècle.* Théâtre Typographique, 1998.

T'AO CH'IEN

T'ao Ch'ien. *The Selected Poems of T'ao Ch'ien.* David Hinton, trans. Port Townsend, Wash.: Copper Canyon Press, 1993.

HSIEH LING-YÜN

Elvin, Mark. *The Retreat of the Elephants: An Environmental History of China.* New Haven: Yale University Press, 2004. (See pp. 335–36.)

Hsieh Ling-yün. *The Mountain Poems of Hsieh Ling-yün.* David Hinton, trans. New York: New Directions, 2001.

T'ANG DYNASTY I: THE GREAT RENAISSANCE

Owen, Stephen. *The Great Age of Chinese Poetry: The High T'ang.* New Haven: Yale University Press, 1981.

Young, David. *Five T'ang Poets.* Oberlin, Ohio: Oberlin College Press, 1990.

MENG HAO-JAN

Meng Hao-jan. *The Mountain Poems of Meng Hao-jan*. David Hinton, trans. New York: Archipelago Books, 2004.

WANG WEI

Wang Wei. *The Selected Poems of Wang Wei*. David Hinton, trans. New York: New Directions, 2006.

LI PO

Li Po. *The Selected Poems of Li Po*. David Hinton, trans. New York: New Directions, 1996.

Varsano, Paula. *Tracking the Banished Immortal: The Poetry of Li Bo and Its Critical Reception*. Honolulu: University of Hawai'i Press, 2003.

TU FU

Chou, Eva Shan. *Reconsidering Tu Fu: Literary Greatness and Cultural Context*. New York: Cambridge University Press, 1995.

McCraw, David. *Du Fu's Laments from the South*. Honolulu: University of Hawai'i Press, 1992.

Tu Fu. *The Selected Poems of Du Fu*. Burton Watson, trans. New York: Columbia University Press, 2002.

————. *The Selected Poems of Tu Fu*. David Hinton, trans. New York: New Directions, 1989.

COLD MOUNTAIN (HAN SHAN)

Cold Mountain. *Cold Mountain: 100 Poems by the T'ang Poet Han-shan*. Burton Watson, trans. New York: Grove Press, 1962. Reprint, New York: Columbia University Press, 1970.

————. *The Collected Songs of Cold Mountain*. Red Pine, trans. Port Townsend, Wash.: Copper Canyon Press, 1983. Revised edition, 2000.

————. *The Poetry of Han-Shan: A Complete, Annotated Translation of Cold Mountain*. Robert Henricks, trans. Albany: State University of New York Press, 1990.

Snyder, Gary. *Riprap and Cold Mountain Poems*. San Francisco: Four Seasons Foundation, 1969. Reprint, Berkeley: North Point Press, 1990.

Waley, Arthur. *Chinese Poems*. London: George Allen & Unwin, 1946. (See pages 105–111.)

WEI YING-WU

Varsano, Paula. "The Invisible Landscape of Wei Ying-wu." *Harvard Journal of Asiatic Studies* 54, no. 2 (Dec. 1994): 407–35.

T'ANG DYNASTY II: EXPERIMENTAL ALTERNATIVES

Graham, A. C. *Poems of the Late T'ang*. Harmondsworth: Penguin Books, 1965.

Owen, Stephen. *The End of the Chinese "Middle Ages": Essays in Mid-T'ang Literary Culture*. Stanford: Stanford University Press, 1996.

─────. *The Late T'ang: Chinese Poetry of the Mid-Ninth Century (827–860)*. Cambridge, Mass.: Harvard University Press, 2006.

MENG CHIAO

Meng Chiao. *The Late Poems of Meng Chiao*. David Hinton, trans. Princeton: Princeton University Press, 1996.

HAN YÜ

Han Yü. *Growing Old Alive: Poems by Han Yü*. Kenneth Hanson, trans. Port Townsend, Wash.: Copper Canyon Press, 1978.

Hartman, Charles. *Han Yü and the T'ang Search for Unity*. Princeton: Princeton University Press, 1986.

Owen, Stephen. *The Poetry of Meng Chiao and Han Yü*. New Haven: Yale University Press, 1975.

PO CHÜ-I

Po Chü-i. *The Selected Poems of Po Chü-i*. David Hinton, trans. New York: New Directions, 1999.

─────. *Selected Poems*. Burton Watson, trans. New York: Columbia University Press, 2000.

LI HO

Frodsham, J. D. *The Poems of Li Ho*. Oxford: Oxford University Press, 1970. Reprinted as *Goddesses, Ghosts, and Demons: The Collected Poems of Li He (790–816)*. Berkeley: North Point Press, 1983.

Tu Kuo-ch'ing. *Li Ho*. Boston: Twayne Publishers, 1979.

TU MU

Tu Mu. *Plantains in the Rain*. R. F. Burton, trans. London: Wellsweep Press, 1990.

─────. *Out on the Autumn River: Selected Poems of Du Mu*. David Young and Jiann I. Lin, trans. Akron, Ohio: RagerMedia Press, 2007.

LI SHANG-YIN

Liu, James J. Y. *The Poetry of Li Shang-yin: Ninth-Century Baroque Chinese Poet*. Chicago: University of Chicago Press, 1969.

Owen, Stephen. *The Late T'ang: Chinese Poetry of the Mid-Ninth Century (827–860)*. Cambridge, Mass.: Harvard University Press, 2006. (See pp. 335–526).

YÜ HSÜAN-CHI

Yü Hsüan-chi. *The Clouds Float North: The Complete Poems of Yu Xuanji*. David Young and Jiann I. Lin, trans. Middletown, Conn.: Wesleyan University Press, 1998.

SUNG DYNASTY: THE MAINSTREAM RENEWED

Chang, Kang-i Sun. *The Evolution of Chinese Tz'u Poetry: From Late T'ang to Northern Sung*. Princeton: Princeton University Press, 1980.

Jullien, François. *In Praise of Blandness: Proceeding from Chinese Thought and Aesthetics.* Paula Varsano, trans. New York: Zone Books, 2004.

Landau, Julie. *Beyond Spring: Tz'u Poems of the Sung Dynasty.* New York: Columbia University Press, 1994.

Lin, Shuen-fu. *The Transformation of the Chinese Lyrical Tradition: Chiang K'uei and Southern Sung Tz'u Poetry.* Princeton: Princeton University Press, 1978.

Liu, James J. Y. *Major Lyricists of the Northern Sung.* Princeton: Princeton University Press, 1974.

Yoshikawa, Kojiro. *An Introduction to Sung Poetry.* Burton Watson, trans. Cambridge, Mass.: Harvard University Press, 1967.

MEI YAO-CH'EN

Chaves, Jonathan. *Mei Yao-ch'en and the Development of Early Sung Poetry.* New York: Columbia University Press, 1976.

SU TUNG-P'O

Egan, Ronald. *Word, Image, and Deed in the Life of Su Shi.* Cambridge, Mass.: Harvard University Press, 1994.

Fuller, Michael. *The Road to East Slope: The Development of Su Shi's Poetic Voice.* Stanford: Stanford University Press, 1990.

Grant, Beata. *Mount Lu Revisited: Buddhism in the Life and Writings of Su Shih.* Honolulu: University of Hawai'i Press, 1994.

Lin, Yutang. *The Gay Genius: The Life and Times of Su Tungpo.* New York: John Day, 1947.

Strassberg, Richard. *Inscribed Landscapes.* Berkeley: University of California Press, 1994. (See pp. 183–94).

Su Tung-p'o. *Selected Poems of Su Tung-p'o.* Burton Watson, trans. Port Townsend, Wash.: Copper Canyon Press, 1994.

LI CH'ING-CHAO

Hu Pin-ch'ing. *Li Ch'ing-chao.* New York: Twayne Publishers, 1966.

Li Ch'ing-chao. *Li Ch'ing-chao: Complete Poems.* Kenneth Rexroth and Ling Chung, eds. and trans. New York: New Directions, 1979.

LU YU

Duke, Michael. *Lu You.* Boston: Twayne Publishers, 1977.

Lu Yu. *The Old Man Who Does as He Pleases.* Burton Watson, trans. New York: Columbia University Press, 1973.

———. *The Wild Old Man: Poems of Lu Yu.* David Gordon, trans. Berkeley: North Point Press, 1984.

YANG WAN-LI

Yang Wan-li. *Heaven My Blanket, Earth My Pillow.* Jonathan Chaves, trans. New York: Weatherhill, 1975.

Schmidt, J. D. *Yang Wan-li.* New York: Twayne Publishers, 1976.

Women's Poetry in Ancient China

Birrell, Anne. "Women in Literature." In *The Columbia History of Chinese Literature*, edited by Victor Mair, pp. 194–220. New York: Columbia University Press, 2001.

Chang, Kang-i Sun, and Haun Saussy. *Women Writers of Traditional China: An Anthology of Poetry and Criticism*. Stanford: Stanford University Press, 1999.

Hou, Sharon Shih-jiuan. "Women's Literature." In *The Indiana Companion to Traditional Chinese Literature*, edited by William Nienhauser, pp. 175–92. Bloomington: Indiana University Press.

Hsüeh T'ao. *Brocade River Poems: Selected Works of the T'ang Dynasty Courtesan Xue Tao*. Jeanne Larsen, trans. Princeton: Princeton University Press, 1987.

Idema, Wilt, and Beata Grant. *The Red Brush: Writing Women of Imperial China*. Cambridge, Mass.: Harvard University Asia Center, 2004.

Larsen, Jeanne. *Willow, Wine, Mirror, Moon: Women's Poems from Tang China*. Rochester, N.Y.: BOA Editions, 2005.

Rexroth, Kenneth, and Ling Chung, trans. *The Orchid Boat: Women Poets of China*. New York: McGraw Hill, 1972. Reprinted as *Women Poets of China*. New York: New Directions, 1982.

Permissions Acknowledgments

Grateful acknowledgment is made to the publishers for permission to reprint work from the following books:

The Late Poems of Meng Chiao, published by Princeton University Press. Copyright © 1996 by Princeton University Press.

Mountain Home: The Wilderness Poetry of Ancient China, published by New Directions Publishing. Copyright © 2002 by David Hinton.

The Mountain Poems of Hsieh Ling-yün, published by New Directions Publishing. Copyright © 2001 by David Hinton.

The Mountain Poems of Meng Hao-jan, published by Archipelago Books. Copyright © 2004 by David Hinton.

The Selected Poems of Li Po, published by New Directions Publishing. Copyright © 1996 by David Hinton.

The Selected Poems of Po Chü-i, published by New Directions Publishing. Copyright © 1999 by David Hinton.

The Selected Poems of T'ao Ch'ien, published by Copper Canyon Press. Copyright © 1993 by David Hinton.

The Selected Poems of Wang Wei, published by New Directions Publishing. Copyright © 2006 by David Hinton.

Tao Te Ching, published by Counterpoint Press. Copyright © 2000 by David Hinton.